About the Author

Janet is married to Michael, and they have a son called Christopher. Their lifelong wish was to buy a dream home in the sun, somewhere they could call their forever holiday home.

This story is about some of the problems they had to overcome when they bought a property in a country that they had never ever considered or visited before.

The author wanted to write something meaningful that made people laugh and also showed them that some dreams can come true.

Licanosh

Janet Gorry

Licanosh
Leka Nosht – means goodnight in Bulgaria

Olympia Publishers
London

www.olympiapublishers.com
OLYMPIA PAPERBACK EDITION

A CIP catalogue record for this title is
available from the British Library.

ISBN: 978-1-80074-713-5

This is a work of fiction.
Names, characters, places and incidents originate from the writer's
imagination. Any resemblance to actual persons, living or dead, is
purely coincidental.

First Published in 2024

Olympia Publishers
Tallis House
2 Tallis Street
London
EC4Y 0AB
Printed in Great Britain

Dedication

I would like to dedicate this book to our dear friends Robin and Barbara (Blodwyn and Knobby), whom we met in Bulgaria.

Robin has a progressive illness and Barbara has recently been diagnosed with dementia. Due to this, I wanted to write a story about some of the wonderful times we had together in Bulgaria.

A happy narrative that they could share with their two sons, grandchildren, family, and friends.

Acknowledgements

I would like to thank my husband, Mick, son, Christopher, and his wife, Jenni, for always believing in me.
Without your endless support, I would have never gotten through some of the sad times.

Sunday Roast

It all started with a trip to the Cumbrian Lakes. Mick, Chris and I were going for a nice day out to Bowness-on-Windermere; nothing special, just a lovely walk along the lake whilst we waited for our Sunday roast to cook in the big oven. It normally took about four hours for the roast dinner to cook; therefore, I knew we had ample time to drive to Lake Windermere, and do some shopping in the lovely village before Mick had to drive us home.

While I was putting the roast beef into the oven, Mick started to pack the car with all the essential things we needed for our day out at the lakes. He gathered our walking boots, two big umbrellas to keep us dry, three lots of hats and winter coats to keep us warm, three pairs of gloves and a few woolly scarfs, because the weatherman on the BBC news had forecast strong winds and heavy rain in the South of Cumbria for most of the day.

Mick packed the car, while I prepared a flask of hot coffee, some orange juice for Christopher, ham sandwiches on brown bread, some fresh cream cakes and three packets of cheese and onion crisps just in case we got hungry. By the time me and Mick had finished putting everything into the Ford Mondeo, it was almost full. We looked at each other for a moment, then Mick laughed at me.

'Where is Christopher supposed to sit, Janet?'

I looked at the back seats of the car but they were full of all the food and clothing. 'Oh my god, Mick, we will have to make room for him, we cannot leave him at home on his own.'

I walked back into the house to set the intruder alarm and lock all of the doors. When I was confident that the house was secure, I made my way back to the car which was now parked at the end of the driveway. To my delight, Mick had managed to squeeze Christopher into the middle of the back seats.

I opened the car door and got into the passenger seat. As I put my seatbelt on, I turned around to smile at Christopher. When I looked at him, I could see that he was sitting in the middle of all the hats and coats.

He looked up at me. 'Look, Mum, Dad has made a special place for me to sit in. It is lovely and warm.'

I smiled at him then turned back around to see what Mick was doing.

I looked to the left side then then the right side of the car, then through the rear mirror. I could see that Mick was trying to close the boot of the car, but he was finding it difficult because there was that much stuff piled into it. I heard him bang the boot a few times before it shut properly. Once he was certain that the boot would not open, he made his way around to the driver's seat. We both settled down into our comfy leather seats and Christopher snuggled into his comfy place.

The route to the lakes would normally be the B5419, then the M62 (North), then onto the M6 (North) and finally the A590, into south Cumbria and the lakes. The B5419 was free of any traffic and our drive along the M62 was great because all the traffic was moving quite fast and there were no delays by IKEA in Warrington; however, as Mick drove towards the M6, there was a bit of a delay getting off of the M62 due to a broken-down car on the slip road.

The delay getting out of Warrington did not bother Mick and me because Smooth Radio was playing some of our favourite songs. We were singing our heads off to the wonderful tunes from the 80s and 90s, while we sat in the queuing traffic. However, through the music, I could hear Christopher shouting from the back of the car, but we both pretended that we could not hear him.

'Mum and Dad, please stop singing. It is hurting my ears; this is child abuse. I am going to phone Child Line and ask Esther (Rantzen) to make you stop!' But Mick and I just started singing louder to all the fabulous tunes.

When the traffic started to move again, Mick drove towards the M6, we joined the motorway just past the Thelwall Viaduct. I looked at the motorway traffic ahead of us and could see that some of the vehicles in front of us were slowing down. My heart sank because I did not want to be delayed for too long again because of the lovely roast dinner cooking in the big oven.

Mick continued to drive north along the M6 towards the lakes. Then suddenly and completely out of the blue, I could see what was making all the vehicles slow down; it was not an accident or a traffic incident as I was expecting, instead, it was a massive sign at the left side of the M6 motorway advertising Holiday Homes in the Sun. I was not surprised that all the traffic was slowing down; the sign was like a big multi-coloured rainbow over the town of St Helen's. As we got closer, Mick and I looked at each other and smiled.

'Shall we go and see what type of holiday homes they are selling?'

Then I heard a loud voice from the back of the car. 'Oh no, not again, Mum!' Christopher was shouting from his comfy seat. 'What about the lakes? I don't want to go to St Helen's, I want to feed the ducks in the lakes.'

I turned around to look back at him. 'Please, Chris, let us

go and have a look. It will only take a few minutes. Dad and I might find our dream holiday home here.'

Christopher smiled. 'OK, Mum, but only for a minute or two.'

Mick signalled to change lanes on the motorway, so that he could come off at the next junction. Once he had navigated his way through all the traffic, he indicated to come off the M6, onto the St Helen's slip road. As Mick drove the car down the road towards a massive roundabout, I realised that I had no idea where we were supposed to be going.

The roundabout was very busy with traffic, Mick slowed down to get his bearings, but then the traffic lights turned green, Mick did not have any time to stop to see where he was going. 'Where are we going, Janet?'

'I am not sure, Mick, I think the sign said the Thistle Hotel?'

'Great, Janet, but where is the hotel?'

I looked around the roundabout as fast as I could to see if there were any signs advertising holiday homes in the sun to help him navigate around the roundabout, but I could not see anything.

Mick was starting to panic. He had been around the roundabout once and I knew he did not want to go around it again. 'Where are we supposed to be going, Janet!'

My eyes were darting everywhere trying to find a holiday sign or the hotel, then Christopher started talking. 'Mum, are we lost? Do you know where we are going? I told you that we should have gone to the lakes!'

Then I saw a little sign on one of the slip roads, I was very relieved. 'Just follow those Holiday Homes in The Sun signs, Mick.' I pointed my finger towards the direction of the signs.

Mick started to slow the car down. 'I cannot see any signs, Janet! Where are you pointing?'

By this time, Mick had started his second journey around the roundabout. 'I am not sure which exit it is, Mick, just keep going around the roundabout until you see the signs for the Thistle Hotel.'

***

Mick and I had wanted to buy a holiday home in the sun for years. It was that bloody Carol Smiley-Smiley's fault. I watched her "Holiday Homes in the Sun" program all the time trying to win the 'own your own home in the sun competition.' It must have cost me an absolute fortune in telephone calls throughout the years.

I remember one Sunday afternoon when I was in the bedroom watching my favourite programme on the portable TV, while Mick and Chris were watching the football on the big TV downstairs. "Holiday Homes in the Sun" came on the television. Carol Smiley was hosting the show. I was delighted because I was on my own and I could watch it in peace. Carol looked amazing in her beautiful yellow summer dress. She did the usual introduction, then she announced the location. 'Today's show is in the beautiful Italian countryside.' She continued to show the viewers lots of beautiful properties in the Italian sunshine.

I lay on the bed daydreaming about living in my very own Italian paradise. I thought, One day, Janet, you will have your very own place in the sun. All you have to do is get today's question right and it is yours. *The moment the competition arrived, my nerves started to tingle.* Come on, Janet, you can do this!

Carol smiled into the camera and asked the question. 'What is the first name of the queen of the United Kingdom?' Once I knew the answer, I jumped off the bed and ran to the

15

house telephone before the competition number disappeared from the screen of the portable TV. I dialled the number. An automated answering service started.

'Thank you for calling Dream Holiday Homes in the Sun. Please listen very carefully to the question, then answer the questions as clearly and concise as you can. Once you have answered the question, please leave your full name, address and contact details, so that we can call you back if you are today's lucky winner.' I could not wait...

Question: 'What is the queen's first name?'

I spoke in my poshest clearest voice. 'The answer to the question is Elizabeth. The queen's first name is Elizabeth.

'My name is Janet Gorry, I live at 96 Cradley, Widnes, Cheshire. My contact telephone number is 0151 424 1003. That is Janet at 0151 424 1003. Thank you, thank you so very much.'

I put the phone down and sat on the end of the bed with my arms, fingers, legs, eyes and toes crossed, hoping to win the competition.

Then suddenly the house phone rang. 'Oh my god, this telephone never rings, it must be Dream Homes in the Sun. Yippee, I must have won!'

'Hello, is that Mrs Gorry, Mrs Janet Gorry, from Cradley in Widnes?' The voice on the other end of the phone sounded familiar. 'Yes, that is me.'

'You have entered today's competition for Dream Holiday Homes in the Sun?'

'Yes, I did, the answer to the question is Elizabeth. I have just telephoned the number for today's competition; did I give you the right answer?'

'Congratulations, Mrs Gorry, you're today's lucky winner.'

My smile must have brightened up the bedroom, I could not believe it.

'Thank you, thank you, thank you so very much.' Then I

heard a little giggle, then a chuckle, then a loud roar of laughter.

'Excuse me, what is going on, have I won a dream holiday home or not?'

Within a second or two, I realised that it was Mick and Christopher on the other end of the house phone pretending to be the producer of the show, telling me that I had won the competition. I almost believed them, in fact I had started to pack my suitcase and unplug the portable TV, then my heart sank!

'You pair of buggers, why would you do that to me, you're horrible.' Then the laughing stopped.

'It was not my fault, Mum, my dad made me do it.'

'Did he now!'

***

Mick manoeuvred the car around the St Helen's roundabout for the second before he managed to navigate his way towards the Thistle Hotel. As he drove into the hotel's car park, I could see the back of the big colourful rainbow sign, the one that Mick and I had seen from the M6 motorway, advertising Dream Holiday Homes in the Sun.

Mick parked the car into the first empty car parking space. I got out of the car as fast as I could to help Christopher get out of the back seat. Once we were all out of the car, we ran through the car park towards the reception area of the hotel.

Dream Holiday

When we arrived at the reception area, we must have looked like we had just been beamed down by Scotty from the Starship Enterprise. We were looking around the building for any signs of life, especially people selling properties in the sun, but we could not see anyone!

Then the receptionist popped up from behind the reception desk, she was going through the post. I could not wait for her to finish sorting out all the mail, because our roast dinner was roasting in the big oven back home. 'Good morning, please can you help me, we are looking for holiday homes in the sun?'

The young woman sat down behind the reception, she looked up from the desk and smiled. 'Hello, the holiday home event is down the first corridor just past the toilets, then through the big white double doors.' Mick and I thanked her, then we were off like two horses in the Grand National.

'Mum, Dad, stop! I am going to stay here if that's OK with you?' Christopher sat down on a lovely comfy sofa next to the fireplace in the reception area to play on his game boy.

'That's fine, Christopher, but do not talk to any strangers, Dad and I won't be long.'

One false start then we were off again; we ran down the corridor, past the toilets then straight through the big white double doors into the big conference room.

Within a split second of entering the double doors, I knew that we were in the right place. One of the many sales representatives came running towards us before any of the other representatives had a chance. As he got close to us, I noticed that he had one of the biggest smiles I had ever seen, his lovely white teeth sparkled in the bright lights.

'Hello, you wonderful people, thank you for coming to this fabulous dream holiday home event here today. I hope you had a lovely journey, and you are excited about buying one of our fantastic Dream Holiday Homes. Have you travelled far?'

I smiled at him. 'We did not intend on coming here today, we were on our way to Bowness-on-Windermere for a nice walk around the lake and a bit of shopping in the village.'

He looked back at me. 'You have got to be joking, the lakes are miles away in Cumbria, why did you stop? Did you see our beautiful big sign on the M6, it's like a big rainbow in the sky? Or did you make the detour because you wanted to buy one of our fabulous holiday homes or are you just browsing?'

Mick started to talk as he moved away from him. 'I don't know why I am here, one minute we were on our way to Bowness-on-Windermere, for a walk around the lake, then Janet saw your sign.'

The rep smiled and winked at Mick then made his way closer to where he was standing. 'Tell me, sir, what are your names and where do you come from?'

As the rep walked past me, I held my hand out to shake his hand. 'We are Michael and Janet, we are from a small town called Widnes, just outside Liverpool.'

The rep held my hand within his warm hands and smiled at me. I started to look around the room at all of the lovely table displays. Some of the tables were set up like miniature islands, displaying holiday homes by the beach or swimming pools. They all looked absolutely amazing to me.

Then I felt the sales representative's warm hands letting go of my hand as he turned to look at who was coming through the big white double door. Within a few seconds, I noticed that all the other sales representatives were like little bees buzzing around a honey pot; every time a new person walked through the double doors, they flew towards them as if they were the queen bee.

Their buzzing around did not bother me, but it seemed to unsettle Mick and I could tell that he did not want to stay in the room (he hated being manipulated by over friendly sales people). But I was in holiday home heaven, the sales rep could have sold me a tent I would not have noticed. Our sales rep had definitely found his pot of honey. Eager to buy my very own dream holiday home in the sun, I grabbed hold of his right hand and headed towards Mick. The sales rep looked at me and winked his left eye.

'Right, Mick and Janet, please look around at all of our beautiful tables advertising fabulous homes in the sun. If you see anything you fancy, please come back to me, don't go to any other rep in the room because I am the very best sales representative here today.' He pointed his finger to all of his colleagues in the room. 'They are all rubbish, but please do not tell any of them what I have just said because they will deny it!'

'Thank you for telling us about the other reps, we won't say a word to anyone, will we, Mick?' I let go of his warm hand and made my way back to Mick, before he left the room.

Mick grinned at me as we made our way to the first table. I spent a few minutes looking through some of the small folders offering beautiful Spanish homes in the sun. Then I looked at one of the big folders advertising one-bedroom apartments, villas with pools and two-bedroom town houses by the sea.

They looked amazing but when I got to the back pages to look at the prices they were all very expensive, and way out of our price range.

Mick and I moved onto the next table which was advertising properties for sale in Greece. All the properties on display looked fantastic, there were lots of whitewashed homes, situated next to beautiful beaches, with extraordinarily bright blue skies and golden sunshine. For a moment or two, I dreamt about being in my very own "Mamma Mia" movie, but when Mick turned to the page of the property folder and we looked through the price list, I realised that all the properties that were up for sale were far too expensive!

'We can't afford any of these properties, Janet, let's go to the lakes.' And he started to walk towards the double doors.

I stood still. 'Please let us look at the rest of the tables, it won't take that long, Mick.' Then I gave him a hopeful smile and an encouraging nudge towards the next table which was advertising gorgeous properties in Cyprus. Every one of the villas and apartments looked stunning. As I gazed through all the brochures, I thought about all the times I could swim around Aphrodite's Rock in Paphos, but once again when Mick and I looked at the price list, even the smallest studio apartment was out of our price range.

I quickly moved onto the next table which was Mallorca, but before I could look at any of the fabulous properties in the brochure, Mick turned to the back page to see the price list first. As I looked down the lists, I could see that the cheapest property was a tiny one-bed apartment for 140,000 euros. My heart began to sink like the Titanic, and all my holiday home hopes and dreams started to fade away like a rainbow on a very wet and windy day.

I looked at Mick and whispered into his ear, 'My God, Mick, we'll never be able to afford any of those homes in the sun, they are all very expensive.'

As I was whispering to Mick, I looked over his shoulder and noticed that our sales representative had not moved very far from us; it looked like he had been hovering behind us as we moved along the tables. He must have just stayed close enough to listen to each and every one of our conversations ready to jump in if we were ready to buy a holiday home.

It did not take me long before I realised that he had heard everything Mick and I had said to each other, because as soon as he saw I had finished whispering to Mick, he came closer.

'Do not despair, Mick and Janet, for one day only I can do you a once in a lifetime deal, but this excellent offer is only available for today.' Then he moved towards us like the candy man giving us a delicious treat. 'How about an easy finance option; it's a great way to buy your new home in the sun today, before you go to the lakes.

'You can pay for it over the next twenty-five years, it is so easy, lots of people have chosen this brilliant option already. All you and Mick have to do is find a property that you love, like one of those you fell in love with, Janet, in Greece.'

I smiled at him then looked at Mick.

'Once you have made your decision, I will take you to one of the big administration tables and then all you have to do is sign along the dotted lines.'

'I would like one of those two-bedroom apartments on the beach in Greece.'

Like a bee to the honey pot, I started to follow him towards the administration tables at the top of the room, as if I were in a trance, then I heard a voice behind me. 'Janet, stop it now, we cannot afford that!'

I turned around and Mick's face was like thunder. Our dream holiday home in the sun had well and truly faded away.

'Let us go now, Janet; I want to get out of here. Where is our Christopher?'

Mick and I had been down the finance option once before, but when we did the sums, it was not right for us because we did not want to go into any additional debt to buy a holiday home. I moved away from the sales rep and moved towards Mick, the holiday home spell had been broken and I was back in reality. We looked at each other, then around the room to find a way to escape the watchful eyes and ears of our sales representative.

Then all of a sudden, Mick shouted, 'I am going to the toilet, Janet; I will meet you in reception, hurry up.' Mick turned and walked towards the double doors as fast as he could.

My smiling face had turned into a frown. 'O all right. Mick, I will see you soon.'

Then I heard a voice behind me. 'That is not a problem, Mr Gorry, come back when you have finished on the loo, I have got all day.' Then he turned towards me. 'I will be back as soon as Mr Gorry returns, I am just going to help those new customers over there,' and he pointed to a man and a woman who had just walked through the white double doors.

While Mick was out of the room, I took one last look around all the tables. I said farewell to Mallorca, Greece and Cyprus, all the dreams I had about owning my own holiday home in the sun had faded away. I decided to make my way towards the big white double doors as fast as I could, and before the sales rep had time to finish with his new customers. I really wanted to make my escape from his ever-watchful eyes and go to the lakes before our roast dinner was overcooked.

Then I noticed that there was a very small table hidden in the corner of the room by the big double doors. As I was rushing past the table, I wondered, *How did Mick and I miss this one?*

Then something inside pulled the brakes on my getaway. The table looked a bit messy, it was not like the other beautiful islands, it just looked like someone had flung a few brochures and documents onto the table, it was definitely not organised or attractive like the other tables. I moved a pile of papers to the side, then I found a folder advertising Amber Sun apartments for sale on the Black Sea coast. I pretended not to be interested just in case the rep was watching me, then I opened the back page of the folder as fast as I could. My eyes rolled down the page like a laser bean. I could not believe it, was I dreaming, or could this be the one and only chance to buy a holiday home in the sun?

Holiday Destinations

To be honest, I did not pay any attention to the location or the destination, I just opened the back page of the folder for a fast glance at the prices, then within a few seconds I realised that the properties were the right price for us. Without any hesitation, I turned around to catch the attention of the sales rep who had followed Mick and I around the room for the last half hour, but to my disappointment, he was still talking to the other new customers.

I knew I did not have a lot of time to waste, the dinner was cooking in the oven and Mick would have finished his visit to the toilet. I raised my arms into the air as high as I could to get his attention, but he continued talking to them, so I stood in the middle of the room like an air traffic controller pointing to the Amber Sun table, then to the toilets, and then back to him. With all the commotion it did not take long to catch everyone's attention including the sales rep. 'Hurry up, I have found the right property, please can you help me now. I am ready to buy this one,' and I pointed to the Amber Sun folder that I was holding in the air.

His face lit up like he had just won the lottery. When he smiled, his lovely white teeth caught the sunlight shining through the window. For the first time, I noticed that he had a gold tooth which sparkled like a diamond in the sun's rays. As soon as he heard me say, 'I have found the right one,' he started running towards me like Steve Austin "The Bionic Man". It was as if he was moving in slow motion, pushing his way through the crowds of people. As he ran past all the other reps, he pushed them out of his way and shouted, 'Move out of my way, this is important. I have got a sale, move out of the way, please move out of my way, this is my sale, not yours.' He rushed past a few of the new customers as they walked through the double doors into the room. 'Sorry, everyone, I have got a sale, you should have come earlier, but don't worry everyone, I won't be too long with Janet. Have a look around all the tables I will be with you soon.'

A few of the new customers tried to stop him to get his attention, but they did not stand a chance. I was his target and nothing was going to stop him from getting his first sale.

When he came close to me, I could not wait for him to get his breath back. 'Please tell me about the Amber Sun apartments?'

He took a few deep breaths then he looked through the information displayed on the table. 'O, err, Bulgaria; it is a lovely place unspoilt by tourism, incredibly natural and not too expensive yet, Janet.'

Without any hesitation, I started to go through our dream holiday home list. 'We want to buy a home close to the sea, overlooking a pool, with lots of nice bars, restaurants and shops. Do any of those apartments offer any of the locations that I have requested, please?' I was beginning to sound desperate, but I knew that Mick had been sitting with Christopher for a while, and if he came back into the room looking for me, I needed to have something to show him.

The sales rep looked at me as if he had just found his first queen bee. 'Yes, Janet, I have got the most wonderful place for you.' He started to move the table from out of the corner of the room, then he pulled out an A4 folder with an information pack inside. 'Here you are, Janet, just what I was looking for, Amber Sun Apollon complex, you have chosen the Apollon 4 apartments which are situated in Old Nessebar.'

I smiled at him and it felt like the Titanic was rising up through the darkest sea.

'Janet, my friend, there is a fabulous ground floor corner apartment, with two bedrooms, two bathrooms, overlooking a fabulous swimming pool and only a hundred metres from the Black Sea coast.'

My heart was pounding out of my chest, I could not control my happiness, it sounded just perfect to me. He carried on reading the information pack then he smiled at me. 'Wow wee, Janet, it comes with a full furniture package as an option if you are interested. Oh my god, Janet, it is just perfect for you and Mick.'

I think he knew straight away that he had sold it to me. Once I had seen the front of the A4 cover advertising the Apollon Complex, I felt like the queen bee again.

'It is just perfect, I want to buy it, where do I sign?' He took me by the hand then he started to pull me back through all the customers and all the other jealous sales representatives.

All I could hear was. 'Coming through, please let me get through, I have got a buyer in my hands. Look at me, everyone, I have got a new lucky buyer.' It felt like he was showing me off to all the other envious reps as he pulled me past the Mallorca, Cyprus, Greece and Spanish holiday home tables.

He continued to hold my hand as he dragged me to one of the big administration tables at the back of the room. When we had finally stopped, I looked over the table. I soon realised that it was not full of dream holiday home brochures like the other

27

tables, instead there were lots of white A4 documents and numerous ball point pens, advertising different holiday locations throughout the world. He pulled out a chair and sat me down.

'Would you like a coffee or tea, Janet, before you sign on the dotted lines?'

'No, thank you.' I was feeling a little bit windswept as a result of being pulled through the room by my hand.

'OK, Janet, let's start the boring paperwork.'

Before I could catch my breath, he handed me a lot of what looked like official documents and a pen advertising Bulgaria.

'Right, Janet, let us make this amazing two-bedroom, two-bathroom apartment, overlooking the pool, close to the sea, yours before anyone else in this room decides to buy it before you.'

Without any hesitation and the fear of somebody else buying it before me, I started to write my name and our address across the first dotted lines. When I had finished writing my name and address, he pulled the sheet of paper away from me and examined it.

'Thank you, Janet, that looks very good to me.'

He completed the section on the apartment and location and handed it back to me. 'O, by the way, Janet, do not forget to put your signature on the last dotted line.' Then he sat down next to me. 'That's all the paperwork for now, Mrs Gorry. Now please let me explain to you the fantastic finance arrangement that comes with your new apartment, but you cannot say anything to anyone else because we can only give it to one lucky couple, and today that is you and Mick, because you are such a fabulous pair.' Then he looked around the room to make sure no one was listening, before he completed the paperwork.

'Right, Janet, we are almost done, please let me explain what will happen next. In the next few weeks, you will have to pay Amber Sun the first of the four instalments. You will pay four payments in total over the next year. The first payment is for the foundations, the second is for the walls, the other one is for the roof and the last payment is for all of the interiors.' Then he laughed out loud. 'Just kidding, Janet, what I mean is, you have got twelve months or one year to pay the full amount to Amber Sun.'

I was so happy that we had finally found a fabulous two-bedroom, two-bathroom dream holiday home in the sun, and that we were the only customers to have been given a whole year to pay for it, and we did not have to pay the full amount upfront because it was off plan. I could not stop smiling to myself. I looked up to see if Mick was on his way back when I noticed a few of the other dream holiday home hopefuls were looking towards me and smiling with a little envy in their eyes. I could also see a few of the other sales reps talking to each other, but they were not smiling at all; they were just giving me a disappointing look!

Nevertheless, I smiled at them and waited for Mick and Christopher to come back into the room. Then it hit me like a lightning bolt. *Oh my God, what have I done? Mick had only gone to the toilet and to get Christopher, he couldn't have been gone for more than ten minutes and I bought a holiday home in Bulgaria. Where the bloody hell is Bulgaria? Oh my God, what have I done? What am I going to do?*

Then the big white double doors opened, I could see that Mick was looking for me, but I was at the back of the room amongst all of the administration tables. I stood up and waved my hand to encourage him to walk towards me. He walked across the room and passed by all of the customers and sales reps as if he was walking up a very steep hill. As he got close to me, he shouted, 'Are you ready to go to the lakes now, Janet? Christopher and I have been waiting in the reception for you, what has taken you so long?' They felt the smile on my face turn into dismay and disbelief.

What have I done?

Mick could see by my face that I was not ready to leave. 'What is going on, Janet?'

My big smile had well and truly disappeared. As I looked across the room, I could see that all of the other dream holiday home hopefuls and the envious sales were all starting to look away, then our sales rep got up to move away. I think he knew it would be a good time for him to disappear, while I updated Mick about the new apartment I had just bought in Bulgaria (where the bloody hell is Bulgaria?).

Before he left, the sales rep whispered, 'Mr G, err, Janet, I will give you five minutes to explain to your husband what has just happened, then I will have to come back to the table because Mr Gorry has got to sign all of the paperwork too.' Then he dashed off like Usain Bolt, breaking the 100-metre world record in the Beijing Olympics (2008).

Mick looked at me as I sat back down on my chair at the table like a deflated balloon. 'What does that mean, what paperwork is he talking about? What has happened, Janet?' Mick looked very worried.

'Please, sit down on the chair, Mick, I have got something to tell you.' Mick reluctantly sat down.

'Michael, while you were gone, I found this fabulous apartment.'

Mick looked at me with anger in his eyes. 'What do you mean you found a fabulous apartment? I have only been out of the room for two minutes, you can't have bought anything, Janet, you've not had enough time! Please tell me what you have done.' I knew he was not happy at all, so I looked down at the table and I tried to explain.

'Well, Michael, I was just about to follow you out of the big white double doors when I noticed a little table in the corner of the room.' I pointed to the table that was advertising Amber Sun apartments. 'It has got some fantastic two-bedroom holiday homes in Bulgaria, at a brilliant price that we can afford.'

Mick looked at me. 'Bulgaria, where is Bulgaria? You have never ever mentioned wanting to go to Bulgaria on holiday before, why now?'

By this time, I could see the blood vessels in his eyes starting to protrude that were once pure white. I grabbed his arm and stood up from the table. 'Please, Mick, come and see the apartment. You will love it; it has two bedrooms, two bathrooms, it overlooks a lovely swimming pool, and it is very close to the Black Sea coast.'

As I was dragging him to the table in the corner of the room, I tried to repeat everything that the sales rep had said to me as quickly as possible to stop him from walking out of the room! When we got close to the table, I could see the Amber Sun brochure. 'Mick, that's the location, and the apartments are out of this world.'

When we got to the table, he could see everything, and he started to calm down. He picked up the brochure. 'Amber Sun, I have never heard of them before, does this place have a golf course?'

Then I heard our sales rep shouting out from behind another table that was close by. 'No, not yet, Mr Gorry, but some of the top golfers are going to design a course not too far from this location.' Then he disappeared again.

I could see by Mick's face and eyes that his mood had

started to soften, so I smiled at him. He looked back at me, but he did not smile.

'Did you say this apartment has two bedrooms and two bathrooms, Janet?'

At that point, the sales rep seized the moment to come back. 'Please come with me, Mick, I will take you to look at the plans, Mr Gorry. You are an incredibly lucky man. The location and the property your lovely wife Janet has chosen for you is simply perfect, but you will have to hurry up and sign the paperwork because they are selling like hot cakes today.'

Mick and the rep walked back to the administration tables, while I stayed for a little while looking at some additional information on Bulgaria. The country looked amazing, it was not what I expected, it was just perfect.

By the time I got back to the table, Mick had just started to go through the information pack, he was talking to the rep about the details and referring to the Apollon site plans as he went through it with a fine-tooth comb. I decided to go and get Christopher from the reception area so that Mick and I could break the good news to him.

Mick and Christopher were both happy with all the information regarding our new two-bedroom, two-bathroom apartment, overlooking the swimming pool by the Black Sea coast. The sales rep poured Mick a very large white coffee with two sugars before he completed all of the documentation and he signed for the fantastic once-in-a-lifetime finance options.

Within a few minutes, all of the legal documents were completed and our dream home in the sun was now a reality. When the sales rep turned to both of us, he had the biggest smile on his face. 'Mr M Gorry and Mrs J Gorry, you are now the proud owners of an amazing holiday home in Bulgaria.'

Mick, Christopher, then I shook his hand and turned towards the double doors and we all walked out of the room with our heads held high in the sky.

When we left the hotel to make our way to the car, it was pouring down with rain. We ran as fast as we could to get into the car without getting soaking wet because we had left all our coats in the car. But the rain didn't bother me. I left the Thistle Hotel with one of the biggest smiles on my face to continue our journey to the lakes, before our Sunday lunch dried up in the casserole dishes.

Mick drove the car out of the car park and he had no problem manoeuvring the car around the roundabout back onto the M6 motorway. Once we were safely driving along the M6. I decided to go through all the documentation regarding Bulgaria and our new property to make sure it was all right. Mick turned Smooth Radio off while I read out all the interesting points about Bulgaria. None of us could believe that we were only just reading about a country where we had just bought our first holiday home.

We were all so happy that we did not realise that we had passed Wigan, Preston, Blackpool, Lancaster, Morecambe Bay, South Cumbria, and before we knew it, we were in Bowness-on-Windermere. When we reached the lake, Mick parked the car in our usual place. When I looked outside the window, I noticed that it was still pouring down with rain. We got out of the car and hurried to put on all of our wet gear before our nice clothes got wet.

The weather was dreadful, the rain was hitting my face and the strong winds were howling and gusting all around us it was a terrible storm, but the weather did not seem to matter to any of us. We just carried on walking around the lake, as if the sun were shining, talking to each other about owning our first dream holiday home in Bulgaria.

After about an hour or so of walking around the lake in the heavy rain and gale-force winds, and when Christopher had finished feeding the ducks what was left of our soggy brown bread. We decided to make our way back to the car to drive home for a lovely hot roast dinner. When we got back to the car, Christopher was delighted because he had all of the back seat of the car to himself, because Mick had managed to squeeze all the wet clothes into the boot of the car. Mick put his seat belt on and drove the car through the local traffic onto the A590, then onto the M6.

None of us could stop talking about all the wonderful things we wanted to do in Bulgaria. Then the car came to a sudden stop, we all stopped talking to see what was going on. The traffic going south towards Lancashire was at a standstill, nothing was moving, the heavy rain was hammering against the car's windscreen and the visibility was so bad that I could not make out if it was a car or lorry ahead of us.

The motorway traffic was at a standstill for about forty minutes, but we did not mind at all, we were all in holiday home heaven. Then suddenly, the traffic started to move along the motorway at a slow but steady pace. As Mick drove towards Lancashire, I could see that several cars had been in a very bad crash and all the emergency services had arrived with their blue lights on and they were all lined up on the hard shoulder.

Mick continued driving along the M6, after a mile or two there was also an overturned lorry on the hard shoulder by the side of the motorway near Lancashire University, it looked like the driver had gotten out safely because he was standing behind the barriers. Mick carried on driving and we all sat in silence because some of the traffic was moving far too fast in the rain and there were a number of terrible drivers breaking the speed limit trying to get to their destination as quickly as possible.

Then suddenly, we came to a standstill again. I looked at Mick. 'Oh my god, I bet one of those terrible drivers has hit something.' Then I saw what had caused the crash. At the left of the carriage way, there was a severely damaged caravan, just outside the M55 slip road to Blackpool. It looked like a car had hit the side of the caravan as it joined the M6, and it had been knocked over onto the hard shoulder.

Mick looked at me. 'No one is going anywhere for a while now, Janet; we will have to wait for the motorway police and the emergency services to arrive before we can continue our journey home.' We all looked at each other. 'OK, what's the first thing you are going to do in our new apartment?'

Christopher leant forward from the back seat of the car. 'I am going to spend all day in the pool.'

Mick and I both said, 'We will join you, son' at the same time.

We each took it in turns to tell each other about the things we would love to do in our new holiday home in the sun.

It was dark by the time we arrived home. As I opened the front door, I could smell something burning, and as I opened the kitchen door there was a big cloud of smoke, the air in the kitchen was covered with a grey haze. As soon as I opened the big oven's door, the oven light came on, and I could see that all our beautiful Sunday roast dinner was cremated, the vegetables had dried up and turned black, the roast beef was like a dehydrated beef burger and the roasting tin and casserole dishes were all jet black! It was that bad I decided to throw it all away, including the casserole dishes and roasting tin before Mick could see it.

I took everything out of the oven as fast as I could, then I opened the conservatory door to let all of the smoke out of the kitchen. I grabbed a tea towel and picked up the burnt casserole dishes and roasting tin and I started to run to the bin to get rid of the burnt offerings, but Christopher caught me.

'Bloody hell, Mum, that looks terrible, we can't eat that. What are we going to have for Sunday dinner now? I am starving.'

I looked at him and whispered, 'I'm not sure, son, what do you fancy?'

He grinned at me. 'Let us have a pizza, Mum, a Mediterranean one to keep us in the holiday mood.'

I continued to run to the bin before Mick caught sight of the cremated roast. 'That sounds wonderful, Chris, please order it while I am busy throwing this away before your dad sees it.'

He made his way back into the kitchen.

'Good evening, is that the pizza takeaway, I would like to order the largest Mediterranean pizza you have, please.'

I was on my way back from the bin by the time he had finished the order. 'How much is it, son? Tell them I will pay for it when it arrives.'

He put the phone down and looked inside the oven.

'That oven will need a good clean before you put anything else in it.'

I looked inside the oven and it was covered in a black mess from the burnt food. 'Please don't tell your dad about the burnt roast, you know what he is like about wasting food, just tell him we did not fancy it any more.'

After buying a property in Bulgaria, we felt like we needed a Mediterranean meal to keep us in the holiday mood.

Roller Coaster Ride

When I woke up the following morning, my first thought was, *Oh my God, what have we done?* I could not believe my emotions were up and down like a rollercoaster ride. *I think we should have gone to Blackpool, instead of the lakes; it was like being on The Big One.*

During that morning, Mick and I were very happy, the next minute we were sad, because we were worried about buying the apartment in a country we did not know and the risk of being ripped off. Despite all our mixed emotions, I decided to telephone the Halifax Bank to make an appointment with the bank manager to sort out our finances. While the phone was ringing, my thoughts started to turn negative again.

'Oh my God, Mick, what are we going to do if the bank doesn't give us the money?'

He walked over to where I was standing and looked at me. 'We have no choice now, Janet, the bank will have to give us the money because you have signed all of the legal papers!'

A voice on the other end of the phone stopped my negative thoughts.

'Hello, you have reached the Halifax Bank, Widnes, how can I help you?'

I put on my poshest voice. 'Hello, my husband and I would like to arrange a meeting with the bank manager to discuss our finances.' I looked at Mick and crossed my fingers.

The woman from Halifax replied, 'You are in luck, the

manager has just had a cancellation. If it is convenient with you, I could fit you in tomorrow at twelve p.m. What are your names and account details?'

I could not believe it.

'That would be wonderful.' I looked at Mick and gave him the thumbs up. I gave her all the information the bank required and I put the phone down. 'We have got an appointment for twelve p.m. tomorrow, Mick.'

He turned the volume down on the TV and smiled.

'Great news, fingers crossed that it all goes well.' Then he carried on watching the golf.

I made my way into the kitchen to clean the big oven. As I opened the door, the light of the day showed me how badly burnt the glass door and the interior walls were. I went to the cupboard under the sink and picked up a large tin of Mr Muscles oven cleaner and sprayed it all over the door, wall and shelves. I spent the afternoon scrubbing the oven clean. I knew what I was doing physically, but my mind was in Bulgaria.

We went to bed quite early that night to get a good night's sleep, but instead of sleeping peacefully I found it very difficult to fall asleep. I kept thinking of all the things that could go wrong. *What if the bank manager says no? What if Amber Sun is not a real company? What if the property does not exist? What if we lose all of our money? What if we don't like Bulgaria? Why didn't I check everything out first? Why did we buy this bloody property?* Every thought created its own hour of sleeplessness.

Good Investment?

The following morning, Mick and I got up quite early. Mick took Christopher to school while I made breakfast. We sat in the conservatory eating our bacon on toast, neither of us mentioning Bulgaria and the "what ifs". The silence was making me feel quite nervous. I washed the breakfast dishes and made my way upstairs to get a shower before our dreaded meeting with the bank manager.

When Mick and I walked into our first ever meeting with the bank manager. (Even when we bought our first home and sorted out the mortgage it was never with the manager, it was always with another member of their team). We were both nervous as we walked towards the help desk, I felt my hands and legs trembling so I held onto Mick's hand to help me feel a little bit stronger.

'Hello, good morning. We have an appointment with the bank manager at twelve p.m.'

The woman from behind the customer service desk smiled at us then looked down at her computer. 'Please can you tell me your names.'

I looked at Mick and he looked back at me, then we both said our names at the same time. 'We are Mr and Mrs Gorry. G-O-double R-Y.'

The woman smiled back at us then clicked the mouse on her computer several times, then she looked up at the both of us. 'There you are, Mr and Mrs Gorry. The manager is just with another customer, please take a seat there next to the glass-framed office.' She pointed to a space at the back of the bank and smiled.

Mick and I sat down and waited outside the manager's office for about five minutes, then the office door opened and two people left. A middle-aged man walked over to where we were sitting. He was quite tall with brown hair, his eyes were blue and he had a nice smile.

'Good afternoon, Mr and Mrs Gorry. Please follow me to my office and take a seat in front of my desk.'

Mick and I sat down on the blue leather chairs. I looked across the table to the manager with a lot of apprehension in mind.

The manager smiled at the both of us then he picked up his pen and asked, 'How can I help you today?'

I started to talk as fast as I could. 'Hello, sir, we have bought an apartment in Bulgaria and we would like to release some equity from our home to pay for it.' I think I had been going over everything during the night and all the following morning, it just came bursting out of me!

I think I caught the manager off guard because he paused for a second or two before he replied, 'Bulgaria, what made you buy an apartment there?'

Without any hesitation, I told him about the information the sales rep gave me. 'It is a lovely place; it is unspoilt by tourism and an excellent investment.' I also went through all the marketing spiel trying to convince him that what we were asking for was a very good financial option. When I had finished blurting everything I could remember, he stopped writing and turned his chair to face his computer, then he switched it on.

'OK, Mr and Mrs Gorry. Let us look at what we can do for you?'

Once the computer had booted up, he found the right document to complete before he could give us an answer. Mick and I had to answer numerous questions about our employment status, weekly/monthly earnings, everyday finances, our social activities and savings. It felt like we were under interrogation, but I knew he was being extra thorough because of the location. For extra evidence, I showed the manager the A4 folder advertising Amber Sun apartments and the Apollon Complex, including the plans for the two-bedroom apartment we were hoping to buy. He looked through the folder as if he was going to buy the property, stopping at a few pages to look at the additional information. When he had finished with the folder, he handed it back to Mick.

'Right, Michael and Janet, you have completed all of the questions, I just have to go into another office to discuss this information with our head office in Warrington. They will have to give their approval first. It shouldn't take too long.'

Mick and I thanked him for his time as he was leaving the office, but before he opened the door, he turned back. My heart sank. 'Sorry, I forgot to ask if you wanted a hot drink?'

Mick replied quite fast, 'Yes, please, Janet will have a white coffee with no sugar, and I will have a white tea with one sugar please.'

My heart missed a beat, but it was not over yet. When the manager had left the room, Mick looked at me. 'My God, Janet, all those questions have made me very thirsty.'

Mick and I both sat quietly for a moment looking out of the office window. I watched all the people shopping on the high street, but I did not pay any attention to what they were doing or buying. All I could think about was *What if he says no?*

Mick looked towards me and I looked back at him. I think we were both thinking the same things, but we did not want to say anything out loud in case it became true. I had my fingers, arms and legs crossed, hoping that the manager would get approval from their head office in Warrington.

After a few minutes, the manager returned with our hot drinks, but he did not say anything; he just put them down on the table and walked away. I think we could have done with two large vodka and tonics to calm our nerves, but tea and coffee was all we had.

Mick and I were both very nervous because we had never done anything like this before and to be honest, I do not think we would do it again! I picked up my cup of coffee and started to drink it, then I heard a loud ding, which seemed to be coming from the manager's computer. We both looked towards the desk as the manager entered the room. He sat down in his big leather chair then he pressed a few keys on his keyboard and the printer started to light up.

'Right, Mr and Mrs Gorry. That sounds like the outcome to your request, please let me take a look.'

He sat facing the computer for a few moments, reading all the information on his computer screen then he looked up, and turned his chair towards Mick and me. I looked at his face, but I could not tell what the outcome was. My heart was beating like a drum. I grabbed Michael's hand and he held mine.

'Congratulations, Mr and Mrs Gorry. Your equity loan has been approved.'

Mick and I stood up at the same time to shake his hand. 'Thank you, kind sir, thank you so very much.'

As we started to leave the room, he shouted, 'Hold on, Mr

and Mrs Gorry. There is one more thing that you will need to do before the money is transferred into your account. You have to set up a new online bank account with one of our "online banking assistants" downstairs. Once this is completed, you will be able to transfer the quarterly payments to Amber Sun.'

Mick and I could not believe it, we left our hot drinks in his office and made our way to the online banking assistant. The manager followed behind us, until we got back into the main area of the bank, then he overtook us to show us where the online assistant was sitting.

'Hi, Mary. This is Michael and Janet, Mr and Mrs Gorry. They want to open an online bank account.' After the manager had introduced us to the young woman, he walked towards the customer services counter to meet his next customer.

The online banking assistant had long black hair, brown eyes and thick black-rimmed glasses covering most of her face. She was medium height with a very slim figure and good looking.

'Good afternoon, Mr and Mrs Gorry. Would it be OK if I called you Michael and Janet?'

Mick smiled at her. 'Yes, please, you can call me Mick.'

She looked at Mick. 'Brilliant, please follow me, Mick.'

I followed both of them to a small blue wooden partition at the other side of the bank, facing the outside window to commence the online banking process.

Mick sat down opposite Mary's desk and Mary turned her computer on. I stood behind Mike, waiting for Mary to get me a chair to sit on, but she did not get a chair for me. Without any hesitation, she started to ask Mick a lot of individual questions which took longer than all of the questions the manager asked, then she turned to me. 'Would you like a seat, Mrs Gorry?' I could not believe it.

'No, thank you!' Then she started asking me all of the same questions as she asked Mick. When all the questions were finished, she asked Mick, then me, to type our secret passwords into the keypad, then we had to set up a security question without either person knowing the answer. By the time we had finished all the online banking applications, my nerves were well and truly shattered.

When we left the bank, the fresh air hit me; it was like a cool breeze on a hot summer's day. Mick suggested going for coffee, something to eat and to catch up on everything before he had to go to work. I found a seat by the window in Cassandra's Cafe, while Mike went to find the menus. When Mick returned, the waitress took our order. When our drinks arrived, Mick and I celebrated with a nice cup of coffee. It all felt quite surreal.

'Well done, Mick, we have finally bought a holiday home in Bulgaria. I did not think this day would ever happen.'

Mick put his cup of coffee down on the table and looked at me. 'Nor did I, Janet, I would have never considered buying anything in Bulgaria.'

Amber Sun

The following week, a woman telephoned, her voice was husky and I could tell she came from London because of the cockney accent.

'Hello, is that Mrs Gorry?'

I hesitated for a moment because I did not know who it was.

'Yes, it's Janet Gorry.'

She continued, 'My name is Sharon and I am the overseas managing agent for Amber Sun.'

I grabbed a pen and paper to write down whatever she was about to tell me.

'Mrs Gorry. I would like to take this opportunity to thank you and Mr Gorry for buying one of Amber Sun's beautiful apartments in Bulgaria. Would it be convenient to go through the documentation you both signed at the Thistle Hotel?'

I got the folder from the bookshelf containing a copy of the information that we had signed at the hotel.

'Yes, it is a good time to go through the information, I have been waiting for your phone call.' I opened the folder, took all the documents out, laid them on the desk and held the pen in my right hand, ready to take notes of our conversation.

'Right, Mrs Gorry, I can confirm that the apartment that you have bought is "off-plan", that means it would take up to a whole year before it would be completed.'

When I had finished writing my notes, I replied, 'Is that

why we got the once-in-a-lifetime offer regarding the finance options?'

She laughed. 'No, Janet, that offer is open to everyone who bought a property off-plan.'

If she could have seen my face, it was like thunder after what the sales rep had said at the Thistle hotel! 'Please, can you tell me about the Apollon Complex, the Bulgarian builders and the quality standards of their work?' I asked her all the questions that had been keeping me awake almost every night since we bought the property.

'The builder's name is Mr Kostov. He was one of the finest builders in the whole of Bulgaria, and the quality standards in Bulgaria are similar to the UK's building standards.'

Then she continued, 'The Apollon Complex is situated in Old Nessebar, it is one of the best apartment complexes on the Black Sea coast. The quality of Mr Kostov's work is second to none. You and Mr Gorry are two incredibly lucky people to buy a two-bedroom, two-bathroom apartment overlooking a pool and such a short distance from the sea for such a low price.'

I thanked her for letting Mick and I buy such a wonderful apartment.

'Mrs Gorry. Do you have time to go through the process of transferring the money through our online banking system, so that you can pay the first instalment today?'

I was a bit shocked by her request, I thought she would want to find out a little bit more about our experience at the Thistle Hotel?

'Sharon, before I made the first online payment, the sales representative mentioned the choice of buying a full furniture package.'

She paused for a moment and I could hear papers shuffling

on the other end of the phone. 'Just a minute, Mrs Gorry, I just have to find the right documentation.'

I held my pen ready to write down what she said about the package.

'Right, Mrs Gorry, the package you mentioned includes a genuine leather two-seater sofa and large sofa bed, coffee table and rug, TV with a stand, two wall cabinets and TV cabinet. Fully fitted kitchen with oven and hob, an extractor van, sink with a mixer taps and bowl. All the utensils, pots, pans, roasting tins, and casserole dishes. A table and four chairs. Fully fitted en suite with shower and wet room with floor-to-ceiling tiling. One king-size bed in the master bedroom with two side drawers and a big wardrobe to match. Two single beds with matching drawers and wardrobes in the second bedroom. Floor tiling throughout and venetian blinds on the windows, and all the soft furnishings including bedding and towels, including hand towels, face clothes and tea towels.' The list seemed to be endless.

After a few moments after finishing off my notes and picturing what everything would look like in the apartment, I was ready to reply. 'Sharon, please can you tell me how much this furniture package will cost?'

I heard papers shuffling in the background again. 'Wait a minute, Mrs Gorry. Right, I have got the list, the cost of all those items I mentioned is £5000.00.' I dropped the pen. 'Wow, that is really good value for money.'

I tried to add everything up in my head but there was just too much to calculate, I needed more time. 'Sharon, would you mind if I spoke to my husband first, I would like to discuss it with him when he comes home from work this afternoon.'

The last thing I wanted to do was to fully furnish the

apartment while Mick was at work and without his agreement.

'That's not a problem, Mrs Gorry. However, you will have to ring me back before five p.m. today, on the Amber Sun, UK office number to make your first payment.'

To be honest, I was a bit worried about making the first payment without Mick. 'That's great, thank you Sharon. Mick finishes work at three p.m.; therefore, I will call you back before four p.m.'

There was no reply. 'OK, Mrs Gorry, I will be waiting to take your first payment.'

When Mick got in from work, I told him about the furniture package and the conversation I had with Sharon. We both agreed that the furniture package was excellent value for money and a good option for us. Our dream home would have everything we needed, and it would be ready to move into within a year's time.

I could not wait to telephone Sharon on the number she provided to give her the approval for the furniture package and make the first payment on the apartment. I dialled the number and she picked the phone up straight away.

'Hello, Mrs Gorry. Are you ready to make your first payment?'

Mick was standing next to me listening to what she said.

'Hi, Sharon, Mick has agreed with the furniture package.' And we gave each other the thumbs up.

'Right, Janet, the extra £5000 will be added to your amber sun finance account, which is fabulous; this means you can pay for the furniture package over the next twelve months.'

I sat down on the chair next to the desk to go through the notes on making a payment.

'Right, Mrs Gorry, are you ready to make your first

payment?'

I looked at Mick and he nodded his head. 'Let's do it, Sharon.'

She took me through all the online banking details again to ensure the first instalment for the foundations and floor tiling were paid. With a little bit of hesitation and with our fingers crossed, Mick and I made our first online bank transfer.

Within a few seconds of the transaction being complete, I became very nervous again. 'Oh my God, Mick, what if Amber Sun is a fake company, what if these apartments don't exist, what if we lose all of our money, what have we done?'

Mick turned and looked at me. 'No, Janet, what have you done!'

With his words echoing in my ear, I telephoned Amber Sun to talk to Sharon again. The phone rang, *ring, ring, ring, ring* what seemed to be for ages, then a man answered. 'Good afternoon, it's Paul here, how can I help you?'

I looked out of the bedroom window, because I did not want to see Mick's face. 'Hello, Paul, can I talk to Sharon, your overseas managing agent, please?'

The man on the phone sounded very professional. 'Good afternoon, please may I take your first name?'

Without any delay, I replied, 'Yes, my name is Janet. Mrs Gorry. I have just spoken to Sharon. She has got our money, where has she gone!'

The man seemed a little bit hesitant. 'Just a moment, Janet, Sharon is on the other line.'

I did not move, I just stood there waiting for her to end her call and talk to me. My first thoughts were *Oh my god, what is she spending our money on?*

After a few minutes had passed, I heard her voice. 'Hello

49

again, Mrs Gorry. It is Sharon speaking, how can I help you?'

Without any hesitation, I spoke, 'Yes, Sharon, it is Mrs Gorry. I am just phoning to make sure the online payment has been transferred to Amber Sun. Please, can you check? And I would like you to send me an email and hard copy of the receipt by post for the first payment that I have made to Amber Sun today.' My voice was very firm.

'Hold on a second, Mrs Gorry. While I go and check with our finance department.'

Time had stopped still for Mick and me.

'Mrs Gorry, it is good news, Janet, your first payment of four instalments has just shown up on our banking system. Is there anything else I can help you with?'

I felt a little bit better and I noticed that the time had started to move on again. 'That is great news, Sharon, please can you send a confirmation receipt by email, and put a hard copy of the receipt in the post and send it to our home address today?'

There was no hesitation. 'That is not a problem, Mrs Gorry. I will do that now. You should receive an email in seconds and I will send the hard copy by first class post tonight.'

'Great news, Sharon, before you go, please would you send Mick and I some pictures of the Apollon apartments as they progress, would it be great to get regular updates from Amber Sun?'

Her voice sounded a bit weary. 'Yes, Mrs Gorry. I will do that tomorrow.'

With my trust in Amber Sun restored, I put the telephone down and ran downstairs into the living room to update Mick about the receipts and the up-to-date pictures.

'Great news, Mick, Sharon has emailed a receipt of the first payment and she is going to send us some pictures of the apartment block as it develops.'

Mick looked relieved. 'I hope it's not pictures of somewhere in Turkey or Spain.'

The following day, Sharon emailed some wonderful overhead photographs of the Apollon apartment block. The photos showed the foundations being laid, there was a big L shape of cement, then a large square attached to a small square on the ground in front of the L shape block which looked like the swimming pools. As I looked beyond the foundations and pool, I could see a long road with several buildings on every side which looked like small hotels and shops. As my eyes crossed the road, I was drawn to the Black Sea coast. The beach was empty, there was no one sunbathing on the lovely golden sand, and there was no one swimming in the beautiful emerald green sea, it looked amazing.

After a while of looking at the wonderful seaside, my eyes took me back to the L-shaped foundations and just behind the building, where I could see what looked like a massive aqua park. There were several cars parked in the car park, but I could not tell if anyone was on the rides, it looked spectacular and it was within walking distance from the apartment. I was so excited; I could not wait to show Mick and Christopher the pictures when they came home.

When Mick's car pulled onto the driveway, I ran out of the front door. 'Look, Mick, Amber Sun has sent some photos, come and see what we have paid for, the foundations have been laid.'

Mick opened the car door and smiled at me. 'I hope so, Janet, I hope you're right and it's not some other building from God knows where.'

My excitement seemed to fade away for a moment.

'No, Mick, you can tell it is the Apollon Complex, because it looks like the picture on the A4 folder. You know the one we got from the sales rep. Come in and look, you can see the L-shaped building and the two swimming pools.'

Mick followed me into the house. I could not wait to show him the photographs. 'Look at the big square,' and I pointed at the photo. 'This must be the adult pool and there, that little square is the kiddies' pool. Look, you can see the two swimming pools.'

When I turned around, Mick was still taking his work jacket off and trying to hang it under the stairs.

'I will look at them soon, just give me a minute, Janet. Will you go and put the kettle on while I get changed out of my working gear?'

While Mick went upstairs to get changed, I walked into the kitchen to make him a nice drink of tea. While the kettle was boiling, I placed all the pictures across the kitchen counter so that he could see them as soon as he walked into the room. From a distance, they looked like someone's holiday photographs. I heard him coming down the stairs.

'Right, Janet, let's see those photos, and can you pass me my cup of tea?'

I was standing waiting for him in the kitchen. 'They are here on the counter, Mick.' I pointed to all the photos and smiled at him.

'Bring them into the living room, Janet, I am going to put the TV on.'

I grabbed the photos and his cup of tea and ran into the living room. 'Look, Mick, you can tell it is the apartment we bought. Look, it has got the L-shaped building, two pools; look, there is the beach and guess what?'

Mick took a sip of his tea and looked at it from above his cup. 'What?'

I smiled at him. 'Our apartment is not only within walking distance of the beach, but it is also remarkably close to an aqua park. Look, you can see it in these pictures.' I passed all the photos to him and he looked back at me.

'This could be anywhere for all you know, Janet.'

'No, you are wrong, Mick, I know this is our apartment, I can tell by those photos because they are the same as ones on the A4 folder.'

He started to laugh at me. 'OK, love, why don't you throw this cup of tea away and pour us a nice glass of wine each to celebrate?'

***

Just before the second instalment was due, I received a few more photos from Sharon. The photos showed the pool being built and the apartment walls going up around the L-shaped building. These photographs of the development looked more like the ones on the front page of the A4 folder, the one that the sales rep provided at the Thistle Hotel. I was ecstatic.

However, this did not last long! After the second instalment was transferred, Mick and I just happened to watch a horrible TV program on the BBC. The programme was about people from the UK being ripped off by overseas development companies, who were marketing new holiday home developments in beautiful locations that did not exist. It showed a middle-aged couple who had invested all their life savings in a luxury apartment in Cyprus. But when they went to visit their new apartment, all they found was an empty building site; there was no development and they could not find anyone to hold to account for the fraud. As a result, they lost all their money, their hopes and dreams. As a reaction to this programme, all my negative thoughts started to resurface!

Mick and I had travelled to so many wonderful places in the world, but we had never visited Bulgaria. I could not understand why we/I had bought a property in a place where we had never visited before and I had never heard of Amber Sun prior to the Thistle hotel. For all I knew, it could be the same sales company as the one on the BBC, which was ripping off loads of people in the UK, and who the hell was this woman called Sharon who had taken half of our money in return for a few photographs? Could Mick actually be right, the buildings on the photographs could be anywhere in the world? Without seeing or touching the apartment in Bulgaria, I would never be convinced that it was real, never mind our holiday home in the sun.

With this constant negativity on both mine and Mick's minds, and too many sleepless nights, we decided to book our very first ever holiday to Bulgaria, to make sure that the Apollon Complex existed, and that the L-shaped apartment block with two swimming pools near the Black Sea coast was actually being built.

Not knowing much about Bulgaria or Old Nessebar, I booked a last minute all-inclusive four-star hotel close to Sunny Beach for one week.

We packed our suitcases. Chris, Mick and I headed to Manchester airport and waited patiently for our flight to depart.

Bulgarian Breakfast

Whilst we were waiting for our flight at Manchester Airport, none of us were excited. This holiday felt quite different; it was not like we were going on one of our normal trips to somewhere wonderful to spend our time having lots of fun in the sun, it was as if we were going on a mission. Our sole purpose was to find the Apollon Complex and visit our apartment before we paid the third instalment.

When we boarded the plane, we all sat together hoping the flight would take off as soon as possible, so that we could finally find out if we had been ripped off. The flight to Bulgaria was only three hours and fifteen minutes' long, but it felt a lot longer because of the anxiety surrounding our visit. I think we all wanted to know if we/I had done the right thing.

When the plane landed on the runway, it felt like it had landed on an old cobbled road because the plane was being knocked from side to side. The safety belt light was flashing and when I looked at Mick and Christopher, I could see they were holding onto their seats to prevent them from swaying. When the plane finally stopped on the runway, everyone started to clap their hands with relief.

Then the pilot came over the Tannoy. 'Good afternoon, this is your captain, please allow me to apologise for the bumpy landing.' Then he gestured. 'The owners of Bourgas Airport will be getting the runway fixed before your return flight home, hopefully!' Then the seatbelt sign went off.

Mick stood up and got our hand luggage from out of the overhead locker. I looked out of the window to see how we were getting off the plane, it looked like the ground crew were preparing some big step ladders at the left hand side of the plane. As I looked down towards the ground, I could see that there were lots of blue and white buses waiting to shuttle all of the passengers over to the airport terminal.

Within a few minutes, everyone started to disembark from the plane. Mick, Chris and I made our way towards the main door. We thanked the air hostesses for their time on the flight, then one by one we stepped from the plane onto the steps. As I walked down the first few steps towards the ground and the waiting buses, I could feel and smell the Bulgarian air for the first time. It was very different from the chilly cold air I had left in Manchester. The air felt nice and warm as it brushed over my face.

Mick grabbed hold of my hand and I held Christopher close to me to make sure we all stayed together. As soon as our feet touched the floor, a very mature bus driver pointed to us to get onto the first bus. We started to run over to the first bus, because all the other passengers were rushing past us to make sure they got to the bus and the airport terminal first.

We were going so fast that we all jumped on the bus together causing a bit of a sticking point between us and the bus's doors. Mick found a pole for all of us to hold on to because there were only ten chairs, five at the front of the bus and the same at the back. The seats at the back had a number of elderly people sitting with their hand luggage and the front seats had a few young mothers with their babies in arms.

As everyone waited for the bus to move, I noticed the bus driver was telling more and more people to get onto this bus.

He crammed so many people onto the bus that by the time he was finished we were all packed like sardines in a tin can. It was as if the bus drivers were having a competition to see who could fit the most people in their bus, or were they saving time and money by doing fewer trips?

The drive from the plane to the airport was very hot and sticky, because we were all so close to each other, I could smell the body odour of some of the holiday makers around me and it was not very pleasant. When the bus finally stopped outside the arrival's terminal, the doors opened and everyone tried to squeeze past each other to get off first. I looked down at my lovely white cotton summer dress and it was full of creases as a result of being that close to so many people in a small space.

When we entered the airport, I noticed that it was vastly different from any of the other European and Caribbean airports that we had visited on our unusual annual holidays; it seemed exceedingly small and it looked like one of those concrete buildings you see in some of those old 1940s war movies. Mick held Christopher's hand as we started to walk forward. When we got near the border control, several lines started to form in front of us. I got our passports out of my bag while we were waiting in the queue.

For the first time, I started to look around the terminal building. I became aware that there were several armed police watching the new arrivals, it was as if they were waiting for someone to step out of line so that they could arrest them. When we got to the passport officer, I handed the young man three passports. The man behind the glass screen had jet black hair, brown eyes and a nice tan. His shirt was white, with perfect creases going down the sleeves (not like my dress).

He looked at each of the passports, then at each of our

faces, then he looked me up and down, then he looked at the passport again, then he stared into my eyes to make sure that I was the same person that was in the photograph. He repeated the same procedure with Michael, then Christopher. When he had finished all his passport security checks, he waved us through the gate and signalled for the next person to come towards him. The whole process felt very efficient and a bit intimidating. I knew that if there was anything wrong with anyone's passport, the armed police would not hesitate to stop you on the spot!

By the time we had gotten through all the security checks, we were close to the baggage collection area. We moved towards the conveyor belts to locate our baggage. Mick told Chris and I to wait by the seating area while he went to find our luggage. Within a few minutes, Mick came back with the three suitcases.

'Wow, Janet, that was unbelievable. Everyone's suitcases had been taken off the plane, and our luggage was just going around on the carousel. There was no mad rush by everyone, it was brilliant.'

Christopher grabbed his suitcase, and we made our way through towards the exit for new arrivals. As I walked through the first double doors, Mick and Chris were behind me. They were talking about how fast the ground crew got our suitcases off the plane and onto the conveyor belt.

I was looking out for the Thomas Cook representative. As I looked through the crowds of people, I could see that she was waiting by the exit door for all the passages from our flight. She had long blonde hair, blue eyes and a fabulous brown tan. Her Thomas Cook uniform fitted perfectly, but her high-heeled shoes looked like they were very uncomfortable, because she had taken one of them off and I could see a plaster where the shoes had rubbed her heel.

I walked over to her and smiled. 'Hello, we are the Gorry family.'

She looked at me, then spoke, 'Sorry, what is your name again? It has been extremely hot here today, my feet are killing me, I should never have worn these shoes.' She fanned her face with the blue Thomas Cook guest board.

I had not noticed the heat since getting off the plane, but nodded my head in agreement with her. 'We are Mr and Mrs Gorry. G-O-double R-Y.'

She looked down her list then stopped and crossed off our names with her pen. 'That's great news, Mrs Gorry. I have been waiting for you three to arrive. Please follow me this way to your coach, your driver is waiting for you.'

Mick, Chris and I followed her out of the main airport terminal doors. When the doors opened and I walked outside, the heat hit me and the whole atmosphere changed. It made me realise how good the air conditioning must have been in the airport.

Outside the main terminal, I noticed that there were lots of taxi drivers walking and smoking along the pedestrian pathway next to the road, and lots of people were standing around looking for their transport. It felt quite frantic in the early evening sunshine. But the one thing that stood out more than anything was the sound of the Bulgarian language, it sounded quite loud and the dialect was very new to me.

With all the hectic behaviour, I had slowed down and the Thomas Cook rep was looking around for the Gorry family again. 'Please come with me, it is this way, the coach driver has been waiting to take you to your hotel in Sunny Beach.'

59

I started to run behind the rep, Mick and Christopher followed with our suitcases and hand luggage. When we all got to the bus, the driver took our cases and placed them in the hold hall at the side of the bus.

By the time we had gotten onto the bus, it was almost full. Mick and I settled onto the two seats behind the driver and Chris sat down next to the Thomas Cook represented baggage at the front of the bus. As soon as we sat down, I could hear everyone else on the coach clapping to celebrate our arrival. I tried to look out of the window to hide my embarrassment, but I couldn't because the windows were covered with an old blue cloth that covered all of the glass. It felt very strange not being able to see outside. After a while, I managed to move the cloth to one side, like a curtain. As I looked outside, I noticed that the sun was starting to set just behind the main airport terminal where the plane had landed. The sun was like a big red glowing sphere in the clear evening sky.

When all the clapping had finished, the Thomas Cook representative sat down next to Christopher. 'Right, Vladimir, you can go now; all of the customers are on board.' The Thomas Cook rep fixed her skirt then took her shoes off. 'Are you looking forward to your holiday, Master Gorry?' Christopher nodded his head and smiled at her, then looked straight ahead towards the front window before he caught my eye.

On our way out of Bourgas Airport, the coach driver drove past a lot of old planes that had been "laid to rest" within the airport's perimeter. It was not a particularly good image, because it just looked like an old scrap yard for ancient aeroplanes. Before the coach left the airport, the driver had to drive the coach towards a security barrier. When he was stopped, the bus driver paid the man some Bulgarian lev. Then he drove the coach along a road that took us out of the airport onto a big roundabout. He turned right at the roundabout, then up a slip road onto a single-track road, either side of the road looked very rural; it was just empty fields for a few miles.

The driver drove along the main road for a while before I saw any buildings or any sign of life, the whole area felt a bit isolated, then he drove past a few unfinished properties and a few old industrial buildings. I was starting to worry about Bulgaria because it felt quite bleak and underdeveloped.

After about ten minutes, we drove past a wine tavern selling local wines and brandy. I looked at Mick and smiled. 'We can try some of the local wine, Mick.'

He agreed then nodded his head. There were a few tiny houses and some fields with crops planted in them, then I saw a police station just set back from the road, it felt like we were heading into civilization.

The coach driver drove on the road for a few more miles before we came to a little village, then a petrol station and a few roadside cafés and a restaurant. I was feeling a bit more optimistic, it reminded me of some of the Greek islands we had visited in the mid-eighties. He drove through a few more villages and towns, then I noticed that there were a small number of holiday resorts. Every time the coach stopped to let someone off, I looked out for the Apollon Complex, but there was no sign of it yet.

When we arrived at Sunny Beach and our hotel, it was dark. The Thomas Cook rep handed us over to the receptionist. The woman at the reception welcomed us to the hotel, she took our names, then requested our passports. She gave Mick a key to our room, then she showed us to our rooms and then she gave Christopher his key before she started to walk away. 'If you need anything, Gorry family, I will be at the reception all night.'

Mick opened Christopher's door first to ensure his room was nice and clean. Christopher was delighted; he had a large double bed, a big comfortable sofa, TV, and en suite.

'Right, Mum and Dad, you can go now. I am going to settle down for the night, see you both in the morning.'

Mick and I made our way out of the door. Our room was next to Christopher's so we knew he would be safe on his own. Mick opened the door and we walked into the room; it was the same as Christopher's. I walked to the window and looked outside; I could see that there was a lovely pool to the left-hand side of the room. Once I had finished inspecting the bed, wardrobes, drawers and bathroom, Mick and I started to unpack the suitcase. It was quite late by the time we had finished so we decided to have a shower then settle down for the night.

The following morning, Mick and I woke up nice and early. I opened the curtains and looked out of the window, the sun was shining on the pool, it looked lovely. We decided to enjoy a few days at the beach before we started to look for our apartment. We put our swimwear on under our shorts and t-shirts to go for breakfast, then the beach. Mick locked the bedroom door while I knocked next door to see if Christopher wanted to join us. When he answered the door, I could see that he was still exhausted from the journey to Bulgaria.

'Good morning, Mum, what time is it?'

'It's around eight o'clock son.'

'Where are you going?'

Mick stood behind me. 'Morning, Chris, we are going for something to eat.'

Christopher's face dropped. 'I'm still very tired. What time do they stop serving breakfast?'

Mick and I looked at each other. 'I am not sure, son. Stay in bed, we will knock for you later, we will let you have a lie in.'

Mick and I made our way to the lift to find the dining room. When we got out of the lift, the reception area looked quite different in the daylight. There was a different woman behind the reception desk. I heard her talking in broken English to a man and his young daughter about something that happened to them when they were eating their breakfast. I could hear that the man was very upset about an incident that had happened to him. And she was finding it hard to understand whatever he was complaining about.

I tried to catch her attention to ask her for the whereabouts of the dining room. But she was having a lot of difficulty trying to explain what she was going to do about the man's "breakfast mishap" or whatever happened to this man when he went to eat his breakfast. By the time Mick and I had located the breakfast room, we were famished. Mick found an empty table in the middle of the room. I put my beach bag down on the chair and we made our way to the food counters.

When I looked at all the food on display, it was very disappointing; I was not impressed! The fried eggs looked like they were made from rubber, the baked beans were so dried up that they were beginning to look like white beans. The fresh tomatoes were so sloppy and they were full of grease, all the scrambled eggs were floating in greasy water, the so-called "English" bacon was so thin I could see the pattern of the dish underneath, and the "British" sausages were nothing like anything I had seen before!

'Sicken tummy came to mind.'

Mick looked at me, I could see the disappointment in his

eyes. 'You call this a four-star hotel; it is more like a one star! Let us play it safe today, Janet, I don't want to become ill on the first day!'

I was devastated and very hungry. 'We paid extra money for this four-star, all-inclusive hotel. I agree this is definitely not four-star food. Let us play it safe with a boiled egg and some dry toasted bread.'

We walked across to the next table, Mick put an egg and two pieces of toast on his plate, then he poured a load of brown sauce next to the toast. 'This will help to soften the bread, Janet.'

I looked at his plate and the toasted bread looked absolutely solid. I put an egg and a piece of dehydrated toast on my plate and I took both plates to the table while Mick went to get some drinks. When Mick came back, we both sat down at the table. I started to drink my orange juice and Mick started to eat his breakfast.

Mick tried to cut a piece of toast with his knife but he was having some difficulty. Then he tried to chip away at the hard-boiled egg. When he managed to get the top off the egg, he tried to dip a small section of his toast into the hard-boiled egg, but it was so solid it snapped the toast into tiny little pieces and it scattered across the table. Mick picked up another piece of the toast and cut a bit of the egg yolk out of the egg with his knife, then he dipped the toast into the brown sauce and put it towards his mouth, as soon as the sauce touched his lips, he spat it out onto his plate!

I stopped drinking my juice. 'What is wrong, is it horrible? I am definitely not eating mine.'

He spat all of the food out onto the plate. 'No, Janet, it is not horrible, it is bloody chocolate sauce!'

I did not believe him. 'It cannot be the chocolate sauce, Mick, we are having breakfast not pudding.'

He looked across the table at me. 'Yes, it is bloody chocolate sauce, Janet, why would they put a bottle of chocolate sauce next to all the cold boiled eggs and toast?'

At that point, we both turned around and looked towards all the food counters to see if there was a waiter that Mick or I could tell! However, it did not take us long to notice why there had been a mix up with the sauces. Hiding behind a pillar by the cold boiled eggs and toast were two little boys. They were messing around with all the condiments. We watched as they were deliberately mixing everything up and laughing their heads off when their hungry breakfast victims did not get to eat what they thought they were eating. Mick and I both looked over at the young boys and we gave them our worst ever evil eyes, but their tears of laughter stopped them from seeing our nasty looks.

Mick took a tiny sip of his drink just in case there was another disaster, but thankfully it was all right. He had to take a massive drink to get rid of the dreadful taste of chocolate, dehydrated toast, and cold hard-boiled yoke.

'Let us go, Janet, I have had enough of this terrible breakfast.'

We both stood up from the table and made our way to the door. However, before we left the dining room, I gave the naughty boys a very disapproving look!

When we got back to our room, Christopher was just coming out of his room, ready to join us. Mick could not wait to tell him about the naughty boys messing around with the food. When he had finished, he went to our room to brush his teeth. While he was gone, I told Christopher about what had

65

happened when the chocolate sauce hit his dad's lip. As I was telling him about Mick spitting the food on his plate, it made both of us start to laugh out loud; it was so loud it made Mick pop his head from around the bathroom door with the toothbrush still in his mouth.

'I don't think it was that funny, Janet, you wouldn't like it if it happened to you!' I stopped laughing straight away. 'That is true, Mick.'

Christopher had also managed to stop laughing. 'Show me who they are dad and I promise to get back at them for you.'

After Mick had cleaned his teeth and swilled his mouth out with some mouthwash several times, we made our way out of the hotel towards the swimming pool. I could see one of the naughty boys messing around with some other children in the pool. Mick recognised the two of them and he pointed both of them out to Christopher. 'There they are, son, those two with the white t-shirts on.'

Christopher looked at the children then back to his dad.

'OK, Dad, leave it with me and I will sort them out for you.' Then he looked and smiled at me. 'Where are we going today, Mum? I am starving now, are you still hungry, Dad?'

I put the beach bag over my shoulder. 'Let us take a walk to the Black Sea coast, we can have a good look around Sunny Beach, it is supposed to be one of the best beaches in Bulgaria.'

Chris walked by my side and I held Mick's hand as we walked towards the busy main road.

'Mum, do you think there will be a KFC or a cafe that does nice bacon rolls on crusty white bread?'

I stopped at the zebra crossing and pressed the button on the traffic lights to stop the traffic. 'I hope so, Chris, your dad is not going to try anywhere that serves Bulgarian food!'

Sunny Beach was about half a mile away from the hotel. The lovely walk provided a good opportunity to look at the shops, cafés, bars and restaurants before we got to the beach. When we arrived at the Black Sea coast, it looked amazing. We stopped at an English cafe for something proper to eat before we made our way to the beach.

When we finished our food, we walked over to the beach. I can honestly say that it was one of the best beaches that I had ever seen. There were miles and miles of beautiful golden sand. The Black Sea was emerald green and crystal clear. As I looked into the distance, I could see numerous hotels, bars, restaurants and shops all along the pedestrian walkway.

I decided to walk on the hot sand along the water's edge to keep my feet cool in the blazing sunshine. After a mile or so, Mick found the perfect location for us to relax and sunbathe for the day. It was close to the speed boats and jet skis for Christopher. There was a bar close by for Mick and a lovely hotel where I could pop in to use the toilets. Mick and Christopher spent most of the afternoon lying in the sunshine, convincing each other that they had made the right decision to buy our dream holiday home in Bulgaria.

Mick lay on the sunbed with his hands behind his head, taking in all the glory. 'I was the one who drove the car along the M6, and I was the first person to see the sign for holiday homes in the sun and it was my skilful driving that navigated the correct way to the Thistle Hotel; your mother nearly had us going around the roundabout over and over again… And I went to the toilet just at the right time so that your mum could spend more time looking around the room before we had to leave for the lakes.'

Christopher sat on his sunbed taking the credit for not

being in our way and allowing us enough time to find the perfect apartment in peace. 'I knew you were going to find the right place, that's why I waited in the reception area, I did not want to get in your way.' Mick agreed. 'And I did not bother you when you went back into the room to find Mum because you had been waiting ages for her.'

I lay on my sunbed listening to the both of them, they were so happy. I was delighted that we were staying in such a lovely location, and we were miles away from some of the underdeveloped areas that we had seen on the journey from the airport. But I couldn't help myself from wondering where the Apollon Complex was located.

Food-Glorious-Food

After a lovely day relaxing in the sunshine, we made our way back to the hotel. As we were walking, we decided to spend that evening in the hotel's four-star all-inclusive restaurant. By the time we got back to our rooms, the sun was just starting to set over the Black Sea coast. Mick and I took a shower and I put on my best outfit, a tailored black evening dress with gold edging around the sleeves and neckline, for our beautiful ala carte meal with unlimited drinks. I was really looking forward to having a family meal together at the hotel, after a long day at the beach.

Mick put on his best black shorts and his designer t-shirt on, he looked very smart. When we had finished putting our shoes on, we left the room to knock on Christopher's bedroom door to see if he was ready. When he opened the door, I was amazed; he looked gorgeous in his new shorts, t-shirt and trainers. I was immensely proud of both of them. Mick pressed the button for the lift, the doors opened and we took the lift down to the reception area. Mick and I showed Christopher the way to the dining room. When we walked through the double doors, we were greeted by a smartly dressed waiter who asked for our room number then he showed us to our table. It was nothing like the breakfast disaster because the dinner service was under the control of the waiters.

Our table waiter introduced himself. 'Good evening, my name is Vladimir and I am your waiter. Please help yourselves to the lovely Bulgarian starters on the counter by the window. When you are ready, I will come back to your table and take your main meal and drinks order.'

I stood up and grabbed Christopher's arm. 'Come on, son, let us go and see what wonderful things they have to eat.'

We headed towards the food counters, but before we got close to the window, Mick shouted, 'Stay away from any brown sauce, son.' Then he looked around to see where the naughty boys were sitting.

As Christopher and I started to look along the food counters, it did not take long before I noticed that none of the Bulgarian starters were what we were used to; not that it was horrible, it was just not what we would normally eat. The starters consisted of cold meats, salad, bread and olives. As I looked around at the other guest to see what they were eating, I knew then that the main meal menu would not offer any nicely battered fish and crispy chips or beautiful beef casseroles, or even chunky meat and potato pies, crispy jacket potatoes, hot Indian curries or spicy Chinese dishes.

Christopher looked at me. 'I am not eating any of that food, Mum, it looks worse than school dinners.'

Mick was not too far away from us; he could also see how bad the food looked! As a result, he shouted, 'What, Chris, you don't want to eat here tonight, where do you want to go?' He stood in front of our waiter pretending it was Christopher's fault that we were not going to eat anything in the restaurant that night.

I could tell by the look on Christopher's face that he was relieved that we were not staying to eat. 'Can we go to eat at Sunny Beach, please, Dad?'

The waiter was waiting to take our order. I made our

excuses. 'Sorry, Vladimir, our son wants to go and have something to eat on Sunny Beach.' I grabbed my handbag and we all left the dining room in such a hurry.

By the time we arrived at the beach, it was very busy, all the nice restaurants were full of holidaymakers enjoying their lovely meals. After a long search along the pedestrian walkway, Christopher found a lovely place with a nice table overlooking the Black Sea coast. As I sat down, I noticed that there was one of the biggest bungee jumps I had ever seen just outside.

As soon as Christopher saw it, he shouted, 'Can we go on that bungee jump please, Dad?'

I could see by Mick's face that he was already regretting sitting next to the biggest bungee jump on the Black Sea coast. 'Later on, son, please let us have something to eat first, I am absolutely starving.'

When we were all settled down, a very thin waiter came to our table with three menus. I took the menus and passed one each to Mick and Chris. They opened the menu and within a few seconds we had decided what we wanted to eat. I tried to place the food order in broken English, to try and help the waitress understand what we wanted. 'We would like three starters. One chick-en so-up. One-king-prawn. One cheesy-garlic-bread.' I used one finger to emphasise the number one. As soon as she had finished writing down our starters, then I ordered three main meals. 'One-well-done-steak-and-chips. One-roast-chick-en-and-chips. One-roast-ed-lamb-with-mixed vega-tables.'

Once she had finished writing down our main meals, I ordered three puddings. 'One-large-straw-berry-ice-cream. One-cho-co-late-cake with ice-cream. One-lemon ice cream-cake-with fresh-fruit.' This was so we did not have to wait to order our puddings later.

As soon as she finished taking the order, she looked at me with disbelief, then she shook her head and stormed off to the kitchen.

Mick and I looked at each other. 'I don't understand why she did that, Mick. Do you think she didn't understand what I was ordering?'

He looked at the menu. 'You only ordered food from the menu. I am sure she is used to taking orders.'

While we were waiting for our starters to arrive, I started watching the bungee jumpers queuing up to go on the ride. I watched a lot of people being transformed into human rockets by letting themselves be catapulted up into the dark starry skies. Some of their screams were so loud that I could not hear the live music playing within the restaurant.

All the hysterical screaming coming from the bungee jumpers had encouraged a large crowd of people to gather outside the restaurant on the pedestrian walkway by where we were sitting. Everybody stopped to watch the bungee jumpers get ready to go for their jump. As soon as the attendant had put the harness around their body, they were catapulted into space. They did not have any time to think about it, it was just 'A Go!' And they were off. The crowd of spectators started laughing as soon as the jumper's feet had left the ground. They were laughing at their pain, discomfort and misfortune, as they made their way to space, then their uncomfortable tilting and spinning journey back down to earth.

I could hear a gang of young English men and women betting with each other about who was going to go on the bungee jump next, so I started to encourage them. 'Go on it don't be frightened. These two are going on the ride when they have eaten their meals.' Pointing at Mick and Christopher.

A few of the men started to talk to Mick and Christopher about wanting to go on the bungee jump. Christopher was made up with the thought of going on the jump as soon as he had eaten his meal. I could tell that he was so excited, and it looked like he had managed to convince Mick to go on it also.

Then suddenly, the waiter tapped me on my shoulder to let me know that our food was ready; however, I could not believe what I was seeing. Everything I had ordered was ready to eat! Three starters. Three main courses and three puddings. I looked at the waiter with despair, as two other waiters brought over extra tables to hold all the plates.

Then Mick looked at me. 'Oh my god, Janet, what have you done?'

The crowd of English men and women, who were talking to Chris and Mick from outside the restaurant, started to notice my mistake. When I looked over at them, they could not stop giggling; it was awful. Three waiters were placing all the plates on the tables. First the starter, then the main course followed by the pudding were all left on the tables. I could hear the crowd of English men and women's laughter getting louder and louder; it was actually blocking out the screams from the bungee jumpers. When they saw the amount of food that I had ordered, they started to have a bet on how much we would be able to eat.

I could not believe what had happened. 'Excuse me, excuse me, please, I did not want all the food together!' I tried to explain to the waiter that I wanted it in three stages. First of all, the starters, then the main course and then puddings to end the meal, but she just walked away shaking her head and waving her hands in the air to the other two waiters about the amount of food I had ordered.

I stood up from the table to follow her! 'Please, please take some of this food back to the kitchen.' But she just walked into the kitchen to bring out more food.

'Oh my god, Mick, what are we going to do?'

Mick started to rearrange a few of the plate tables, to make sure the right meals were next to the person who ordered it.

'Don't worry, Mum, I am starving; I will eat it all.' Christopher grabbed a piece of his cheesy garlic bread and started to eat it. Mick picked up one of the spoons from a stack of cutlery at the end of the tables and he started to eat his chicken soup.

'Sit down, Janet, everyone is looking at us. Eat your starter before it goes cold!'

As I returned to the table, I sat down. 'Bloody hell, Mick, I am not going to order any food again!'

One of the waiters placed a few paper napkins as close as he could get to each of us. We all tried to eat our starters as quickly as possible to prevent our main meals from going cold and our ice-cold puddings from melting in the heat of the night.

Mick started to eat a spoonful of his soup, then a slice of his steak and a few chips. Christopher was trying to consume his garlic bread, roast chicken and chips all at the same time. I tried to eat the roasted lamb gravy with my king prawn starter but it did not taste good together. But none of this mattered; all our "speed eating" did not make a lot of difference! By the time we got to our puddings, Christopher's large strawberry ice cream had melted all over the plate and the tablecloth, Mick's chocolate cake was just a brown mess surrounded by what looked like milk, and my lemon ice cream cake with fresh fruit was like a yellow drink with bits of orange floating in it. They had also become a horrible mess over the table cloths.

I had had enough food for one night and the tables were in a terrible state, so I signalled to the waiter for the bill. Within a few seconds, the waiter came with the bill. While I was reviewing the bill, three other waiters came over to empty the tables.

Mick got his wallet out of his pocket to pay for the food. 'How much is it, Janet?'

I looked at the bill. 'It is 110 Bulgarian lev, Mick.'

Christopher started to count the lev as Mick took it out of his wallet. '90/100/110 lev, are you going to leave a tip, Dad?'

Mick looked at me then Christopher. 'Yes, son, I think they deserve one, but do not let your mum order our food again!'

As soon as Christopher put the lev down next to the receipt, the waiter came to take it away. Christopher got up from his seat and started to walk out of the restaurant. 'Please can we go on the bungee jump now, Dad? I have finished eating my meal.'

Mick rubbed his tummy with his hands. 'Sorry, son, I cannot do a bungee jump now. Do you know that you are not supposed to do any exercise after you have eaten a full meal? Never mind doing a bungee jump on a full stomach, I would be sick over everyone below. Let us do it tomorrow night instead, before we have anything to eat?'

Christopher looked a bit disheartened. 'Well, OK, Dad, I cannot wait till tomorrow; it will be brilliant.'

Mick looked at me, I could see the relief in his eyes. I gave him a supporting smile. 'OK, Chris, tomorrow it is; you and Dad can go on the bungee jump and I will take some photos.'

Mick put on his bravest face and stood up. 'That's great, son. It is not our fault your mother ordered too much food, and that is why I cannot go on the bungee jump with you tonight.'

Desert Storm

The following morning, Christopher wanted to stay in bed a bit longer, then he was going to stay around the pool to prepare himself for the evening's bungee jump. Mick and I decided to miss the four-star all-inclusive breakfast at the hotel to go to one of the English beach bars in Sunny Beach, for a full English with HP brown sauce.

The walk to the beach did not seem as long as the previous day and it was not as hot without the midday sunshine. When we arrived at the beach, Mick found a lovely English cafe for breakfast. When we walked into the café, a waiter came towards us. I asked the waiter for a table overlooking the beach so that I could watch the holiday makers as they walked by.

The waiter showed us to a little table at the corner of the room overlooking the beach, he passed two menus for us to look at. Mick did not even look through them, he just ordered two full English breakfasts with one white coffee and an orange juice. While we waited for our breakfast, I sat quietly watching all the people walking past, some of them were going onto the beach and others were shopping in the small kiosks that lined the walkway.

When our breakfast arrived at the table, it looked a million times better than the food at our four-star hotel all-inclusive restaurant, and it had real HP brown sauce! It did not take Mick and I long to eat all our lovely breakfast. Mick cleaned the plate with his last piece of toast then he asked the waiter for the bill.

When the waiter returned with the bill, he paid in Bulgarian lev and left a big tip. For the first time on this holiday, we left our meal feeling full and content.

Mick and I walked along the golden sand until we found a lovely quiet location by the Black Sea. We planned to top up our suntans. I settled down on the sunbed to relax in the midday sunshine. While I was relaxing, I watched some of the families playing with their children in the sand. It reminded me of the fun Mick and I had with Christopher when he was younger. Some of the parents kept walking in and out of the sea to help their children cool down, a few took their children for a little swim along the edge of the coastline, while others built sandcastles; it was wonderful to watch.

I turned to Michael to talk to him about all the times we played on the beach with Christopher when he was younger; however, as I turned, I felt a very cold breeze all over my body. Without any warning, the wind started to gust and swirl around the sunbeds and umbrellas. Within a few seconds, we were all getting sand blasted. It was like being in a desert storm without any camels to rescue you. As I looked up, I noticed the sun bed owners were starting to take down all of the umbrellas before they were blown away. One of the men started to stack all the unused sun beds on top of each other to prevent them from flying off or getting broken.

Some of the parents started to hold onto their children while they gathered all their belongings, then they made a run for it. But this little sandstorm did not deter Mick and I; we stayed on our sunbeds because we were determined to get a nice tan before we returned home. With good sun tans on our minds, we held onto our beach towels while trying to stop the sun beds from taking off into the sky.

After a few minutes, the storm started to get worse, with every gust of wind my sun bed lifted up into the air then fell back down onto the sand. I had to hold on tight just in case the strong winds tipped me off, I looked over at Mick and he was lying on his front, shielding his eyes from the sand. As the sand gust over my body, it felt like a cyclone had started. The howling sandstorm was starting to remove the skin from the bottom of my feet; as it gusted up my legs, it was like a hard sheet of sandpaper removing any imperfections from my ankles; as it made its way towards my knees, it felt like it was sanding around and over my skin until it started to hurt.

The heavy gust of sand and wind continued to rub down the tops of my legs until it gusted over my bikini bottoms onto my stomach, with the heavy force of nature, as it hit my chest so hard it nearly blew my bikini top off. I had to let go of my beach towel to protect my dignity. Within a few seconds, it had started to polish my chin, then my nose and cheeks, and last of all my forehead; it felt like the sandstorm was buffering away every imperfection on my face and body; it was not a good feeling.

After a while, I decided to take my sunglasses off to take a look around the beach and see what had happened to all the people. When I opened my eyes, my vision was quite blurred, it had diminished because I had closed my eyes tight to prevent the sand from getting through my eyelids. When my vision finally returned, I could hardly believe my eyes. There was no one left on the beach, the whole of the beach looked empty. The sand had covered everything in sight, all of the seats and beds at the local bars were tipped over and sand was gathering over them like a big sand dune. After seeing the state of the bar furniture, I decided to put my sunglasses back on to protect my eyes and turn over to get the back of my body sanded down.

Mick and I stayed on the beach for a few hours longer, without either of us realising that we were putting our bodies through an extreme exfoliation. When we decided to leave, I had to dig my beach bag out of the sand while Mick hunted for our shoes in the newly formed sand dunes.

When we returned to the hotel, Christopher was waiting by the pool in his shorts and t-shirt to go on the bungee jump with his dad. As we walked towards him, he looked shocked.

'Mum, Dad, what is the matter with your faces? They are red raw, you look like you have gotten a terrible red rash, except for Mum's white eye patches where her sunglasses have been.' Then he burst out laughing.

Mick and I could not believe what he was saying; we hurried to our room as fast as we could to see for ourselves. Mick opened the door and I ran to the mirror in the bedroom. When Mick turned the light on, I could not believe it, the whole of my face was bright red. I ran into the bathroom and covered my face with a load of cold water and after sun, and waited for it to cool down. We both sat on the bed waiting for the after sun to work, but after an hour and half, both of our faces were still red raw. 'What are we going to do, Mick, I am not going out like this.'

Christopher knocked on the bedroom door and he was determined to go on the bungee jump. 'Wow, how red are both of you, your faces look like two big red tomatoes.'

Mick did not look happy. 'No, we don't, it's just sunburn. It will settle down once we have had a shower. Go and watch TV in your room and we will knock for you in about half an hour.' Mick turned the shower on cold and he washed his face with after sun. 'Bloody hell, Janet, look at my sun tan.'

I turned to look at him. 'Do you think you can get sunburn in a sandstorm?'

He smiled at me. 'Absolutely, can't you see, I'm going to have a great tan by the time I return home!'

When he was finished in the shower, I turned the shower to warm and I stood under the lovely running water until the pain of my extreme exfoliation had stopped. I covered myself in after the sun cream and got dressed, ready to go out for the night.

I decided to give the hotel's four-star all-inclusive restaurant a miss, because I knew the lights were too bright and everyone would notice our "crimson faces" and I did not want to give those naughty boys something else to laugh about! With a lot of luck, we managed to get out of the hotel without anyone noticing our red faces. Mick suggested walking along the other side of the beach to allow us a bit longer to cool down, and to see if there were any nice Indian or Chinese restaurants. I knew that he was using the restaurants as an excuse to go as far away from the bungee jump because his "exfoliation" was still quite tender.

We walked along the main road until we came to a big hotel at the end of the road, we turned left and walked down another small road that led to some hotels, shops and supermarkets. Mick took a right towards the beach, and as we walked along the pavement, we came across a small bridge that took us on to the far side of the golden sands.

After a while, Mick found a lovely restaurant overlooking Old Nessebar. The waiter showed us to a table by the window, then she brought us three menus and waited for our drinks order. This time, I decided to order our drinks first, then one dish at a time to avoid any indigestion! 'Please, can I have a small beer for Christopher, and a large beer for Michael and a small rose wine for me?'

She wrote the order down on her notepad, then she walked over to the bar to place the order. Within a second or two, she was back for the food order. 'Would you like anything to eat?'

Mick and Christopher had decided what they wanted for their starters. 'Please can we have one portion of salt and pepper chicken wings and one portion of BBQ ribs.'

She made a note then looked at me.

'Please, can I have a bowl of hot and sour soup with some prawn crackers?'

She wrote my order down. 'Would you like anything else?' We all looked at each other and Mick turned to answer her. 'Not yet, thank you.'

She looked a bit upset. 'No more to eat?'

I looked at her. 'No, not yet, we will order more after we have eaten our starters.'

She looked confused. 'You can order it now, no?'

Christopher looked at her. 'Don't worry, I will call you when we want to order our meal.'

She took the menus and walked off into the kitchen, talking to herself.

When our starters arrived, they were lovely and hot. When we finished our starters, Christopher shouted to the waiter. She frowned then walked over to take our empty plates away. Christopher passed her his plate with leftover chicken bones on it. 'Please, can we order the main course now?'

The waiter ran back to the bar for three menus. Mick looked at the menu and within a few moments he had decided. 'Please, can I have chicken fried rice with chips and curry?'

Christopher wanted to order his food next. 'Please, can I

81

have beef in black-bean sauce and chips?'

While she was writing down the order, I had decided. 'Please, can I have roast duck with spring onion and Chinese vegetables?'

She took the order and smiled, then she walked into the kitchen singing the song that was playing on the radio.

When our meals arrived, we took our time eating it because it was so nice. Mick, Chris and I spent most of the evening talking about Bulgaria and looking over the bay at Old Nessebar, the place where our apartment was being developed. When the waiter came for our empty plates, I ordered three ice cream desserts and two more beers, one large and one small and as a special fruit cocktail for me.

At the end of the night, Mick ordered a large Bulgarian brandy, another small beer for Christopher and a special fruit cocktail for me. We ended the night with a lovely walk along the beach back to the hotel. No one mentioned the bungee jump, I am not sure if Christopher had forgotten about it, or Mick had just been given a little more time to come up with another excuse to get out of doing it tomorrow?

The Stars and Back

The following morning, I woke up incredibly early. When I got out of bed, I was feeling a bit unwell and not my usual self. While I was on my way to the bathroom I wondered if I was feeling ill because of the sandstorm yesterday afternoon, or was it something to do with all the lovely food at the Chinese restaurant or could it be something to do with those two special fruit cocktails? Whatever it was, I knew something was wrong and I was not feeling quite right.

When Mick woke up, the first thing I asked him was if he felt all right. He said he felt great and there was nothing wrong with him. I went into the bathroom to get dressed. While I was putting my bikini on, I ruled out the Chinese food and the sandstorm because Mick was feeling OK, then it clicked; it must have been the two special fruit drinks Mick and I had ordered. Then I remembered something I read about Bulgaria, the article advised tourists not to have any ice cubes with their drinks, because the ice water may have come from the tap water and there were lots of minerals in Bulgarian tap water. The special fruit cocktails I had last night were made up of fifty percent ice!

When I returned to the bedroom, Mick was waiting on the balcony to go to the beach. Nothing was going to stop me from sunbathing after yesterday's extreme exfoliation had blown away what little tan I had. Mick knocked on Christopher's bedroom room. When he answered, he said that he wanted to stay in bed for a little bit longer. I asked him if he felt OK and he said he felt fine. He just wanted to stay in bed a little longer. Mick asked him to join us when he was ready so that they could go for a nice chicken kebab and chips from the kebab shop on the beach. My stomach turned with the thought of eating anything greasy.

When we got to the reception area, I made Mick avoid the hotel's restaurant, the smell of the breakfast food was turning my stomach. We left the hotel to make our way down to the beach. Mick managed to get the same two sunbeds as we had the day before. The sunbed owner came over to collect his payment and he laughed at us. 'You pair are mad, you stayed out here in the sandstorm, you are *loco.*'

Mick agreed. 'It's her fault, she wants a good suntan for when she gets back home.' Then he pointed at me and winked.

I pulled the sun cream out of my beach bag and passed it to Mick. 'Can you make sure to cover the whole of my body with this cream, it is still quite red from yesterday's sand storm.'

The sunbed owner looked at me. 'You are *loco*, missis.'

I was not feeling well enough to answer him back. I just lay down on the sun bed while Mick poured the sun cream all over my red raw aching body. I enjoyed the morning sunbathing and it seemed to reduce some of the illness that I was feeling earlier on.

While Mick and I waited for Christopher to join us for lunch, I watched as the jet ski riders rode into the Black Sea. As their jet skis cut through the waves, the once-tranquil crystal green waves turned white then pale blue as they shot off into different directions. I could hear the raw of the engines as they made their way to the edge of the horizon.

When Christopher arrived, I got up from my sun bed to

give him a big hug. 'Can I go on one of those jet skis, Mum?'

I sat back down on my sun bed. 'Of course, you can, son.'

Mick stood up and started to put his t-shirt on. 'Not until we have had a chicken kebab; I am starving. Come on, everyone, let's find a nice place to eat.'

I pulled my sun dress out of my beach bag and tucked the towels into the sun beds so that they did not blow off. As I came back up from tucking Mick's towel in, I felt a little dizzy. I took a deep breath and sat back down for a second or two.

'Come on, Mum, Dad, I'm starving.'

I stood up and put my bag over my shoulder. 'I'm on my way, son. You and Dad go ahead and I will catch up with you.' I did not want to rush, I just needed to take my time in the midday sunshine.

As I made my way off the golden beach; I could see that Christopher and Mick were slightly ahead on the pedestrian walkway. It looked like Christopher had found a place where they sold kebabs and they were waiting for me to catch them up. Christopher pointed at the kebab house then to his dad.

I shouted, 'Great, son, you both go in and I will see you soon.'

Mick sat on the wall. 'It's OK, Janet, we will wait for you, you have got my wallet.'

It was good to spend our lunch time together away from the beach. Mick and Christopher ordered a kebab and chips each, and two small beers. I ordered water and some soup. While everyone was eating and drinking, I sat in the shade watching some of the sun seekers enjoying their beach activities. After an hour or so, we made our way back to the sun beds. Mick and Chris went jet skiing while I fell asleep in the afternoon sun.

85

I must have been asleep for a few hours. Mick woke me up around five p.m. to go back to the hotel. As I got up to put my sun dress on over my bikini, I noticed that I was still feeling quite unwell, but I did not say anything to Mick or Christopher, because I did not want to spoil their day. I picked up my beach bag and placed all the beach towels into it. Mick and Christopher were at the edge of the golden beach by the time I had caught them up. I took my time walking back to the hotel; it felt like the sun had drained all of my energy.

When I got back to our bedroom, I was feeling extremely hot and sweaty. I got undressed then I took a shower to cool down. As the warm water ran down my face, I felt my body burning up. I started to worry that I might have sunstroke after yesterday's sandstorm, but that should have happened yesterday. Then I started to think my symptoms could be as a result of falling asleep in the afternoon sun, or was it because of the ice in those special fruit cocktails?

When I came out of the shower, Mick was sitting on the balcony holding a can lager in his hand. I noticed that he had poured a glass of rose wine and he had left it on the table for me. I did not want to spoil his wonderful day and tell him about my illness, so I joined him in the evening sunshine.

We both sat on the white plastic sun chairs overlooking the swimming pool, drinking and talking about the lovely day we had had together until it was time to get dressed for the nights' activities. To be honest, after a few wines I did not want to move, but I knew Christopher was looking forward to going on the bungee jump with his dad. I went back into the bedroom and chose a dress that was comfortable, and not too tight around my stomach, I put a pair of comfy beach sandals on and grabbed my going out bag. Nothing was going to stop me from helping

Mick to go through what could be a terrible ordeal or a wonderful experience.

Mick took his time getting dressed, he was not sure what to wear. I think he wanted something comfortable and loose fitting, but not too loose that it would fall down or get caught in the harness. While I was waiting for Mick, Christopher knocked at the door. As I got up to let him in, I felt a little giddy.

'Hello, son, you look amazing. I like those new shorts and t-shirts.'

He walked into the bedroom. 'Where is my dad?'

Mick was in the bathroom having his last "just in case wee" before the jump! 'I'm in here, son, I won't be long.'

Christopher looked around the bedroom. 'This is similar to my room, only my room is bigger because it's just for me.' Then he giggled to himself.

When Mick finally came out of the bathroom, Christopher and I were sitting on the balcony watching the sunset. 'Right, everyone, I am ready to go for something nice to eat.'

Christopher stood up. 'I am not eating until after my bungee jump.'

Mick walked towards the balcony. I thought he was going to stop for another drink, but he picked up his wallet and made his way to the door.

By the time we arrived at the bungee jump, it was getting late into the night, because Mick had made us stop at every bar on the way to the beach to build up some "Dutch courage". As a result of the pub crawl, there were lots of people waiting to go on the jump.

Christopher and Mick took their place in the long queue and waited for their turn to jump. I sat on the wall near the restaurant where we had our first evening meal, the one that gave us indigestion. Within a minute or so, I heard the Bulgarian man who was taking the payments for the bungee talking to Mick. 'Sorry, mate, it is going to be around twenty minutes before your jump.'

Mick's face lightened up. 'Let us come back tomorrow, Chris, there are too many people waiting, it's going to take ages.'

I looked at Christopher and it looked like he was willing to wait all night. 'No, Dad. Let us wait in this line, it won't take that long, please, Dad, just wait here with me.'

I think Mick knew there was no way he could escape the bungee jump this time. He turned to look at me. 'It's going to be a while, Janet. Are you OK, are you still feeling ill, do you want to go back to the hotel?'

I stood up. 'No, I am fine now, Mick.'

He looked a bit annoyed. 'I thought you said you were feeling a bit unwell this morning?'

'I'm OK now.'

I wanted to go back to the hotel, but I did not want Christopher to miss out on the bungee jump, and I could not leave Mick to suffer without me. I sat waiting on the wall, and every now and again, Mick would shout, 'Are you OK, Jan, do you need to go back to the hotel?'

I tried to ignore him by watching all the people in front of him go through the pain then the "glory" of being catapulted to space and back.

Before long, it was Mick and Christopher's turn, they were at the front of the queue. Christopher looked so excited, not like his dad. 'You go first, Dad.'

I think Mick was expecting Christopher to go first. 'No, Christopher, you're younger than me, you should go first.' Then none of them had a choice, the Bulgarian man who sold them the tickets told Mick that he was the first to go.

I shouted over to Christopher. 'Watch how your dad does it, son.' Then I looked over to Mick. 'Please hold on tight, love.'

Mick put on his bravest face as he made his way towards the man holding the bungee cord, the man started to place the harness around Mick's body. As he pulled the harness up to the top of Mick's legs, he had to loosen the strap to get it over his hips and waist, then the man tightened the harnesses around Mick's lower regions, which looked very painful. He fastened the harness to the bungee cord and told him to hold on tight. Within a second, he had launched Mick into space. I am sure I heard him scream in horror. But was it the pain from the very tight harness around his lower regions, or was it the fear of coming back down to earth with a big bump?

When Mick had finally stopped *screaming*... I mean bouncing up and down, the man held on to him to stop the bungee cord from getting caught on the railings. By the time Mick had found his feet again, the man was removing the harness; however, the harness support for Mick's lower regions had climbed that far up his body, it was just under his chest now and his lower regions were looking very delicate from the force of gravity and the tightness of his harness. Mick's painful predicament did not seem to matter to the man, he just pulled the harness down past his chest, then he ripped it off from his lower regions with unlimited force. I could see that Mick was in a bit of discomfort as he started to walk towards Christopher; he looked like "John Wayne" after a few days and nights out riding his horse without a saddle.

I looked towards Christopher to see if he still wanted to do the bungee jump. Within a second or two, I could tell he was still going ahead with it because his face was full of excitement. The Bulgarian man tightened the harness around Christopher's body then he shouted, '5-4-3-2-1.'

Christopher was off into space like the speed of light. I could hear him laughing aloud as he bounced up and down in the dark black sky. When he had finished the initial bouncing up and down, he did an extra somersault in the night sky, it looked amazing.

When Christopher was firmly back on the ground, the man undone the harness, then within a few seconds, he ran towards me. As he ran through the crowd, I could see that he had the biggest smile ever on his face.

'That was brilliant, Mum, can I go on it again?'

I smiled at him. 'Absolutely, son, where's your dad?'

Then he turned around to look for Mick. Mick was walking gingerly towards me.

'Dad, do you want to go bungee jumping again tonight?'

Mick's face dropped. I don't think Mick had gotten over the first jump jet. 'Not tonight, son, maybe tomorrow, I want to get myself a large brandy and something to eat. Do you fancy a small beer?'

Christopher was not disappointed. 'OK. Wasn't the bungee jump great, Dad?'

We started to make our way down the pedestrian walkway. I could hear Mick and Christopher sharing their bungee jump experiences with each other. It sounded like they had watched the same film, but they had both experienced quite different beginnings, middle and ends.

Mick's conversation was all about the harness being a bit too tight around his body; therefore, he could not really enjoy the ride because he was in too much pain, especially when he went up into the sky. Christopher spoke about all the fun about putting the harness on, and the man having to tighten it after Mick's ride. Then he spoke of all the joy of going up and down in the sky, then somersaulting before he landed. 'It was the best bungee jump ever.' Christopher was so excited. Mick needed to have a large drink or two to soften the pain.

I stopped at a lovely restaurant overlooking the Black Sea coast, it wasn't too far away from the bungee jump. Mick and Christopher went to the toilet and I "strategically" ordered three drinks and our first course. I was determined to order one dish at a time to avoid any confusion and indigestion. When they returned from the toilet, I carried on listening to Mick and Christopher chatting about the fun they had on the bungee jump. However, as they were talking, I noticed that my illness was getting worse; the pain in my stomach was getting stronger and more uncomfortable. It felt like I had been thrown to space and back without the bungee cord!

When my starter arrived, I could not eat it. My appetite had taken a tumble for the worse. Mick and Christopher hardly noticed that I was not eating, they enjoyed their starter so much that they ordered their main meal before the waiter had the time to take their plates away. I waited for them to eat their meal and drink their drinks before I asked them if we could make our way back to the hotel. I did not want to ruin their night, so I made the excuse that I wanted to watch a good film on TV.

The walk back to the hotel was quite difficult for me, I felt like I was never going to make it back to the hotel. The pain was that bad. I could not say anything to Mick and Christopher, they had both had such a good evening, even Mick was celebrating his fantastic bungee jump achievement.

When we got back into our bedroom, I got undressed and

ready for bed. Mick and I watched TV for a while then he fell fast asleep. I think all the evening's excitement had exhausted him. But I could not settle down or even fall asleep, because I had terrible pains in my stomach. I got up to go to the bathroom to see if it helped, and as soon as I turned the bathroom light on, I vomited everywhere. The sickness was pouring out of me and I could not stop it! My temperature went from very hot to freezing cold as I stood on the marble floor in the midnight air.

I had never experienced anything like this in my life; I was feeling all alone and very scared.

You Only Live Once

I was very relieved when the daylight appeared through the bathroom window. I sat on the marble floor holding my stomach to stop the pain. Thankfully, the vomiting came to an end with the early morning light. I pulled myself up from the bathroom floor and I managed to get into bed before Mick woke up. As my head hit the soft white cotton pillow, the morning light disappeared and I fell into a deep sleep.

When I woke up, Mick was no longer in bed next to me. I looked over to the balcony and I could see that he was wearing his beach shorts and t-shirt ready for another day in the sunshine. I wished that I were back at home in the UK, where I would be safe and secure. As soon as Mick saw that I was awake, he smiled at me.

'It's a beautiful day, Janet, let's leave looking for the apartment until tomorrow so that we can go to the beach and you can top up your suntan. You're looking a bit white today.'

I was relieved that we were not going all the way to Old Nessebar to find the apartment. I convinced myself that another day in the sunshine would make me feel better. I got out of bed and walked into the bathroom to see if I looked as bad as I felt. When I looked into the mirror, I could see big black circles around my eyes, I looked like a panda. My complexion had gone from crimson red to white overnight.

I whispered to myself in the mirror, 'Come on, Janet, you are on holiday, you need to make the most of every day, and you will have to find that apartment on the Apollon Complex tomorrow so pull yourself together!'

I turned away from the mirror and I started to get undressed. As I moved my arms and legs, every part of my body felt sore, as if I had been in a boxing match with Mick Tyson. I grabbed a bottle of sun cream and covered my tender flesh and bones with the lotion to try and ease the pain. I pulled my bikini bottoms to just below my stomach to avoid any tenderness, then I slowly placed my bikini top over my chest, trying not to tie it too tight in case of any soreness around my chest. When I left the bathroom, I was not feeling up to doing anything except falling back to sleep again. But I put on my bravest face and smiled at Mick as I walked slowly towards the balcony.

'OK, gorgeous, are you ready to go to the beach?'

I thought to myself, *It would be much better to sunbathe in the lovely sunshine, then staying in bed all day on my own.*

The walk to the Sunny Beach felt much longer than usual, because I had to stop a few times to ease the pain. I told Mick I was looking at a restaurant's menu or a clothes shop window. When we arrived at the beach, the heat of the sun made my temperature go even higher and the sweat started to pour down my body and I started to shake. I grabbed Mick's hand and held on tightly.

'Are you OK, Janet? Your hands are roasting and you are dead sweaty.'

I looked down towards the golden sand. 'Yes, I'm fine, it is just very hot today.'

Mick managed to find two sunbeds near a posh hotel, which I knew had clean toilets just in case I needed to go in there. I gently placed my bottom on the sun bed, but the sunshine was shining directly at me. 'Mick, please, will you move my sunbed under the shade?'

He looked quite shocked. 'That's not like you, Janet, you're as white as a ghost.'

He moved my bed towards the shade then turned towards me. 'At this rate, nobody will think that you have been away on holiday.'

I just smiled at him, then I laid my body under the safety of the big sun umbrella. Mick hung the beach bag under the umbrella then he settled down onto his bed. 'Christopher will be joining us for lunch, he is having a lazy morning.'

I lifted my head up from the sunbed. 'Oh my god, I had forgotten about Christopher!' It's a good job Mick had remembered. I felt really guilty.

I closed my eyes and tried to catch up on some of the lost sleep before Christopher joined us. My intention was to try and feel better by lunchtime. I kept dozing off, but the heat from the sun kept making me feel extremely sick. I used all my energy to get up and walk across to the posh hotel to use the bathroom! When I walked into the reception area, the cold air conditioning hit me and I felt my stomach churn. I pushed the toilet door open and ran into the cubical. Within a second or two, I was feeling slightly better after pouring out my illness. I walked to the sinks and rinsed my face with cold water, making sure not to swallow any of it! I caught sight of myself in the tall mirror by the toilet door.

'Bloody hell, Janet, you look rough. Get some help!'

Our dream holiday apartment was the last thing on my mind because all I really wanted was to go home on the next flight to Manchester.

Throughout the morning, I tried to make myself feel a little better by listening to the laughter of children playing in the sea with their parents. However, the sound of the sunbathers having lots of fun in the sun had made me feel so sad. I could not get up from the sun bed, never mind going for a swim or playing games in the sun. I just lay on the bed praying that the pain would go away so that I could go for lunch with my family.

When Christopher arrived at the beach, the first thing I heard was, 'I am starving, Dad, can we go for lunch right away?'

I opened my eyes and looked up to the sky. Christopher stood in front of my sun bed, in a position that protected my eyes from the bright sun rays. I felt so proud of him; he looked gorgeous, he had a lovely sun tan, and he was smartly dressed. Then I saw my reflection in his mirrored sunglasses and I looked like an albino panda!

I sat up as fast as I could. Christopher raised his arm to protect my eyes from the sun. 'Hiya Mum, are you ready to go for lunch? I am starving.'

I looked at Mick then Christopher, they were both eager to get something nice to eat, but that was the last thing I wanted! Without any hesitation, I told them to go for their lunch without me because I wanted to stay in the sunshine to top up my tan. They both looked down at me for a short while, then Mick got his wallet out of the beach bag. He gave me a kiss on the forehead, then they both walked away.

While they were gone, I managed to fall into a deep sleep. While I was sleeping, I dreamt about finding our dream apartment and it was everything we wished for. Mick and I had moved in and I was swimming in the pool then I heard familiar voices. 'Hi, Mum, we are back, you should have come with us. The food was lovely, wasn't it, Dad?'

I jumped up and looked towards the sunlight. My eyes were

blurred for a moment then I got my vision back. Christopher and Mick both looked fabulous in the sunshine. I smiled at both of them.

'Mum, do you want to join us?'

Without saying anything, I fell back into a deep sleep. When Mick woke me up, it was getting late. The walk back to the hotel from the beach was dreadful. Christopher and Mick did their best to support me, but I kept on saying that I was feeling fine. As soon as I got into the bedroom, I lay on the bed and fell asleep.

Then I heard Mick taking a shower. When he came out of the shower, he was dressed in his lovely blue evening shorts and white shirt.

'You look very nice, Mick, why don't you take Christopher out for a "boy's night out"? There is a girly film on TV tonight that I would like to watch on my own.'

He looked surprised. 'Are you sure? You never want to stay on your own at home, never mind on holiday.'

I looked up at him. 'I know, but I have been wanting to watch this film all year.'

He shook his head and kissed me on the lips. 'I will go and see if Christopher is ready.' And he walked out the door.

To be honest, I was too frightened to leave the room just in case I did not make it back, and I really didn't want to spoil their holiday.

That night while Mick and Christopher were at Sunny Beach, enjoying their boy's night out together, I thought I was going to die, the pains in my stomach were absolutely terrible. I was unable to sleep, eat, drink, or stand up without support. Then a little voice inside my head started saying, *Janet, you have travelled all this way to make sure that bloody apartment*

exists, and now you are going to die unless you get this sorted;
you're a stupid fool. Call for a doctor. My inner survival
thoughts started to get louder and louder as the daylight faded,
and I fell into a deep sleep.

Dr Who?

When Mick returned home from Sunny Beach, the sound of the bedroom door opening woke me up.

'Good evening, gorgeous, Christopher and I have had a brilliant time together. We had a few pints and a lovely meal at the Big BBQ Bar.'

As I opened my eyes, the pain in my stomach was excruciating! Within an instant, I knew that there was something very seriously wrong with me. Whatever it was, all the sunshine in the world and any additional sleep was not going to make it go away. I looked across the bed towards where Mick was standing.

'Please, Mick, will you go down to the receptionist and ask her to phone a doctor for me, I am not feeling very well.'

He looked at me for a moment then he walked out the door. Mick knew by the look on my face and the tone in my voice that something was very wrong. I would never ask him to call the doctor at home, never mind in Bulgaria.

When he came back into the room from the receptionist, he stood at the side of the bed looking at me. 'The receptionist has called the doctor, she said he would be here soon.' Then he sat on the bed next to me. 'Christopher and I would have never left you on your own if we knew that you were feeling poorly.'

I lifted my head up from the pillow. 'I was feeling all right before you went out, I thought I would feel much better if I had a good night's sleep.' He snuggled up next to me. 'But I was wrong, Mick.' Then tears started to roll down my face.

He held my hand close to him, then gave me a big hug. 'You silly woman you should have told me that you were not well.'

There was a knock on the door, Mick got up from the bed to see who was knocking. When he opened the door, I heard a Bulgarian man talking. '*Zdraveite*, the hotel's receptionist has called me.'

I looked to see who it was. A tall grey-haired man, in a white coat, was standing in the doorway. He was holding a brown leather bag and a mobile phone in his hand. '*Zdraveite.*'

Mick let him into the room. 'Please come in, my wife is in the bedroom.'

The man in the white coat walked across the room towards the bed, he stood at the bottom of the bed looking at me as I lay under the white cotton sheets, then he sat down on the edge of the bed and held my left hand for a while. Then he took my pulse. After he had taken my pulse, he picked his leather bag up from the floor and opened it. After a while, he pulled out several documents and handed them to Mick. 'Please take them.' He took my blood pressure, looked into my eyes, then he turned towards Mick. 'She is not very well; you will need to sign all of those documents now please.' He handed Mick a pen from the top pocket of his white coat.

'What is wrong with her?'

The man stood up and walked towards Mick. 'She is very sick, please sign the forms I gave to you.'

Mick started to sign all of the documents.

When Mick had finished signing the documents, he handed them back to the man. The man checked them thoroughly. 'Can I see a copy of your holiday insurance please?'

Mick took the holiday insurance certificate out of the safe. The man noted down the name of the insurance company and the reference number. 'Please you have to come with me, please follow me to the ambulance.' Without any hesitation, he placed the documents back into his leather bag and turned to walk out of the door as if it was an emergency.

Mick helped me to get out of bed, then he supported me to pull a big baggy t-shirt over my bed top and night shorts, then I pulled a pair of leggings over my shorts. We made our way towards the doorway. As I walked out of the bedroom, I could see that the man was on his mobile phone. When Mick had locked the bedroom door he guided us to the elevator and pressed the button for the lift to come to our floor. He carried on talking to the other person on the phone. When the lift doors opened he held them open until we had gotten into the lift then he pressed the button to take us down to the reception area.

He continued to talk on the phone. His voice was quite loud and it echoed around the metal lift. I tried to work out what he was saying, but he was talking in Bulgarian. When the lift stopped, we all got out. Mick had to hold me up as I walked outside the hotel towards the man who was standing by a little white van that was parked in the hotel's parking area.

This white van was not like any of the ambulances in the UK. It reminded me of the 'Scooby Doo Where Are You Mystery machine Fred Jones drove when Shaggy, Velma and Daphne chased ghosts in their cartoons.' However, this vehicle did not have any colourful pictures over it, there wasn't even a red cross. The man stood at the passenger side of the van.

The driver was holding the back door open. 'Please Mr, bring her here.'

Mick helped me up into the van then onto the long black

plastic seat, then he sat down next to me. The doctor opened the passenger door and sat down, he spoke to the driver in Bulgarian, then the driver sat down and closed his door, he started the engine and he drove off into the night.

The inside of the van was empty. There wasn't any medical equipment, oxygen tanks or emergency trolleys for the sick. There were only two plastic seats for me and Mick to sit on. I could not hear any sirens or see any blue lights, there was just a driver, a man in a white coat holding a leather bag and a mobile phone.

After about twenty minutes of pure agony in the back of the van, the driver finally stopped. He got out of the van and opened the back door. Mick helped me onto the pavement and as I looked up I could see that the doctor was waiting for the both of us, he looked at Mick and pointed to a black door that was closed. 'Please come this way.'

As I stepped forward, I felt extremely weak. Mick had to support me from falling. With Mick's help, I started to walk towards the black door. When I looked up, I thought we would be outside the new hospital in Sunny Beach, the one the Thomas Cook coach drove past on our way to Sunny beach from the airport.

I struggled to get my bearing, I did not recognise the location or the place. I just assumed that the four-star hotel's receptionist would have called for a doctor from the nice new modern hospital with all the up-to-date equipment. But I was very wrong. There was no A&E or hospital. The white van had stopped at a small building behind one of the main roads. I held on to Mick's hand. 'Where are we, Mick?'

He looked at me with a reassuring smile. 'I'm not sure, Janet. We are about two miles away from the hotel.' I looked at the building in front of us for any signs of a hospital, but there was nothing, not even a pharmacy sign. There was only the van driver. He was holding the black door open, encouraging Mick and I to go inside before anyone saw us! A part of me was extremely nervous about what was going to happen to me when I got inside the building. The other part of me was far too sick to care.

Mick helped me to walk towards the black door. The driver closed the door shut when we walked through, then he showed us into a small grey room. As I walked into the room, I noticed that there was a large red hospital stretcher pushed up against the wall on the left-hand side of the room. There was a narrow glass cabinet with a few white medication boxes and some small bottles of clear liquid on the glass shelf. On the opposite side of the room, there was a black chair and wooden desk, the light from the PC provided little evidence that this man may have been a professional. I looked around the room with a lot of despair. Mick held me up to prevent me from collapsing on the cold white marble floor.

Then the man in the white coat put his phone down on the desk. 'Please come, please put her onto the bed.'

I hesitated before I looked up at the man in the white coat. Mick helped me to walk to the bed then he supported me to sit on it. As I lay down onto the bed, I looked up at the ceiling. There was a single fluorescent light that flickered in the dark. But to add to my excruciating pain and despair, I noticed a squadron of mosquitoes circling around the light; it looked like they were waiting for their next meal.

Mick held on to my hand. 'You'll be all right, love, don't worry about anything the receptionist from the four-star hotel called this man so he must be good.'

Then I heard the man's Bulgarian voice. 'Please pull your panties down, I did not have the energy to move, 'please help her to pull them down now.'

The fear in my face must have been terrifying. 'No, Mick, I am not pulling my pants down here.'

Mick looked at the man then back to me. 'Come on, Janet, this will make you feel better, love.'

The man was standing near the glass cabinet. Mick held my hips up while I tried to pull my shorts down to the top of my pelvis. As I looked up, I could see that the man in the white coat was standing at the bottom of the red bed.

He looked at me. 'Please Mrs, pull them down more. I need to give you an injection.'

I used the last of my life to sit up on the bed. 'An injection, what injection, no one mentioned an injection, I don't want any injection!'

Mick held my hand, then he pulled me back down onto the bed. 'Just do it, Jan, trust me, it will be OK!'

I reluctantly pulled my shorts and leggings down on the right-hand side, I only showed the man a tiny bit of my bottom. Then I heard the loud noise of buzzing from the mosquitoes above me. The sight of my white flesh seemed to further the advances of the hungry mosquitoes, and they started to dive towards me like sharp arrows from a crossbow. Mick noticed the squadron of mosquitoes forming two lines ready to dive into my flesh from above. He stood up to protect my bottom, as the flying insects made their attack, Mick tried to squat them by clapping his hands around them. I hoped that he would kill them before they had a free meal from my white juicy bottom.

Mick carried on clapping to stop the mosquitoes from dive-bombing my bottom for their supper, but the squadron changed their formation and they were starting to break through Mick's defences. With the possibility of being eaten inevitable, I turned my head to look for the man with the white coat to try and hurry him up before all of the mosquitoes got their free meal and Mick's hands got tired from fending them off.

In my sheer panic, I noticed that the man had opened the glass cabinet and he was holding one of the small bottles in his right hand. I watched in slow motion as he turned the glass bottle upside down and he drew the clear liquid from inside with a large stainless-steel needle. 'Oh my god, Mick, look, what is he going to give me in that massive needle?'

Mick stopped clapping for a moment. 'It will be OK, Janet, trust me!' Mick tried his best to calm me down, while he continued to protect my bottom from a relentless squadron of hungry mosquitoes. The man in the white coat must have thought Mick was mad, because all he could see was Mick clapping his hands together above my naked bottom. I don't think he had noticed that numerous mosquitoes had invaded his treatment room. But that did not matter to me, I was just so thankful that Mick was killing all the hungry mosquitoes before they got their knives and forks into my juicy white bum.

The man with the massive injection approached the bed. 'Please, Mr, move over to the door and stop your clapping. She will be OK.'

Mick stopped killing the mosquitoes, then he reluctantly walked over to the other side of the room and everything went silent. Then there was a loud ouch as the needle went into my flesh. I pulled my knickers and leggings backup as fast as I could. Then I lay on the bed for a moment or two, unsure whether I was going to live or die. Then I started to get bitten again by the bloody mosquitoes as a result of my only protection being told to move across the room.

With tears in my eyes, I looked across the room to get Mick's attention before the next squadron of mosquitoes landed on their helpless meal. But the man in the white coat was making him sign more medical claim forms. Then to make matters worse, by the time all the forms were completed, he requested an upfront payment in Bulgarian lev for the treatment. I felt like charging him for feeding his insects.

When the doctor was paid and all the paperwork was signed, the Bulgarian driver pointed towards the black door. Mick walked over to the bed and rescued me from the feeding mosquitoes. He helped me off the bed and together we made our way through the door. Before we left, I turned around to thank the man, but I could not get his attention because he was counting the money. Mick helped me to get into the back of the Scooby Doo van, the driver closed the door. We left the man and the squadron of mosquitoes waiting for their next unfortunate patient.

By the time we arrived back at the hotel, the sun was starting to rise. We decided not to say anything to Christopher about our mystery ride in the Scooby Doo van, the man in the white coat and the squadron of mosquitoes dive-bombing my bottom just in case he thought that we were going mad.

Mick and I made our way to the bedroom to get a few hours' sleep before Christopher woke up. When I opened the bedroom door, I could feel the chilly air from the air conditioner, it cooled my temperature down as soon as it hit my body. The curtains were still closed which made the room nice and dark. I got undressed and lay on the bed.

However, as soon as my head touched the pillow, there was a loud knock on the bedroom door. Mick jumped up out of bed just in case it was Christopher, but when he opened the door it was the man in the white coat.

'Hello, Mr Gorry. I have just called to check on Mrs Gorry.'

I could tell by the tone in Mick's voice that he was not expecting another home visit! 'My wife is in bed, she is trying to get some sleep; I was not expecting you back so soon.'

The man in the white coat walked through the door and he made his way to the side of the bed where I was laying. 'That is very good, Mr Gorry. I will check to see if she is OK now.' He sat on the bed, he looked into my eyes, then he checked my pulse. He turned towards Mick. 'Mr Gorry, you will have to go to the pharmacy when it opens to get this medication for your wife.'

He handed Mick a prescription, then requested some more Bulgarian lev to pay for the second home visit.

While he was talking to Mick, I lay on the bed thinking about the amount of money we had been charged for this bloody illness, and how lucky we were in the UK to have such a wonderful NHS. As soon as the man in the white coat was paid, he walked out of the door. Mick ran after him to see if he knew where the nearest pharmacy was in Sunny Beach, but he had gone.

Mick did not go back to sleep; he went looking for a pharmacy instead. While he was out, I decided that I would have to get over this illness as soon as possible. To ensure that there were no more home visits from the man in white coat, and there were no more rides in the Scooby Doo van to the mosquito habitat. I convinced myself that I would get back to normal once I had had a day's rest and good night's sleep. I had to get better before we ran out of money, and we ran out of time to find our dream holiday apartment.

When Mick returned from the pharmacy, he opened the medication boxes to see what had been prescribed. The first box contained some Imodium tablets (which I already had) and the second box held some pain killers (which I also had). 'Bloody hell, Janet, these are the most expensive tablets I have ever bought.'

I felt sad. 'I know, Mick, I have got the same medication in our first aid box which I brought from home!'

He looked at me. 'Never mind, they may be different over here.' I took both medicines with a little bit of water and I fell asleep.

When Christopher woke up, he came into the room. 'Good morning, Mum and Dad, do you fancy going to the beach again? I am looking forward to going on the bungee jump again.'

Mick's face dropped, he had been up all night with me, and now Christopher wanted him to go on the bungee jump again. 'Come on, lad, I will go to the beach with you for something nice to eat, but there will be no bungee jump for me today.'

While the lads were out for the day, I tried to sleep as much as I could. I continued to take the medication as prescribed throughout the day and all through the night. When I woke up the following morning, the sun was shining through the half open curtain, Mick was still fast asleep. Bless him. He had had a rough twenty-four hours.

I made my way to the bathroom to get a nice shower. As I washed the warm soapy water over my body, I felt a tiny number of mosquito bites on my bottom, where Mick had not managed to protect me and the mosquitoes had a feast on my face, legs and arms. It looked like I had caught the measles. However, I was feeling a little bit better overall. I covered my body with antiseptic cream, then I decided that I was going to join the world of the living again.

I put a long sundress and cardigan on to hide all of my bites and returned to the bedroom. 'Right, Mick, let us get started.'

He sat up in bed, looking a little bit bewildered. 'I thought you were ill?'

I sat down on the bed and smiled. 'I am feeling a little bit better today, we only have a few days left in Bulgaria to find our apartment in Old Nessebar, I do not want to go back home without knowing that it is actually being built!'

Mick got out of bed and opened the curtains to check on the weather, then he turned and looked at me. 'Why do you want to go to Old Nessebar, that's miles away.'

I followed him onto the balcony. 'Because that is where the sales representative from the Thistle Hotel said the apartment was located.'

He walked towards the bathroom. 'OK, let us wait for Christopher to get up, Janet, then we will get the bus to Old Nessebar. It should not be that hard to find our apartment there.'

Old Nessebar

When Christopher woke up, he said that he was hungry and that he wanted to go and have breakfast at the cafe on Sunny Beach, because it made one of the best full English breakfasts on the Black Sea coast. I was still feeling quite weak, but I knew we all needed to have something nice to eat before we travelled on the bus to Old Nessebar.

The walk to the beach was very nice, the sun was shining and we were all talking about finding our new apartment. When we arrived at the cafe, the waiter remembered Mick and I and he smiled. As soon as he saw the three of us approaching he grabbed some menus then asked us to sit at the table nearest the pedestrian walkway.

It did not take Christopher long to order sausage on toast with an orange juice. Mick and I ordered a full English breakfast with hot white coffee. Once the orders were taken, the waiter took them into the kitchen. I sat watching all the people going in and out of the shops in the big shopping square, it all looked quite frantic to me. I did not have the energy to walk far, never mind shop. The waiter brought Christopher's sausage on toast first. I could see his face light up. 'Wow Mum, that looks just like the breakfast you make.' He picked up the toast and started to eat it.

When the waiter placed my breakfast in front of me, I looked at it and my tummy turned. 'I'm not sure I can eat this, Mick.'

He was just starting to eat his. 'Listen, Janet, if you don't eat anything, we will not be able to go to Old Nessebar.'

I drank my coffee and ate a dry piece of brown toast.

'Mum, if you are not eating that sausage, can I have it?'

I picked up the sausage with my fork and passed it over to Christopher. 'Thanks, Mum, I'm still hungry.' He looked gorgeous and his smile made me feel so happy inside.

'Have you had enough to eat, Janet?' Mick had eaten all of his breakfast.

'Yes, love. I feel much better now that I have eaten that toast.'

Mick got up from his seat and paid the waiter while I went to the toilet.

When I came out of the toilet, I could see that Christopher and Mick had started to walk towards the main shopping square. As I was leaving the cafe, I asked the waiter where the bus stop was for Old Nessebar. He pointed to a small bus stop across the road from the main square. I thanked him and made my way to them.

By the time I had caught up with both of them, my energy levels had started to dip again. 'Right, lads, the bus stop for Old Nessebar is just across the main road.'

We walked over the main road and waited at the empty bus stop for about ten minutes which was brilliant for me.

'Are you sure this is the bus stop for Old Nessebar, there's no one waiting.'

I looked at the sign on the bus shelter. 'Yes, it says that the bus is due now, they run every fifteen minutes.'

Then a blue and white bus approached the bus stop. When it stopped, I could see a little sign with Old Nessebar written on it in the corner of the window. We moved away from the front door to let all the people get off the bus. Christopher and Mick got on the bus but before I could step one foot onto the bus, lots of people came from everywhere and they all jumped on the bus in front of me.

Fortunately for me, Mick and Christopher had managed to get three seats at the back of the bus, so I walked past all the people who nearly knocked me over to join them. I sat down near the window and within a few seconds the bus conductor was asking for a payment.

'How much for two adults and one child?' Mick got his wallet out of his pocket. 'Six Bulgarian lev.'

When he paid her, she handed him three tickets. I watched as she took payments from everyone on the bus. My eyes started to go blurred, everything and everyone around me seemed to be going so fast, but I felt like I was in slow motion. I stopped looking at all the people on the bus and I started looking out of the window at all the shops, bars, and restaurants. I realised that we would not have enough time to visit any of those places today, but I knew we would have loads of time in the future.

The journey to Old Nessebar took around twenty minutes, we went past so many lovely places including the new hospital. The bus drove along a lovely, beautiful causeway, which provided a peninsula into the Old Nessebar. The bus stopped just outside the stone walls surrounding the old village. It looked amazing. I could not wait to find our apartment.

The bus completed a 360-degree turn, then it stopped. I stood up and within a few seconds everyone had piled off. I took my time getting off the bus because I did not want to get caught up in the mad dash of people; however, as soon as I tried to step down from the bus a crowd of people started pushing past me trying to get the best seats on the bus. It was terrible, it felt like I had just been hit by a whirlwind. When they had all rushed past me, the bus driver left. I stood still on the pavement.

'Bloody hell, Janet, you looked like you have just been through a stampede.'

Still dazed, I looked around to see where Mick and Christopher were standing. The two of them were sitting on the wall behind the bus.

'Stop laughing at me.' I was not amused. 'Right, lads, the rep from the Thistle Hotel told me that our apartment was near Old Nessebar, so this is a good place to start.' Pretending that I was OK, I walked along the pavement towards the old stone wall, then I came across a sign and I started to read it (which allowed me a little time to get my breath back).

The ancient City of Nessebar is situated on a rocky peninsula on the Black Sea, the site is more than 3,000 years old. Nessebar was originally a Thracian settlement at the beginning of the 6th century BC; it is linked to New Nessebar town by a long and narrow neck of land. There are twenty-three churches and monuments, from an early Christian cathedral to a domed Byzantine church, reflecting the archaeological and artistic influence of the Greek and Roman period.

The sign was really informative. I was delighted that our apartment was being built in such a wonderful location. Mick decided to start our search from the right-hand side of the peninsula facing New Nessebar. We made our way past several beautiful restaurants until we came to a little harbour which had lots of small fishing boats tied up for the day. As we walked away from the harbour, we came across a big amphitheatre. We all stopped on the steps to take in the magnitude of it. I looked at Mick and Christopher.

'This must have been a glorious setting in its day, can you

113

imagine how many wonderful concerts have taken place here.'

After we finished walking around the theatre, we made our way down some steps towards a pathway along the right-hand side of Old Nessebar, which overlooked the coastline of New Nessebar. I looked up and down, and across the Black Sea to the new town, to see anything that resembled the pictures Sharon had sent me of the Apollon Complex, but there was no sign of the apartment or water park in sight.

When we reached the top of the peninsula, we continued to walk up and down all of the cobble pavements in search of the complex. I kept hoping that it would be located next to one of the wonderful churches or even at the side of a Roman ruin, but the Apollon Complex was nowhere to be found. We carried on walking until we came to the left-hand side of the peninsula.

'Look, Mum, you can see Sunny Beach from here. Can we go back there now, I have had enough walking for one day?'

Every part of my body was crying out to go back to the hotel, but my head was saying this is your last chance to find the apartment. 'Sorry, love, not yet. Please let us carry on until we find the apartment, it will not take long.'

We carried on walking up and down the peninsula until we were back at the bus stop. I sat on the wall with no energy left in my body. When I looked up towards Mick, he frowned at me.

'The man from the Thistle Hotel must have got the location wrong, Janet, because we have searched every corner of Old Nessebar. The Apollon Complex is nowhere to be found! Therefore, the rep must have meant New Nessebar.' He pointed his finger. 'Look, you can see hundreds of hotels and apartments from here, let us have a look around there.'

I stood up and looked towards New Nessebar town. Mick was right, there were hundreds of apartments and hotels. The

Apollon Complex had to be over there! I gathered what inner strength I had left and started to walk towards the pathway that joined Old Nessebar with the New Nessebar. Mick held my hand and the three of us walked along a narrow pathway by the side of the marina that led to a coastal pathway, which lay below most of the big hotels. I looked along the steps leading up to some of the hotels, I could see that there were lots of beautiful locations just above us, but when I looked at their names, none of them were called Apollon.

The midday sun was beaming down, and the heat was becoming unbearable. As a result, I had to stop for a rest at a large wooden pirate ship that was docked at the end of the walkway. Christopher was excited because they had real pirates on board who had turned the ship into a drunken sailor bar. As I sat down, a drunken pirate came to take our drinks order. Mick ordered a large bottle of still water, a lager for him and a small Fanta for Christopher. When the pirate brought the drinks, I took my time drinking the water, so that I could rest my tired body.

I looked into the distance from the port side of the pirate ship, and ahead of the ship, just past the long golden beach I could see some sand dunes in the distance, my heart started to beat faster. 'Look, Mick, can you see those sand dunes ahead of us? They look like the ones from the photos Sharon sent.'

Then the sound of lots of people playing games along the beach in the glorious sunshine made me smile. I thought to myself, *It is not far now, you can make it.* I heard the clinking of glass on the table, Christopher and Mick had finished their drinks. I looked across the table to where Christopher was sitting, he looked at me and smiled. His smile was like a ray of sunlight, it gave me the energy boost I needed to get up and continue looking.

Mick paid the bill and I left the pirate ship, Christopher said goodbye to the drunken sailors and we walked along the sandy beach until we came across a massive restaurant, with lots of big wooden chairs and tables outside, it looked fabulous. There was a large fire pit in the middle of the floor and there were lots of big pictures hanging around the walls showing local people dressed in traditional Bulgarian gowns dancing in and around the fire pit. It all looked quite scary to me; I was glad that Mick and Chris did not want anything to eat in there.

We continued walking up the pathway, then Christopher turned around the corner to look at a toy shop that sold footballs. Mick discovered some steps by the side of the shop that took us to the top of the hill where all the hotels were located. The walk up the steps was very challenging due to the heat of the midday sun. Christopher and Mick kept looking behind to make sure that I was keeping up with them and to give me the encouragement I needed to finish the hundreds of steps.

When I got to the last step, I looked up and I could see the main road that led down to Old Nessebar straight ahead of me. There was an old hospital to the left-hand side and a school just across the road. Mick did not bother walking to the right side, he knew that the Apollon Complex would not be down there, because we had seen all the names of the hotels from the beach walkway below. We all walked together past the hospital hoping we would see the complex, but there was no sign of Apollon, so we carried on walking along the main road towards the sand dunes that I had seen from the pirate ship. They were the only things that resembled the photos that Sharon had sent us.

It felt like we had been walking for several miles, but we did not see anything that resembled a complex or a water park.

I looked along the left-hand side of the road towards the sand dunes and along the sandy beach, but I could not see the name Apollon anywhere. All my negative thoughts started to come to the surface again. *What had I done, we have been robbed by Sharon! It was a big rip off, just like the ones we had seen on the TV.*

I did not believe that Mick and I could have lost all our money and our dream home in the sun was just a fabrication of someone's imagination. As we walked along the never-ending road, I kept going over and over what the sales representative had said at the Thistle Hotel. 'The location is perfect; it is only a hundred metres away from the beach.' I knew that from the pictures Sharon had sent to me were the same. Therefore, the complex had to be somewhere along this coastal road.

Suddenly, Mick stopped. 'Right, Janet, we are at the end of the New Nessebar town and that so-called complex is not on this road.' I looked at him and my heart sank, then my eyes started to fill up with tears and I just wanted to collapse on the floor. I knew that I was the one who got us into this mess. And now we were going to go home without our dream home in the sun, no money and an unexpected medical bill!

Then out of the corner of my tearful eyes, I saw a plan of the Apollon Complex in the window of a tiny shop selling homes. It looked like the same plan that the sales rep had shown Mick and me at the Thistle Hotel.

'Look, there it is.' Mick and Christopher looked all around them for the complex. 'No, it is in that window.' Mick looked through the glass window at the plan. 'There it is, Christopher, look, can you see it?'

With all our hopes raised again, I walked towards the shop. Mick opened the door and we both burst into the shop like two lottery winners. Mick was talking and I was pointing my finger at the Apollon Complex plans in the window. The two estate agents looked at the both of us, as if we were from another planet, never mind another country. In our excitement, we both kept asking them questions in English regarding the Apollon Complex, as if we were in England, and they could understand every word that we were saying. It must have taken us about five minutes before we realised that they did not understand a word of English, never mind our excited gibberish. One of the agents managed to get a word in. 'Stop, no English.'

I could not believe it. 'What do you mean, no English?'

The other agent smiled and pointed at the plans. 'Apollon, *dobre* (good), *nyama* problem (no problem), *li polucha tova* (I have that).'

During all of this confusion, Mick and I did not realise that they thought that we wanted to buy a new apartment on the Apollon Complex. As a result, they were starting to sell us something we had already bought. Before we could do or say anything, another man from a big office at the back of the shop had come to see what was going on. They all started to talk to each other in Bulgarian.

The man from the office started to smile at Mick and me then he rubbed his hands together and spoke, 'Yes, that is very good, excellent, come with me.' Then he showed us the keys to his car, then he pointed to the main road. 'Please come with me, I will take you to the apartments.'

I stopped smiling. 'No, no, no, thanks, we have already bought an apartment, it is on the Apollon Complex, but we don't know how to find it.'

The man carried on walking towards us. 'Yes, very good, please come with me, I will show you.'

Mick started to make his way out of the shop. 'No, no, thanks, please can you tell us where to find those apartments, the ones you have in the window.' Then he pointed to the plans. But this did not stop the man, it just encouraged him more.

'Yes, please come with me, I will take you there now.' He dangled his car keys in front of both of us and grinned. I could not believe what was happening.

'No, no, thanks, I am so sorry, but we do not want to get in the car, we only wanted to know where the complex was so that we could walk there.'

The man picked up his leather case and he walked towards us. The two other members of staff got their bags and started to move us towards the doorway. 'Please stop, we do not want a lift!'

Mick and I rushed past the three of them and ran out of the shop. As we passed our Christopher, Mick shouted, 'Hurry up, son, run, we are leaving here now!'

Christopher looked a bit startled. 'But Mum, Dad, my feet are hurting.'

Mick looked back at him. 'Hurry up, son, your mother has just nearly bought us another apartment.'

'Oh no, not again, Dad, we have not found the first one yet.' Then he started running to catch us up.

We carried on running until we came to a crossroads on the main road. Our hopes of finding our dream home were now the least of our worries because we had three estate agents chasing agents after us!

I had to stop for a while. We all hid behind a little kiosk so that I could catch my breath. Mick looked up the main road to make sure no one was following us.

'Wow, Janet that was close, you nearly bought another

apartment.'

I just burst out laughing, I don't know whether it was nerves or just pure exhaustion. 'The complex has got to be somewhere around here, it can't be far, please let us keep looking.'

Mick looked at me with disbelief. 'Janet! That man was closing the shop and getting ready to drive us to the Apollon Complex, so it must be too far to walk.'

I did not want to believe him, but inside I knew he may be right. 'No, it cannot be that far, that man looked like he was too big to walk anywhere.'

Mick looked at Christopher. 'What do you think, son?'

Chris looked at me. 'It's OK, let us continue to walk along the road for a little while longer.'

Christopher and Mick carried on walking along the main road and I walked behind them, hoping to find the complex before my energy levels faded and their support ended. I caught up with both of them when we started to walk through some undesirable areas with lots of empty buildings, which made me wish that we would not find the complex there, because it was in such a terrible location. After a while, we came to a big hill and the landscape started to change, the area was becoming increasingly desolated. There were only two shops and a small bus stop. It looked like we were walking along a road to nowhere.

There was no way we were going to turn back because of the misunderstanding in the estate agent's, we knew we could not stay where we were, so we had to carry on walking forward because we had to move away from the area because it was derelict. As we made our way to the bottom of the hill, I noticed a car park leading to a beach.

'Mick, this looks like that beach I had seen from the pirate ship.'

He stopped walking and turned to look at me. 'Great, Janet, but it is not what we are looking for.' On the left-hand side of the road, there was a lot of barren land and what looked like big sand dunes. 'Why don't you go have a look over there, Janet? The complex might be over that ridge of sand.'

My heart skipped a beat, it looked a little bit like a photo Sharon sent from Amber Sun. I walked across the main road to the edge of the sand dunes. I had to make my way through some overgrown bushes to get onto the actual sand dunes. As I made my way to the top of the dunes, I was hoping to see the complex and the water park, but when I looked across the land, all I could see was lots of sand and barren land for miles.

Reluctantly, I made my way back through the bushes then across the road to Mick and Christopher, to give them the unwelcome news. 'Sorry, lads, the complex is not over there.'

Mick looked at Christopher. 'Well, there's a surprise, son, what did I tell you? I knew there wouldn't be anything over there.'

I could tell that they had both had enough of walking in the midday sunshine and they were fed up with searching for the apartment. 'All right, Mick, let us just carry on to the other side of the hill and if it's not there, we will go back to Sunny Beach!'

Christopher's face brightened up again. 'That sounds good to me, Mum.'

The walk to the top of the hill was horrible, because all my physical and emotional energy had gone away with my hopes of finding the apartment and my inner thoughts were turning negative again. Not only had I bought an apartment that we could not find, Mick and Christopher were also losing what little hope they had and I was dragging them along a pavement in the midday sun, on a road to nowhere.

When we finally got over the brow of the hill, I could see a massive green building on the left-hand side of the road. It was the biggest building that I had seen in Bulgaria so far. I almost ran down the hill to see what the name was on the building. Wouldn't it be great if it was called the Apollon Complex? I could hear Christopher talking to Mick. 'Wow, Dad, we are heading back into civilization.'

Unfortunately, when I got to the bottom of the hill, I could see that it was a hotel, and it was called the Nessebar Sol. It looked like one of the major hotels on the Black Sea coast. However, to my delight, it was remarkably busy. There were so many holiday makers popping in and out of the reception area, the car park was full of coaches and there were lots of staff helping happy families with their luggage, it looked lovely. Mick walked over to me. 'That is a good sign, Jan, we must be coming into the posh area of Old Nessebar.'

Christopher overheard what Mick was saying. 'That is great news, Dad. Can we stop at the next decent cafe to rest for a while because my feet are hurting me?'

I gave Christopher a big hug. 'That is a great idea, son.' My energy levels had passed the point of no return and I was walking on empty. I think the only thing that was keeping me from collapsing was the thought of seeing our dream home before we had to go home.

While we were walking towards a little village, I noticed that there were a few hotels on the right-hand side of the road, and the coastline was on the left side. When we got into the village, Mick spotted a lovely little bar set back from the main road overlooking the Black Sea. It looked very inviting, so we decided to rest there for a while to get something to drink. We all sat down on the old wooden chairs around a big pine table and waited to be served. When we looked out across the sea, Christopher spotted something.

'Wow, Dad, look at that shipwreck.'

Mick looked across the table at me. 'Great, son, that is just like us, it's just our luck, this whole bloody holiday has been one big shipwreck from the start!'

My head dropped and I looked at the ground below my feet and prayed that he was not right, because I knew that it would take me a lifetime to make up for this mistake!

When the waiter arrived, Mick ordered our drinks. I sat back in the big wooden chair and listened to the noise of beautiful emerald green waves rolling along to golden sand. This amazing moment ended when the waiter started to pour our drinks. My glass of orange juice was one of the nicest, coolest, softest drinks that I had ever swallowed. We all seemed to take our time drinking the wonderful cold drinks in the hot sunshine.

We were sitting in one of the most idyllic locations in silence. I knew that none of us wanted to move or say what the other one was thinking because none of us wanted to spoil the moment. After a while, when we had finally finished our drinks. I gathered what was left of my hopes and dreams and we walked out of the bar, ready to find a taxi to take us back to the hotel.

We walked past a few hotels that were situated along the golden beach, then Mick spotted a little pathway that took us back onto the main road. When we got to the road, I saw a bus stop like the one we had stood at in Sunny Beach. We waited for the traffic to pass, then we all walked across the road towards the bus stop to see if there were any buses going to

Sunny Beach. When we crossed the road there was a little corner shop and a small beige building in front of us. Then I saw a sign partially hidden behind some overgrown rose bushes inside the building's garden and I could not believe my eyes. 'Mick, look, does that sign say Apollon Complex apartments?'

We all ran across a small dirt road towards the sign as if it were a pot of gold. When we got to the sign, I noticed that it was the same sign that the rep had shown us at the Thistle Hotel. I was ecstatic! 'It's here, we have found our dream holiday home.'

There was a tall man wearing white shorts standing in the garden. He was watering all the beautiful rose bushes by the side of the sign. I could not wait to talk to him.

'Hello, Mr, can you help me, where is Apollon Complex?'

He stopped watering the flowers, then he pointed his finger towards a newly constructed road to the left of the building. When I looked ahead, I could see that there were some builders working on a new development.

'It is here, Janet; I knew it would be around here.' Michael looked very relieved.

I smiled at Christopher and winked. 'Our new home in the sun is just up this road, son.'

But he did not smile back. 'Oh no, not more walking, Mum, my trainers are worn out, you said that we were going to get a bus or taxi.'

I was so relieved. 'Come on, son, it is not that far now.'

We walked a short distance along the new road then Mick pointed out another sign advertising not only Apollon 1, 2, 3 but 4, 5 and 6. We all looked very reassured! Mick looked at me then Christopher. 'I told you it would be around here, didn't I, son?'

Christopher had had enough. 'Great news, can we go and get a taxi now, Dad?'

I had almost killed myself trying to find the Apollon Complex, I was determined that I was not going back to the hotel or home until I had touched it. 'Just a few more minutes, son, we have not come all this way to walk away now, I have to see the inside of our apartment, don't you want to see the swimming pool?'

With Christopher convinced to stay, we walked to the end of the dirt road on to the new road of the development. We walked along a small pavement to the left-hand side of the road. Then I noticed that there was a small gate leading to a sun area and swimming pool. Mick and I looked through the railings next to the gate, we could see a few people sunbathing by a pool, it looked like a wonderful little oasis.

'This is the dream, Mick, one day that will be us.' We both looked at each other and Mick kissed me on the cheek.

Christopher started coughing. 'Find a room, please.'

Feeling a bit embarrassed, I managed to catch the attention of two sunbathers relaxing by the pool. 'Hello, hello, I am sorry to bother you, but we are looking for the Apollon 4 complex, do you know where it is?' They did not move an inch. We must have looked like two noisy outsiders trying to get into their little oasis. 'Excuse me, please, can you help us to find our apartment on Apollon 4.'

The man looked up at me then pointed to some foundations at the top of a field, then he returned back to his sunbathing position.

'Thank you, kind sir. I am so sorry to bother you. Mick, Christopher, I think that is Apollon 4?' Then a wonderful Irish woman's voice replied.

'Yes, it is, but you will need to talk to Ploughman first.' The woman who was laid next to the man had gotten up from her sunbed to help us.

'Who's Ploughman?' Mick and I both shouted together.

Then the man sat back up. 'He should be in the old train carriage in the middle of that field.' He pointed to a big grass field, then he lay back down on his sun bed.

'OK, that is brilliant, thank you so very much.'

We started to walk through the grass field until we came to an old train carriage, situated at the side of a new development. Mick knocked on the door, but there was no answer. I walked up the steps and I knocked repeatedly on the metal door, but there was no one in the carriage. I was devastated. 'We will have to go and find him; he can't be far away.'

Christopher was standing at the side of the carriage. 'I can't believe this, Mum and Dad! We have travelled on a busy bus from Sunny Beach, we have walked around the whole of Old Nessebar, we have sat on a pirate ship, we have walked through Nessebar New Town and lots of little villages, we walked over a hill and all along the Black Sea coast to find our apartment and now there is no one at home, and now we are standing in the middle of a field up to our ankles in mud and you want to start looking for somebody called Ploughman!'

I knew he was right, but I carried on walking past the train carriage towards a fence in the field just in case he was working on the building site in front of us. As I looked through the fence, I could see a new structure being built that looked like a new apartment block. 'Come over here and look closely at that building. Is it the same shape as the photographs Sharon had sent us from Amber Sun.'

Mick and Christopher started to walk towards me, and they

looked through the fence. 'Is this Apollon 4, Mick, could this be our dream home?'

Mick looked straight at me. 'It could be Janet; it looks like some of those pictures from Amber Sun!' Within a few seconds of standing in a muddy field we had convinced ourselves that this building was Apollon 4, and our dream holiday home in the sun was actually being built.

Although we could not touch the apartment, swim in the pool or talk to Ploughman, we could finally see that it was being developed.

'Right, Christopher, this is our new dream holiday home in the sun, let's go.' I turned to see the expression on Christopher's face.

'Great news, Mum, can we go and get a taxi now; I have had enough house hunting and walking to last me a lifetime.'

I held Mick's hand. 'Bless him, he has had a long day.'

'He's not the only one, let us go and get a taxi.'

We walked through the muddy field back to the main road to get a taxi back to Sunny Beach. When we arrived at the hotel we packed our suitcases ready for the flight home to the UK

Good News

The journey back to Bourgas Airport was great. However, I was still not feeling one hundred percent. But I knew my GP would sort everything out as soon as I got home and I had made an appointment. I was confident that the apartment was being built, because I had seen a building's foundations, and I had actually stepped foot on the Apollon Complex, which looked like a little oasis albeit within a big muddy field. It was good to know that our dream holiday home was no longer a fabrication of someone's imagination!

When the plane landed at Manchester Airport, I was so relieved to be home. The taxi ride from the airport felt quite cold, compared with the lovely heat from the sun in Bulgaria. When we arrived home, Mick opened the front door and he dropped the suitcases off in the hall. I walked behind him and picked up the house phone to make an appointment with my GP. I wanted to make sure whatever illness I had in Bulgaria was not something more serious and the medication provided by the man in the white coat was legal.

When the doctor's receptionist answered the phone, I explained to her what had happened to me on holiday and how sick I had become. I told her about the trip in the "ambulance" and the massive injection in my bottom. As a result, she asked if I could come into the surgery first thing the following morning to see the GP. I agreed then I put the phone down.

That night, Mick and I looked through the photos from

Amber Sun to see if we could recognise some of the buildings. We found the bar where we had a lovely drink, the beige building and the pool where we asked the lovely Irish couple for directions, then we realised that it was Apollon 2.

The following day when I arrived at the doctor's, the receptionist asked me to wait in a little room on my own, which was a bit strange because I was normally made to wait with the rest of the patients in the waiting room? I waited in the room for around ten minutes before the GP opened the door.

'Hello, Janet, I believe you have been away on holiday to Bulgaria, and while you were away you became quite ill?' I looked up at him.

'Yes, Doctor, that is true.'

He sat down on his chair then turned towards me. 'Please can you try to explain to me what actually happened?'

I sat up in the blue plastic chair. 'Well, Doctor, it all started when I ordered too much food in a restaurant in Sunny Beach, and we didn't have enough time to eat it all before it melted on our plates.' He started to take notes. 'Then Mick and I went to the beach to sunbathe and there was a sand storm. Mick and Christopher did a bungee jump and I watched them, then I started to feel terribly ill. I could not eat or drink because my stomach felt like it was going to explode.' He did not look up at me, he just continued to write down what I was saying... so I continued.

'When Mick and Christopher came back from a boys' night out, I had to ask Mick to go down to the receptionist to ask her to phone a doctor for me, which he did. Then this man in a white coat knocked at the bedroom door and Mick let him in, he sat on the bed and looked at my eyes then he took my pulse and then he told Mick that I needed to go with him because I was very sick.' The doctor continued writing.

'I thought we were going to go to the new hospital in Sunny Beach, but when we got outside the hotel, the man in the white coat made us get into a little white van. The Bulgarian driver had driven us to one of the backstreets, then we got out. We went through this black door into a room with a bed against the wall and one glass cabinet. The man in the white coat made me pull down my knickers while Mick was trying to kill the squadron of mosquitoes that were trying to bite me as I lay on the bed. Then the man in the white coat told Mick to move away, then he gave me a massive injection in my bottom.'

The doctor looked a bit bewildered. 'Right, Janet, tell me how did you feel after he gave you this injection?'

I remembered all of the mosquitoes' dive-bombing my bottom. 'Well, Doctor, I was worried about all the mosquitoes biting me and I was wondering how we were going to get back to the hotel.'

He stared at me, then shook his head. 'No, Janet, that is not what I am asking you, how did the injection make you feel?'

I stopped talking and thought back to being on the trolley in the grey room. 'I am not too sure, Doctor, I was so worried about being bitten to death by the insects that I could not tell you, but I did have tears in my eyes because it hurt so much.'

He looked down at his notes. 'OK, Janet, what happened when you got back to the hotel?'

I leant forward in my chair. 'When I got back to the hotel, I got undressed and got into bed, then the man in the white coat came knocking again.'

He looked up from his notes. 'Did he give you any more injections, Janet?'

I smiled at him. 'No, thank god, there were no more

injections. He gave Mick a prescription for some additional medication.'

He held his pen towards me. 'Do you know what was on the prescription, Janet?'

'Yes, Doctor, Imodium and something else.' I bent down to pick my bag up.

'Do you have it with you, Janet?'

I grabbed the box from my bag. 'Yes, Doctor, here is the box of pills, I kept it just in case you wanted to see it.'

The doctor looked at the writing on the medication box, then he took out the document that was still inside, he looked through it and made a note.

'Please lay on the bed because I want to examine your stomach.' After he had examined my belly, he checked my eyes, heart, and blood pressure. 'Right, Janet, here is a prescription for a week's supply of antibiotics. Please can you go next door to the phlebotomist nurse for some routine blood test, to make sure you have recovered from the illness.'

I left the doctor's surgery with a sore left arm and a large box of antibiotics. I waited for a week, then I phoned the surgery for the results of the blood test. I was very happy because they all came back normal.

Mick and I continued to receive regular updates from Sharon at Amber Sun. When I had paid the third instalment, she supplied the name of their Bulgaria solicitor to guide us through all the legal requirements for buying a property in Bulgaria. I phoned Anastasia, the Bulgarian solicitor, as soon as Sharon had emailed me her contact details because I wanted to introduce myself.

When I called her, I thought she would struggle to understand my English accent, but she was brilliant, she actually spoke the queen's English better than me! Anastasia provided advice on all the legal procedures that Mick and I would need to complete before we could finalise the sale. But most of all, she confirmed that the apartment development was going to plan and that it would be ready in time for the fourth and final instalment. Mick was so relieved when I told him that I had spoken to a Bulgarian solicitor. This meant that the sale was going through and we were not getting ripped off. Our dream holiday home was finally for real.

Before we made the final payment, we decided to tell my little sister, Michelle, and her husband, Paul, about our new holiday home. None of us wanted to tell any of our family or friends before, just in case it did not happen. I invited my sister and her husband around to our house for a nice meal and a game of cards, to break the good news to them.

Mick went to pick them up from their home in Halebank, I could not wait to see my little sister, Paul and their daughter Cerys. When the car pulled onto the drive, I ran to open the front door. Cerys got out of the back seat and ran towards me. I gave her a big hug, then she went upstairs to see Christopher. Michelle got out of the car and walked towards me.

She took her Everton tracksuit jacket off and placed it over the staircase bannister. Paul and Mick walked into the kitchen, Paul placed his lagers and Michelle's ciders into the fridge. Mick passed him two glasses before I told them the good news. 'Guess what, Michelle. Mick and I have bought an apartment in Bulgaria. It has two bedrooms, two toilets and two swimming pools.'

Michelle stopped pouring her cider and sat down on the chair in the conservatory. 'That's fantastic news, sis, but where is Bulgaria?'

Mick came walking into the conservatory. 'It's next to Greece and across from Turkey.'

Paul came into the conservatory from the kitchen. 'What made you buy a property in Bulgaria?'

I sat down next to Mick. 'Because the price was right.'

They were so happy for us. Paul offered to book some time off work to help us move into the apartment once we had got the completion date. Michelle was so happy because Paul and her had never been on a holiday abroad with their daughter Cerys; she could not wait.

When we sat down for the meal we all celebrated buying a holiday home, their first holiday abroad with Cerys and lots of fun in the sun. It was a wonderful evening. We laughed and joked about all the wonderful times we would have together sunbathing by the pool and relaxing by sea.

Before they left to go home, Michelle gave me a big hug. 'Good night, sis. We will buy our new passports when Paul gets paid at the end of the month, and then I will start to save for our flights over to Bulgaria in the next few weeks. It is going to be great, I can't wait to see your new apartment.'

I hugged her back, then we stood in the hallway waiting for Paul and Cerys. Everything was going so well; Michelle and Paul were looking forward to a well-deserved holiday with Cerys.

The following week, Mick and I received an email from Sharon regarding the furniture package. We spent the weekend choosing one of the beautiful bathroom fixtures and tiles, we decided the colour of the kitchen worktops and units, all the living room furniture and soft furnishings, including the bedding and bathroom towels. It was all beginning to feel so real then unexpectedly, I received an email from another unknown buyer telling us not to pay any more money to Amber Sun, because the development was ending, and all the payments would be lost.

I could not believe what I was reading. This unknown person had emailed a warning to Mick and me about our worst fears! I must have read the email several times before I called Sharon at Amber Sun. As soon as I got through to her, I told her about the email from this man. She informed me that there was an issue with one of the Bulgarian developers about Amber Sun's "commission" but it did not affect the Apollon Complex. She continued to tell me that our apartment was almost complete and all they were waiting for was for Mick and me to confirm a few more items on our furniture package. I felt a little bit reassured by Sharon's advice, but I was not a hundred percent certain.

When Mick came home from work, I showed him the email from the unknown buyer, he was extremely disappointed. Then I explained to him what Sharon had said and he claimed down. We spent the next few hours completing the furniture package then I emailed it to Amber Sun. I phoned Sharon shortly after to confirm that they had received the final furniture package options and to make sure that Amber Sun was still operating. And I had to go through all the negative thoughts I was having once again with Sharon for some more reassurance while Mick was listening.

Sharon confirmed that everything was going to plan with the Apollon Complex development. She advised Mick and me that a Bulgarian furniture company that they worked in partnership with were out buying all the furniture packages that day and that the kitchen would be fitted within a week's time, this included all the fixtures and fittings. The bathrooms would also be fitted into the apartment within a month to make sure it was completed on time. I put the phone down and looked at Mick.

'What do you think?'

He looked outside the window. 'It's hard to trust someone when you can't see or talk to them in person.'

Although we were both delighted with the thought of everything being fitted and the apartment being ready for the complexion date, I could not forget about what the unknown buyer had written in his email and his terrible situation, which just made me worry even more about all the things that could still go wrong.

With all of this fresh in my mind, I decided to telephone Anastasia, the Bulgarian solicitor. I informed her about the information within the email from the unknown man and the conversation with Sharon. Within a few seconds, she confirmed that there was a big issue with Amber Sun's commission.

I could not believe what she was saying and all of my uncertainty came gushing out! 'Mick and I knew that these apartments were too good to be true! I knew that our dream home in the sun was just a fabrication of that bloody Sharon's imagination.' All the negativity that had built up over the years had come to the surface! Mick left the room to make a cup of tea.

After about five minutes, Anastasia managed to calm me down. 'Mrs Gorry. An urgent email will be sent to you and your husband today advising both of you not to pay any more money directly to Amber Sun, because the Bulgarian builders on the Apollon Complex (Kostov) were in dispute with them over their high commission charges.' She also advised us that the final instalment had to be paid directly into the developer's bank account. I put the phone down and waited for the email to arrive before I could call her back.

I could not believe what was happening, I sat down by the computer and waited for the email. When the email arrived, I read it as quickly as I could. Then I scrutinised every written word on the screen before I spoke to Mick, because I was worried about how he would react to the disturbing news. 'Anastasia has sent an email confirming everything that Sharon had said on the phone except that the final payment has to be paid to the developer, someone called Kostov.'

He looked at me. 'You need to phone her back again; I want to listen to what she is saying about the final payment.'

I phoned her number. 'Hi, Anastasia, thank you for your email, but we are still not convinced about the final payment with everything that is going on with Amber Sun. We have only just ordered all of our fixtures, fitting and soft furnishings with Sharon!'

It took her a long time to convince Mick and me that everything was going to plan and all the payments that we had paid through Amber Sun were safe.

She confirmed that the apartment was complete; however, we had to pay the final instalment to Kostov the developer for all the outstanding internal work and the furniture package, which included the kitchen and bathroom fixtures and fittings. Mick and I had to trust her; it felt like we had no choice! Amber Sun had taken too much commission and the developer wanted the rest of the money to complete the apartment.

The next day, Anastasia emailed the new bank details of the developer and she supplied the completion date for the final payment. Mick and I had so many uncertainties about what was happening with the apartment and if we were still at risk of being ripped off.

The next day Mick and I decided to make sure that the Bulgarian building company existed before we paid the last instalment. Without any hesitation I printed the email off that Anastasia sent and we took it to our bank to check out the new developer's Bulgarian bank account, and to check what had happened to all the money we had paid to Amber Sun.

The journey to the bank was a bit of a blur; we both wanted our dream home to exist, but we did not want to pay any more money to any building developers until we were certain. When we walked into the bank, I made sure that we spoke to the assistant that had taken us through the online banking registration.

Mick told her about the situation with Amber Sun and the Bulgarian developers then I handed her the email from Anastacia, our Bulgarian solicitor. As she read it I noticed that she looked a bit concerned then she started to type some information into her keyboard. Within a few minutes, she smiled at me then she confirmed that the bank account on the email existed, and that the account was in the same name as the developer's company, which was Kostov.

I felt more confident knowing that the bank had some tangible information, she also advised Mick and I that Halifax would have a financial audit of all the online payments and where they had been processed. Therefore, to safeguard all the payments including the final payment transfer to the new account we needed to ask the Bulgarian solicitor and developer to confirm in writing that they had received each and every one of the financial transactions, which I did as soon as I got home.

When we made the final transaction Anastasia sent Mick and me the Contract of Ownership that needed to be signed by a notary solicitor and ourselves. She also provided the name of one of her local contacts (Nikolay) who would help with any problems or issues when we were ready to move into our new apartment.

Our dream home in the sun was almost ours, but we needed to find someone to sign the notary. I tried all the legal professionals in our local area, but none of them specialised in notaries. After a few days, I finally found a specialist in Southport. I phoned the solicitor's office and spoke to the administrator about the whole process, which seemed simple enough, so I made an appointment for the next weekend.

The following Saturday Mick, Christopher and I got all the documents ready and we went to Southport to get the notary signed. It felt a lot more secure with the notary being signed by an English solicitor. It took us a while to find the office of the notary solicitor. I expected a big law firm, but it was just a small office just off the main shopping area. As I walked into the reception area, I could smell the polished wood and the sense of oldness, as if I had just walked back into the 1940s.

The receptionist was very mature, and she spoke with a quiet manner. 'Good afternoon, can I assist you? Are you sure that you are in the right place?'

I felt like a naughty school child who had wandered into the head master's office. 'Hello, we are Mr and Mrs Gorry. And this is Christopher, our son. We are here to see the notary solicitor.'

She looked me up and down as if she was not expecting two young parents and their son. 'Mr and Mrs Who?'

I smiled at her. 'We are Mr and Mrs Gorry, G-o-double r-y.'

She looked down at the large diary on the desk. 'Yes, that

is correct, please take a seat by the front door.'

We waited by the door for around fifteen minutes. Christopher was becoming very bored and Mick was dying for a nice cup of tea after our long journey. Then a big white wooden door opened in front of us. A small lady stood in the doorway, she reminded me of Miss Hathaway from the Beverly Hillbillies.

'Sorry to keep you waiting, please come through.'

The very posh lady made her way across the dark red carpet to her desk. As we walked forward, she requested that we all sat down in front of her big oak desk. It really did feel like being back at school.

'Good afternoon, how can I help, Mr and Mrs Gorry?' She sounded very professional.

I looked at all the law books she had on the bookshelves behind her. I was delighted to see a number of books on European law.

'Good afternoon, Ms Solicitor. My husband and I have purchased an apartment in Bulgaria, and we need someone to sign the notary, and you are the only person we could find.'

She looked across to me, then to Michael and Christopher. 'What on earth made you buy a property in Bulgaria?'

Mick and I informed her about the information the sales representative provided at the Thistle Hotel, but she did not seem to be overly impressed. She got a number of documents out of her desk drawer and she talked us through the entire process, which took quite a long time because she was very thorough. I felt more confident with her involvement, knowledge and experience. She was worth more to Mick and I than any of the Amber Sun representatives and the Bulgarian solicitor, because we trusted her words of wisdom and we could actually see and talk to her in person.

When we came out of the solicitor's, it was one of the most confident times any of us had felt since the day we signed the legal documents at the Thistle Hotel. With this renewed confidence, Mick decided to have a celebration lunch knowing that one day soon we would be the proud owners of our very own dream holiday home in the sun.

Birthday Surprises

Once the notary was signed and completed, it was sent to the Bulgarian solicitor for approval. We waited for a few weeks before we received the official documents of Ownership. We were now the proud owners of apartment A12, Apollon 4, Apollon Complex. The completion date was set for June 2009. Mick arranged to pick the keys up for our new apartment from Ploughman the builder at Apollon 4.

This was fabulous news because it was Mick's fiftieth birthday in June. Without any hesitation, I phoned Anastasia to confirm the completion date and our arrival time at the Apollon Complex. While I was on the phone, she advised me to complete a snagging list on the fixtures and fittings, and to go through the furniture package that we had ordered from Amber Sun, to make sure that everything we had paid for was in the apartment. And if there were any problems with the interior of the apartment or the furniture package that we should contact her straight away. This final piece of information provided all the reassurance Mick and I needed.

I could not wait to tell Michelle and Paul that we had confirmed the actual moving-in date, and that we could finally book our flights. Mick, Chris and I got into the car and we drove over to Halebank where they lived. I could not wait to tell her the good news.

When we arrived at their house, Michelle opened the porch door. 'Hiya, sis, what are you doing here?'

I ran towards her. 'Great news, Michelle, we can move into the apartment on Mick's fiftieth birthday.'

Then the smile on her face dropped. 'Come in, everyone, I have got something to tell you.'

As I went to walk through the doorway, Christopher ran past me to give Michelle a big hug, then he went into the kitchen to find one of the many bags of sweets she kept in the cupboards.

'Are you all right, sis?'

She went into the living room and sat down on the chair by the table, then Cerys sat on her knee. 'Sorry, everyone, but we won't be able to come on holiday because Paul's car had broken down and he needed to get it fixed for work, so we had to use the money we had saved for our flights and new passports to get it repaired.'

We were all devastated, we had spent so many wonderful weekends talking about moving into the apartment, enjoying a great holiday in Bulgaria and how much they had been looking forward to spending their first holiday abroad with Cerys. (I think we all needed to have lots of fun in the sun). Before we left, Mick and I both promised Michelle, Paul and Cerys that we would be going back to Bulgaria again, and as soon as they had saved enough money for their new passports and flights, we would all go to the apartment as planned.

My older sister Lillian and her husband Melvin had never been on holiday abroad before, they were both aware that Michelle and Paul had offered to help us to move into the new apartment in Bulgaria. When they had found out about Paul's car breaking down, they were upset because Michelle and Paul were no longer able to make it. They were also aware that we would be moving in the apartment on Mick's fiftieth birthday, which they did not want to miss, so they asked if they could come on holiday with us instead of Paul and Michelle?

Mick and I had spent weeks talking to Michelle and Paul about moving into the apartment and they knew what to expect. We tried to explain to Lillian and Melvin that it was not going to be like a typical holiday abroad, with a lovely hotel, lots of sunbathing and relaxing around the pool, because we would be moving into a new apartment and we did not want to spoil their first ever holiday abroad, but moving into a new apartment did not put them off; in fact, they offered to help us move in. Mick and I were delighted because we had some additional support and we could share his fiftieth birthday with someone from our family.

Christopher had decided that he did not want to come with us while we were moving in, he wanted to stay at home with Lillian's son, because for the first time, they were both old enough to be home alone.

When we arrived at Manchester Airport, everyone was ready to have an enjoyable time moving into our new holiday home. We were all looking forward to having lots of fun in the sun and celebrating Mick's fiftieth birthday. When we walked into the departure terminal, Mick found our flight number and he located the check-in desk, and we all waited in the line to be checked in, with our tickets and passports in hand.

Mick and I checked in first to reduce any anxiety for Lillian and Melvin. Mick placed the heaviest suitcases onto the belt first, and I felt a sense of relief because I had packed so many extra "moving-in items" that both cases were ready to burst open. The women at the "check-in desk" put a red warning sticker for "heavy luggage" on both of them. Mick and I looked at each other and smiled as the two heavy suitcases made their way towards the aeroplane.

We both stood away from the check-in and waited while Lillian and Melvin checked in their luggage and to make sure everything was OK? We did our best to make sure that they were coping well with their first ever check-in. I watched as Melvin put the first suitcase onto the belt. I noticed that he looked a little bit nervous, so I smiled at him to give him some reassurance, but he seemed to be a bit preoccupied. Lillian passed him the second suitcase and he placed that one on the belt, she seemed to be a bit anxious.

The women at the check-in desk asked them both a few questions which made Lillian look even more nervous, so I went over to them to give them both some moral support. As soon as they got their passports and tickets, Melvin said that he needed a big drink, and Lillian agreed. We all walked through to the departure gate with our little suitcases in hand, as if we were only going for a lovely long weekend away.

When we finally got through all the security checks, Mick and Melvin found us a nice place to sit until our flight was called. We settled down at the bar, I ordered the food and Mick asked for two pints of lager for him and Melvin, and a bottle of wine for myself and Lillian to calm her nerves.

Melvin started to laugh. 'I could not believe it when the man at customs asked me to take my belt off, because I was worried that my jeans would fall down to my ankles.' We all burst out laughing at the thought of Melvin's jeans falling down.

When we had finished our meals and well-deserved drinks, Lillian and I had a last-minute look around the duty-free shops for some nice perfume and a bottle of decent aftershave for the boys. Then I heard our flight being called over the tannoy. I looked at Lillian to give her some reassurance, but I could tell by her face that her nerves were getting the better of her.

'Come on, sis, let us make our way back to the boys, then we can go to the boarding gate. Everything is going to be OK, this is the easy bit.'

As we all made our way to the boarding gate, I could tell that Lillian was getting more and more nervous with every step she took towards the gate. The passenger check-in area was very busy. Mick and I went first then we waited at the other side to ensure that they both got through without any holdups. They managed to get through without any delays to their delight. Then we all took our positions to board the plane. Mick and I held hands then he looked at me. 'This is it, Janet, we will soon be back in Bulgaria.'

I squeezed his hand gently. 'I know, I can't wait to see our new apartment, love.'

When I stepped on the plane, the air hostess helped all of us to find our seats. Mick and Melvin put the small cases in the overhead lockers and we all settled down into our seats. Then the light came on to fasten our seat belts. I looked behind my seat to where Lillian and Melvin were sitting to give her some assurance, I could see that her nerves had turned into stress and she was getting worse. When I looked down, I could see that her hands were shaking and I could hear her voice quivering as we waited for the plane to take-off.

The air hostess did her final checks, then I could hear the engines getting louder as we made our way towards the runway. I gave Lillian another supportive smile to reassure her as the plane started its journey on the runway. As the engines got louder and louder and the plane finally left the ground, I could hear her saying to Melvin, 'Fucking hell, oh fucking hell.' And she never ever swears!

Mick shouted, 'You will be OK, Lillian, it is only the take-off and landing that is bad.' He looked at me and whispered. 'God help her when we land in Bourgas Airport, she will think the wheels have fallen off the plane.'

Then I heard her shaky voice from behind me, saying, 'Thanks, Mick, I heard that. I will spend the whole of the flight worrying about landing now!'

Once we were up in the sky, Melvin managed to calm her down, we were all relieved that her "nervous swearing" had stopped, and her lovely smile had returned.

We started to laugh and joke together with a few more well-deserved drinks of wine and larger. While we were drinking, we talked about all of the lovely things we were going to do together in the sun once we had moved into the apartment, then the seat belt sign came on. Mick grabbed my hand.

'Your Lillian is going to hate this landing.'

We both sat waiting for the plane to land. And as soon as the wheels touched the runway at Bourgas Airport, it felt like the wheels were falling off as the plane travelled over the cobbled stone.

Then we heard Lillian starting to swear again. 'Fucking hell, Melvin, are the wheels falling off this plane.'

Mick turned to look at her. 'Lillian, last time we flew the pilot said that this type of landing was normal for Bourgas, because the runway needed resurfacing, and the airport had not managed to save enough money to get it done yet.'

This comment did not help her at all! 'Oh my God, Mick, I do not want to fly home if they haven't resurfaced the runway.'

Mick looked back at her again. 'You will be fine, Lillian, just don't eat or drink anything heavy before we take off or you will eat and drink it twice!' I kicked Mick's foot to stop him from making her worse.

Then Lillian shouted, 'Thanks, Mick, but you are not being helpful!'

Then within a second or two, the plane came to a standstill and we all waited for the seatbelt sign to go off so that we could stand up ready to get off.

When we got off the plane, the bus drivers crammed most of the tourists onto one bus again, then the driver made his way to the airport terminal. We looked like hundreds of jelly babies squashed into a moving container. When the bus stopped at the terminal, we all scrambled off the bus and made our way up the steps to the new arrival terminal.

When I entered Bourges Airport, I noticed that there had been some massive improvements since our last visit. For some reason, it felt a little bit more relaxed, because there did not seem to be as many armed police around. However, as we started to go through customs, I noticed that Lillian and Melvin seemed to be a bit more anxious than usual. I was starting to get a little bit worried about them. 'What is the matter, sis?'

She whispered, 'Nothing, sis, we will be OK as soon as we get our suitcase and we are out of this airport.'

When we had finally passed through passport control and customs, we all sat down on one of the big benches waiting for the sign to say which conveyor belt would deliver our big heavy suitcases. Then all of a sudden, a light started to flash on the nearest luggage belt, then it slowly started to move.

Mick and Melvin got up at the same time to collect the suitcases. Within a second or two, everyone who was waiting in the luggage area of the airport started to make their way to the same baggage collection area, it was like the crowd gathering at the beginning of the London marathon. Lillian and I watched in amazement as all the people started to battle with each other to get their suitcases off the only conveyor belt that was moving. I could not believe the chaos; it was like watching numerous mini Rugby Union scrum downs, because everyone wanted to get to their suitcase first.

Mick and Melvin came out of their scrum without too much trouble, they managed to get all the heavy suitcases off before another load of new arrivals got to their bags. When Mick returned, he looked at me. 'I knew all those years of playing rugby would come in handy one day, Janet.'

I burst out laughing. 'I am so proud of you and Melvin, have you seen how many more new people are trying to get to their cases?'

Mick grabbed hold of the handles on the suitcases. 'Let us get out of here before there's a fight, we have got our suitcases.'

We all grabbed our suitcase handles and followed the signs to the exit point to find Nicolay, the Bulgarian friend of Annastasia who was going to drive everyone to the apartment and help us to move in.

Apollon 4

Nikolay was an acquaintance of Anastasia the Bulgarian solicitor, he had started to communicate with Mick and I as soon as Anastasia had informed him that we were the new owners of apartment A12 Apollon 4. I was delighted to have someone from Bulgaria to help us move in. Nikolay spoke very good English, he was very knowledgeable about the complex and he had lots of experience in supporting other new owners to move into their apartments.

Following a number of *"getting to know you"* emails, Nikolay offered to sort out all the wall and ceiling lights in the apartment and buy some additional soft furnishings to ensure everything was ready for when we arrived in June, which was brilliant and one less job for us to do. Mick and I had to provide written permission to Vanya, the site manager, to allow him access to the apartment, which made us feel safe and secure.

Throughout our conversations, Nikolay had mentioned that he also provided taxi rides for some apartment owners to and from the airport, which was great news for us, considering how long it took Mick, Chris and I to find the complex for the first time! As a result, I arranged for him to meet all of us at the airport.

When we made our way to the exit point, I told everyone to look out for a sign with Mr. Mrs. Gorry written on it. It did not take Mick long to find Nikolay, because he was standing at the arrival doors holding a big white sign with our surname written in black.

I walked up to him and he smiled. 'Hello, Nikolay, I am Janet.'

It was great to finally put a face to the person that I had been communicating with. He was quite tall with light brown hair, green eyes and olive skin.

I introduced Nikolay to Michael, Lillian and Melvin. He said hello and shook hands with everyone, then he asked us to follow him to the car park. We made our way out to the pedestrian crossing which led to the car park. When we got to the car park, we stopped at a green people carrier. Nikolay took the big heavy suitcase from me, I think he regretted this, because when he tried to lift it into the boot of his car it nearly pulled his arm from his socket. He went to grab hold of Mick's suitcase but Mick stopped him.

'Please let me put this one in the boot, it's heavier than the one you have just lifted.' Nikolay looked a bit relieved.

On the way to our apartment, Nikolay provided a lot of additional information regarding the Apollon Complex. He advised us that the builders would be calling to make sure that all the water in the kitchen and shower rooms were working correctly. He also informed us that Vanya was the complex manager and she was very efficient. Before we pulled into the complex, he mentioned that he had bought all of the items that we needed to ensure that our move went smoothly. Mick and I were delighted, because we wanted to spend as much time with Lillian and Melvin on their first ever holiday abroad.

When Nikolay drove the car towards the complex, it looked absolutely amazing; the muddy field had been replaced by a new tarmac road, there was a brick wall all around the complex with wrought iron gates and black railings, and a new paved walkway which led to the different apartment blocks. When Nikolay stopped the car outside the Apollon 4 complex, I could not believe my eyes; the apartment complex looked fantastic. It was a lot bigger and better than I expected it would be.

Nikolay asked Mick and I to come with him to the old railway coach that was now in the middle of a field opposite the apartment, so that he could introduce us to Ploughman. He knocked on the metal door and a tall man opened it. Nikolay spoke to him in Bulgarian, he smiled at me and Mick then he handed Mick a document to sign, then he gave him the bag of keys to our dream home in the sun. We were finally ready to open the door to our new apartment. We thanked Ploughman and Nikolay, then we made our way back to the apartment.

Mick and Melvin got the suitcases out of the car, then they pulled the suitcases through the gates then across the paved area to the first double doors. I could see that our apartment was straight ahead of us. They carried the suitcases up a few steps and dropped them at the door of Apollon A12. Mick put the key in the lock, he turned it twice and the door opened.

As I walked into the apartment for the very first time, I was very impressed with the floor tiles, kitchen cabinets, TV stand and wall cupboards. They all looked exactly like what I had ordered from the furniture package. Everything looked great, but then I noticed that there was no oven. I walked to the space where the oven should have been and opened the double doors. When I looked inside the unit, I could see two roasting tins and three casserole dishes.

'Mick, there is no oven.' I turned around to see what Mick was doing. 'There are no tables and chairs, they are missing too.' I walked into the big bedroom. 'There are no soft furnishings either?' I carried on looking around the apartment to see what else was missing?

The two-seater couch and bed settee were lovely, but they were not made of leather like we thought it would be. All the bedroom furniture was great, but there was no bedding. The wet room and en suite were far much better than our bathrooms at home, but there were no towels. I went to find Nikolay to ask him for help. Fortunately, he was still talking to Ploughman. I explained the situation to him as we made our way back to the apartment. I pointed out the missing items and asked if he could talk to someone? He told me that he would phone the furniture company right away to try and sort out the missing furniture, bedding and towels. It was really good to have someone local who spoke the language and understood my dismay. I could hear Nikolay talking to the other person on the phone, he seemed to be talking for a long while, before he told me it would all be sorted tomorrow.

To cheer me up, Nikolay informed me that he had bought some additional bedding, towels, mattress protectors, as well as the wall and ceiling lights before we arrived to make sure that Mick and I had everything we needed, just in case something like this happened. I thanked him, then I asked him if he would bring them around to the apartment when it was convenient with him.

Mick thanked Nikolay for all his time, then he turned to walk away, but just before he left, he asked if we were hungry. And we all said yes at the same time. He recommended a local fish restaurant near our apartment, he told us that the owners went out fishing every morning to catch the "fresh fish of the day" for all their customers, he advised us that it was one of the best fish restaurants in Ravda, then he left.

When I opened the blinds in the living room for the first time. Mick opened the brown patio door and we all walked out onto the balcony. The view outside the apartment was stunning. I could see two beautiful swimming pools, a small one for children and a big one for adults. There were a few people sunbathing on the sunbeds around the pools. We all stood together on the balcony watching everyone having lots of fun in the sun. After about five minutes, the doorbell rang and I went to see who it was. When I opened the door, it was Nikolay; he had a load of sheets, towels, mattress protectors in his hand and a receipt for all the additional items that he had bought. I thanked him for all his help and support. Mick paid him the money that we owed him, then he left so that we could finish settling into the apartment.

Without any hesitation and the thought of having some fun in the sun, Lillian and I started to make the beds and unpack the suitcases, while the lads sorted out the fridge, freezer, CD player and the big Bulgarian TV, which was as wide as it was high. Once Lillian and I had made the beds, I unpacked the rest of the kitchen utensils, while Lillian sorted out the bathroom towels that Nikolay had bought. Mick and Melvin had started to arrange all the living room furniture.

'Janet, do you like furniture like this?'

When I turned around to see what the lads had done, my face lit up, because the apartment was starting to look quite homely. 'Come and see the living room, Lillian, it's beginning to look like home.'

When she walked into the room, she had a big smile on her face. We all looked at each other, then Melvin walked towards the window.

'Let us go out for a walk in the sunshine to buy some

birthday beer and wine for Mick's birthday.'

We all smiled, Mick grabbed the keys and we all walked outside into the midday sun, it felt wonderful. Mick locked the apartment door for the first time and we started to walk around the complex.

We walked along the new tarmac road until we arrived at Apollon 1. As soon as we stopped, I realised that this was the small apartment block where I first saw the man watering the rose bushes when Mick and I were searching for the Apollon Complex with Christopher over a year ago. I noticed that there was no pool at Apollon 1 and it was quite small compared to the other apartment blocks that we had passed on our way in.

There was a little shop on the other side of the road, then a main road that led to the beach. We turned around and walked along the pavement until we came to Apollon 2. I remembered that this was the complex that I called the little oasis, when Mick, Christopher and I came on our first visit to the complex. I started to tell Lillian and Melvin about when we interrupted two lovely sunbathers to ask them for directions to our apartment. I showed them where they sent us to find Ploughman, and what happened when we could not find him.

We carried on walking until we came to Apollon 5, this complex was situated in a wonderful location, it had two lovely pools. There was a sign for the complex manager Vanya, her office was situated under a little walkway. The complex supermarket was located next to Kostov's office, the developers. We did not stop to thank them for building our apartment. We just rushed into the shop to buy some food, snacks and party drinks for Mick's birthday.

When we had finished the shopping, Mick decided to walk back towards Apollon 5, as we walked through the gate and it didn't take long before Lillian spotted a lovely children's play area, which was next to the tennis courts.

I could not believe what I was seeing; the complex looked absolutely amazing! I walked past the tennis courts towards Apollon 3. This development looked like the biggest apartment block in the complex. It had a lovely restaurant called Cats situated at the top by the tarmac road and there was a lovely bar situated next to the snooker room, spa centre, gym and a beauty salon. I looked at the beautiful swimming pools, the midday sunshine was sparkling on top of the crystal clear water. It looked like something out of one of Carol Smiley's holiday shows. The pool had a lovely adults swimming area with fabulous water showers squirting up into the air from around the children's pool. This was far more than I ever expected.

Mick carried on walking along the pathway until he came to a small number of steps then he shouted. 'Come and see this, Janet.'

I walked up the steps which led to the Apollon Hotel, then back to Apollon 4, swimming pools. As I turned the corner, I could see our ground-floor apartment. It looked fabulous because it was situated in the corner of the block facing the swimming pools. This location felt much quieter because there were no bars, shops or restaurants. As we made our way back to the apartment for some well-deserved drinks, I noticed that there was a large piece of barren land behind the Apollon 4 apartment block that led to the Aqua Park that I had seen in the photographs from Amber Sun.

When I got back inside the apartment, Lillian and Melvin kept smiling and giggling with each other like two naughty children. I looked at Lillian. 'Now that the beds are made, the living room is sorted, and we have been to the shop to buy food, snacks and drinks, do you think it is time to celebrate Mick's significant birthday?'

Everyone stopped what we were doing. 'Most Definitely! The apartment looks amazing; now it is time to celebrate and have a party.'

Melvin got the glasses from out of the cupboard. Mick started to pour the celebration drinks, while Lillian and I got the table and chairs ready on the balcony. Melvin brought the drinks out and we all sat down for well-deserved birthday drinks.

While Mick and Melvin were talking about the complex, Lillian looked across the table towards where I was sitting and whispered. 'I'm not being funny, sis, but I noticed that the towels and bedding Nikolay had bought for you don't look brand new to me; in fact, all of those towels have Apollon 3 written on them.'

I thought for a moment and then the penny dropped. 'I agree, sis, we have just walked past Apollon 3, I think he must have bought too many towels for those apartments, and that is why he is selling them to us.'

She smiled and picked up her celebration drink. 'Cheers, Mick, happy birthday.'

Lucy in Disguise

Mick and Melvin started laughing about Lillian's behaviour on the flight, I told them about how worried I felt when they were going through customs, because they both looked so incredibly nervous, then Melvin jumped up out of his chair.

'Mick, would you like to open one of your birthday presents?' Mick looked a bit shocked because I don't think he was expecting any birthday surprises. 'Why not? It's my birthday.'

Melvin had a big smirk on his face. I looked at Lillian to thank her, but she had the biggest naughty smile on her face. Melvin left the balcony and he started walking through the living room into their bedroom. While he was in the room, all I could hear was the sound of his laughter coming through the open window.

While Mick was waiting for his birthday present, I poured everyone another drink to ensure that our glasses would be full when he returned. As soon as I put the wine bottle on the table, Melvin handed Mick a card and a large box, then he shouted, 'This is your very own little Lucy, Mick.'

I looked at Lillian and she burst out laughing, then the tears started rolling down both of their faces. Mick looked a little bit apprehensive as he opened the card, he read out the lovely verse and birthday wishes then he put the card on the table next to the wine then he looked up at Melvin before opening the box. 'What is Lucy?'

Melvin stopped laughing for a moment. 'Open the box and you will find out.'

Mick removed the wrapping paper then he opened the top of the box very slowly, just in case anything popped out. He held his finger under the top of the box then he opened it. Within a few seconds, he pulled out a little plastic doll, then he looked at Melvin and Lillian. 'What is this?'

'You have got to blow it up first, Mick!'

Mick had hold of the plastic doll's legs. 'You have got to be joking, Melvin, I am not blowing it up. Something might happen!'

I looked over to Lillian, to ask her what it was, but she could not stop laughing. Her tears had fallen down her face onto her t-shirt. 'Bloody hell, sis, how did you get that through customs?'

She managed to stop laughing for a second, then she dried her eyes with her T-shirt. 'I know, sis, Melvin and I were really worried when we got to Manchester airport. I wanted to tell you about Lucy, but we did not want to get you into any trouble if we were caught.'

I laughed at Melvin, then Mick. 'Did you carry Lucy through customs without her passport?'

Lillian and Melvin stopped drinking their wine. 'Well, it was like this, Melvin put Lucy into one of the big suitcases to prevent anyone from stopping us at customs, but we thought that they may have found her when we were waiting ages to board the plane at Manchester. I think some of the swearing when we finally took off was pure relief that we did not get caught.'

Then Melvin stood up from his chair. 'That is true; however, when we started to go through all the customs checks at Bourgas Airport, we thought that they were going to stop us from coming into Bulgaria!'

Mick and I laughed at both of them and we both shouted together, 'Wow, no wonder you both were very anxious!'

Then we all looked down at the plastic doll lying across Mick's knee. Melvin could not hold back his excitement. 'Go on, Mick, blow Lucy up, it won't take you long, she's only a little lady.'

Mick found the place on her back where he had to blow her up, then he started to blow, with a few big puffs, Lucy started to appear. It was so funny.

With every puff of air, Mick had to stop for a while to join in with all the laughter. At this point, none of us were worried about the people around the pool hearing all of our laughter or looking over the balcony to watch as little Lucy started to appear, we were all just enjoying having the best fun in the sun.

We just could not stop ourselves from laughing, after a while Mick continued to blow Lucy up. With two more big puffs, her legs started to grow, then after another few more puffs her stomach popped out, as he blew a little bit more her left arm popped out than her right hand popped out.

Melvin shouted, 'Go on, Mick, you can do this!'

Mick did two more massive big blows and her head popped up like something you would see in a "*Men in Black movie.*" As she got bigger and bigger, her appearance started to evolve. She had long blond hair which stopped at her shoulders, she had lovely big brown eyes and the biggest red lips that I had ever seen on a plastic doll. Her body was small, but well-proportioned, she looked like a miniature woman.

After Mick had finished blowing, he had to close the valve on her back to stop her from going down on him. Then he turned her the right way around to get a good look at her face. However, when he tried to stand her up on the table by her own two feet, to keep her upright he quickly realised that she could not stand up without his support. Every time he let go of her, she kept falling towards him as if she wanted to be close to him, which made us all laugh out loud. Lucy was one of the funniest birthday presents Mick had ever received.

It must have taken us about thirty minutes before we could finally stop laughing and joking about little Lucy. Mick smiled at me. 'Janet, please, can you take her inside the apartment out of the hot sun, because I don't want her to get sun burnt.'

I got up from the table and he handed her to me. 'Be careful with her, she's not used to this heat.'

I wondered where it would be best to keep her safe and cool. As I walked into the living room, the sun was shining on the sofa through the window, it was far too hot for her. I decided to close the blinds in our bedroom and place her on the bed. I put her head between the pillows to keep her comfortable until we decided to get her out for a bit more fun later on.

When I returned to the balcony, Lillian was waiting to give Mick his second birthday present. This was a small box. Mick looked quite hesitant then he looked at me. 'Thank God, you're back, I don't want to open this present on my own, because I don't know what I will have to do with this one!'

Lillian grabbed his hand and looked him in the eyes, then in an exceptionally soft voice, she said. 'Open it slowly, Mick; it's only a little manicure kit for your tiny bits and bobs.'

Melvin just burst into fits of laughter again, then we all started laughing out loud. When the laughter had finally calmed down, Mick took a big sip of his beer for Dutch courage, then he slowly opened the little box. As he turned the lid upwards towards his face, he just burst out laughing again. None of us could contain ourselves, the tears of laughter started falling down everyone's face again.

After a while, I looked up towards Mick, then I asked him to pass the miniature manicure kit to me. When I looked inside the box, I could see that it was actually a miniature grooming box; it contained a small magnifying glass, a tiny pair of tweezers and the smallest pair of scissors that I had ever seen, they were all line up within the box to help keep Mick's little bits and bobs well-groomed. We all howled with laughter as I pulled each of the miniature manicures out of the box.

Then, all of a sudden, the apartment bell started to ring. We all stopped laughing, and Lillian looked at me.

'Who could that be, sis? Do you think someone has complained about all the laughter?'

Mick stood up and whispered. 'Quickly, Janet, go and put Lucy in the wardrobe and hide that grooming kit somewhere safe while I open the door.'

I ran into the bedroom and I flung Lucy into the wardrobe, then I placed the grooming kit on one of the shelves. As I left the bedroom, I could see that Mick had opened the front door.

A very tall Bulgarian man was standing in the doorway with a smaller guy. Mick smiled at the both of them. 'Hello, can I help you?'

In broken English, the small man started to speak. 'I come to sort out your aqua.'

With all the fun and laughter, I had forgotten that the builders were coming around to check on all of the water; this was one of the jobs Nikolay had mentioned when we were on our way to the apartment from the airport.

Mick opened the door fully and asked them to come in. The

tall man walked into the kitchen and turned the sink tap on, then he looked at Mick. 'This is working well, yes?'

The smaller man looked at Mick and pointed his finger. 'Please, I need to check the other two rooms.'

He made his way into the wet room first. As he entered the room, he flushed the toilet and turned the taps on in the sink. 'This is working well, yes?' I agreed and smiled. Then he walked over to the shower and pulled the single tap up; the water came rushing out of the shower head. 'This is working well, yes?' I smiled and nodded my head.

When he left the wet room, he started to walk towards our bedroom. 'Now I check the en-suite, please.' I opened the bedroom door. As he entered the bedroom, I followed him into the room. As we walked past the wardrobe, I noticed that Lucy's head was hanging out of the door, because I did not close it properly after putting the grooming kit on the shelf. I tried to guide him past the wardrobe as fast as I could. When he entered the en-suite, I stood outside looking at him, while my right foot was trying to close the wardrobe door. I tried my best to hide Lucy but every time I turned around, I could see her blonde hair, big brown eyes and rosy red lips popping out of the door as if she had wanted to see what was going on.

It soon became impossible to hide her, because every time I pressed my foot on the door, she made a squeaky noise as her plastic body squashed against the door. Each time it happened, the man kept turning to look at me to see what was making the awful sound. Every time she made a noise, I tried to pretend that it was coming from outside. As he turned the sink taps on, I tried to hide her again, but I didn't want to press too hard in case I popped her or she made the terrible sound of hot rubber popping, like a very loud balloon.

After a few turns of the tap, the water started to pour into the sink, then he flushed the toilet and moved towards the shower and opened the door, he pulled the tap up and within a few seconds the water started to run from the shower head. 'Everything is working good, yes?'

I could not wait to get rid of him. 'Yes, yes, it is all good with me.'

I think he knew that I just wanted to get him out of the bedroom as quickly as possible. I pointed towards the bedroom door, and he smiled at me as he walked past the wardrobe, then he stopped for a moment as if he had forgotten something. I am not sure whether he could see Lucy's head hanging out of the wardrobe, but he never said anything.

Mick showed the builders to the door and they left the apartment. I closed the front door as fast as I could and turned the lock. 'You would not believe what has just happened when I took the small builder into the bedroom.'

Mick looked towards me. 'Did you forget to flush the loo after lunch, Janet?' I could not believe him!

'No, nothing like that; this is the worst! When the builder walked into the bedroom, Lucy's head was hanging out of the wardrobe door. I had to guide him past her head as best as I could. While he was turning the taps on, I tried to use my right foot to close the wardrobe door, but every time I pressed my foot on the door, she started to make some very loud noises because I was quashing her head in the door and I did not want to press too hard just in case she popped.'

Mick turned to look at Melvin. 'Bloody hell, Kev, does Lucy come with a puncture kit? I have only just finished blowing her up, now Janet is trying to pop her.'

Everyone burst out laughing again. Mick checked on Lucy to ensure there were no punchers, then we made our way back to the balcony to finish off Mick's birthday drinks.

Fresh Catch of the Day

Thank God, Mick's fiftieth birthday surprises went without a bang. The apartment was starting to look like home. Lillian and I had made sure that we had nice clean beds to sleep in. The builders had ensured that we had lots of hot running water for a shower and Lucy was back between the pillows on the double bed.

By the time we had finished the last of the wine, I noticed that the sun was starting to set behind Apollon 4. Mick was beginning to feel a bit hungry so we decided to go for a nice birthday meal at the fresh fish restaurant Nikolay had recommended. He told us that it was only a few meters away from the apartment, and it was run by a local family who went out fishing every morning to catch beautiful fresh fish for all of their customers. We could not wait to order our very own fresh catch of the day.

We left the balcony and everyone went to get ready for the evening. Within thirty minutes, we were all showered and changed into our best party clothes. Mick closed the apartment door and walked along a pathway past the restaurant on the Apollon 3 complex, then up towards the supermarket at Apollon 5. As we walked along the road, I noticed that there were a few residential homes opposite the shop. Mick walked across the road towards what looked like a very small community, then he stopped in the middle of the residential estate.

'Where did Nikolay say this restaurant was located, Janet?'

I looked at him with a little bit of bewilderment. 'He never really said where it was, he just pointed to these houses.'

We walked up and down the pavement for a little while longer, then Mick saw a small sign in front of one of the houses. Then I spotted a very small bar with a few chairs in the middle of the garden.

'It must be in here, Mick, because it has got a fish sign restaurant in the garden.'

With the sign in sight and the bar a few yards away, we all made our way up past the house and along the driveway into the garden, then we sat down as fast as possible before anyone could stop us.

Within a few seconds of sitting down, a young girl came out of the house and she walked towards us. I did not know if she was going to ask us all to leave her garden, call the police or take our food and drinks order. Everyone looked very nervous as we waited for her to get closure. As soon as she reached the table, I spoke to her in my best broken English Bulgarian voice.

'Hello-we-ha-ve-come-to-eat-yo-ur-fre-sh-fish-of-the-day. Nik-o-lay-yo-ur-fri-end-told-us-to-eat-here.'

She stood looking at me as if I had just been transported into her garden from a "Star Trek" movie, then a mature woman came running out of the house towards the table where we were sitting. We all looked at each other to see who was going to be the first to run off. When she got to the table, she smiled.

'*Dobra vercher,*" *She smiled at* Lillian.'

'What does that mean, Janet?'

I tried to talk to the women with my poshest English accent. 'Hello, good evening. Nikolay, your friend, told us we could eat here.'

Everyone knew what I was trying to say except for her. Mick looked at me.

'Listen, Janet, you need to make sure that we are in the fish restaurant and not some local Bulgarian's back garden.'

The women looked at me again. '*Dobra vercher,* please take a seat over here.' She spoke very good English.

I was still unsure if we were in the fish restaurant, but I got up and followed her to another table nearer the bar, then we all sat down slowly just in case we needed to do a runner.

The mature woman turned towards the house and shouted something in Bulgarian to the young girl, then the girl ran back into the house. Lillian looked at me, then at Mick and Melvin. We were all worried about her calling the police. When she came out of the house, we all gazed at her as if we were on starters orders at the Grand National. Then she held up what looked like a number of homemade menus and she ran towards us. We all laughed with relief, Lillian took the menus from her hand, then I thanked her.

We spent some time reading through the menus to see what we could order for Mick's birthday meal. I was very surprised because they had a wide range of food to eat besides the fresh fish. Melvin was the first to put his menu down on the table.

'I am going to have the fresh catch of the day; it looks good to me and the prices are very inexpensive compared to the UK.'

Mick ordered some drinks from the mature women, while I continued to look through the menu to see what I could order for a birthday pudding.

When the woman returned with our drinks, she placed them on the table, then she asked us what we wanted to eat. Melvin and I ordered the fresh fish of the day with chips and salad. Lillian ordered fresh chicken breast with chips and Mick asked the woman for a nice piece of rump steak, with homemade chips and peppercorn sauce for his special birthday meal.

While we waited for the food to cook, we talked about how easy it was to move into the apartment with Nikolay's support. We laughed about all the fun we had on the balcony, when Mick opened his surprise birthday presents. Then Mick asked. 'What would you have done, Janet, if Lucy would have popped out of the wardrobe in front of the Bulgarian builders?'

I stopped laughing. 'I would have felt so embarrassed, if the builder would have caught me with her, I would have said that she was our daughter, Mick.'

Melvin laughed. "Illegal Daughter Janet." We all burst out laughing.

When our meals arrived, they were not what we expected; they smelt delicious, yet they were just like something you would have made in your own kitchen at home. There were no frills or special designer plates, it was just good home-cooked food. Mine and Melvin's fish still had their heads and tails, and the fish's eyes were wide open. Lillian's chicken looked like it needed some golden colouring because it was pale white, and Mick's rump steak was not as large as he expected. I think we were all expecting five-star quality food in someone's back garden! Nevertheless, we did not let the local home cooking spoil the evening; it was Mick's birthday and nothing was going to stop us all from having a really good time.

Melvin and I picked up our fish knives and forks and we started to cut into our fresh fish. Lillian and Mick tucked into their meals and we were all very surprised, because the food actually tasted much better than any of us expected. When all of the plates were empty, the young girl came over to take them back to the kitchen.

Mick tried to whisper to me. 'They will need those dishes for their breakfast tomorrow.' But everyone heard him and we all started to laugh out loud.

As soon as the young girl walked into the house with the empty plates, the mature woman came out. It looked like they were taking it in turns to watch Bulgarian TV, while each of them were trying to keep an eye on the four strangers in their garden. The woman made her way over to the table, she looked at Mick then asked him if we wanted the same drinks.

'Yes, please, it is my birthday today.'

The woman congratulated Mick, then she returned to the kitchen and the young girl came out of the house to watch us.

With all the drinking and constant laughter, I needed to go to the lady's toilets; however, as soon as I stood up to find out where they were, the young girl turned around and ran into the kitchen to get the woman. As I made my way towards the house to ask where the toilets were, the woman was on her way out of the house. I felt a little bit worried because I did not want to use the toilet in the house. The woman stopped just in front of me. I smiled at her and then asked her where the ladies' toilets were. It took her a little while to work out what I was asking for, then she pointed to a tiny door next to the homemade bar in the garden. I had not noticed that there was a small door with toilets written on the sign, because it just looked like a tiny wooden door (similar to the one in the *Alice in Wonderland* movie).

She smiled then led me towards the little door, it felt like she was taking one of her little children to the toilet. When I got to the doorway, I opened it before she had a chance. Then she pushed past me to turn the light on. When the light had stopped flickering, I discovered one of the smallest toilets in the world.

I closed the door on her, then I tried to manoeuvre my body into position for a much-needed wee, but I could not do anything without bagging my head on the ceiling. When I finally managed to stoop down, my head hit the door and it opened up exposing my stooping body and bare bottom. I tried to rotate my right arm to get some loo roll, but that made the door open again because my left leg was hanging out. I had to grab hold of the door as fast as I could to keep my modesty intact, then when I finally managed to get my hand on the toilet roll, it was impossible to reach the parts of my body that needed some attention without banging my head on the door or the ceiling. And if this was not bad enough! I was also trying to prevent some of the big splitters from sticking into my arms, elbows and bottom because of all the untreated timber surrounding me.

After a few minutes of delicate positioning, I gave up trying to sort myself out, and I turned to wash my hands in the mini sink. Then my feet got tangled up and I fell out of the tiny door with a massive big bang. It was so loud that Mick, Lillian and Melvin all turned around to see what was happening.

Mick looked over towards me as I tried to get up from the floor, then I heard him shout, 'What's all that noise, Janet? Be careful, you will wake the neighbours up.'

Lillian stood up and came walking towards me. 'Is everything OK, sis, are you all right? There were an awful lot of loud sounds coming from the toilet.'

I stood up and brushed myself down. 'Lillian, that is the smallest toilet in the world.' I started to fix my underwear before making my way over to the table. I was still trying to get my dress out of my knickers when I sat down at the table. 'Listen, everyone, you do not want to go into those toilets because they are so tiny! It has got to be one of the smallest toilets in the world. Look at me, I have got splinters in my elbows and my bottom as a result of bending over to have a wee, and you don't want to know what happened when I tried to reach for the toilet roll or wash my hands, if that was not bad enough the bloody door kept opening on me.'

Lillian sat up in her chair. 'Oh my God, we had better leave soon because none of us want to get stuck in the loo on Mick's significant birthday.'

We all decided that that was a great idea. Mick asked the mature woman for the bill. She ran into the house to get the receipt and the young girl came out to watch us. Melvin and Mick paid the bill and we all made our way back to the apartment for another drink and a well-deserved sleep in our new beds, with the clean sheets from Nikolay.

When I woke up the following morning, I looked out of the bedroom window. It was a glorious day, the sun was shining and the swimming pool looked very inviting. I woke Mick up and we got dressed ready to sunbath on the sun beds just outside the apartment. We did not want to go too far because we had to wait for the rest of the furniture package to arrive. As I walked past Lillian's and Melvin's bedroom, I could hear them laughing and joking with each other about all the fun they had had together. When I walked into the living room; it looked amazing in the morning sunshine. I picked up four new beach towels and made my way to the pool with Mick.

When we got to the swimming pool, Mick arranged four sunbeds just outside the apartment so that we could hear the doorbell when the furniture arrived. I put my sun cream on, then I sat on the sun bed and settled down in the wonderful morning sunshine. After a short while, Lillian and Melvin joined us. When Lillian sat down, she said her sunbed was lovely and warm from the heat of the sun. It was so hot, I wanted to go swimming in the pool to cool myself down; however, as I started to walk towards the steps of the pool, Nikolay came walking around the corner. I made my way back towards Mick, then I sat down on the sun bed to talk with him.

Nikolay stood under the shade of the umbrella to keep himself cool, he informed me and Mick that he had spent the morning talking to the furniture people about all the missing furniture, he said that he had managed to sort everything out and that they would be bringing everything to the apartment that day. Mick and I were delighted with the good news, Mick thanked him for all of his time and support, then Nikolay walked away.

After about an hour or so of relaxing in the sun, Melvin heard a van pull up outside Apollon 4. Mick and I got dressed and we made our way to the double doors that led to the apartment. I stood in the shade watching the man getting out of his van. He made his way towards where Mick was standing. When I looked at him, I could see that he was holding a white sheet of paper in his right hand. I smiled at him, then I asked him if he had the missing furniture. He looked at me, then to the white piece of paper, then he just nodded his head.

Mick got the apartment door keys out of his pocket, then he walked towards the apartment, as soon as the man saw that Mick was opening the apartment door, he banged his hand on the back door of the van, then it opened. Two other men jumped out of the back of the van, then together they pulled a new glass table to the edge of the van's floor, then they carried the table through the double doors, up the steps then into the dining room. I was so delighted that the table looked just like the one I ordered from the furniture package.

While Mick and I were admiring the glass top on the table, two of the men went back towards the van, and within a few seconds they brought one chair each then placed it under the left-hand side of the table by the wall, then the first man asked Mick to sign the white piece of paper. I did not want Mick to sign for anything. I asked the man in broken English. 'Whe-re-

171

are-the-oth-er-two-cha-irs-ple-ase?'

He looked a bit confused. I pointed at the two chairs that the two men had just put under the table then I put four fingers up to him, then two fingers and I shook my head from side to side, then I put four fingers up then nodded my head up and down (not realising then that 'no means yes' and 'yes means no' in Bulgaria).

The man did not say anything, he just pointed to the sheet of paper and offered Mick the pen to sign it.

Mick shook his head. 'Sorry, mate, I am not signing anything until we get the four chairs we paid for.'

I looked at the man. 'Where are the other two chairs?'

Then Nikolay came to the door. 'Hello, Janet and Mick, I saw the furniture van outside your apartment, so I have come to make sure that everything is good with you.'

I looked towards Nikolay. 'No, it is not good, Nikolay, we should have four chairs but they have only delivered two.' Nikolay looked at the two chairs along the wall, then he had a long conversation with the delivery man. When they stopped talking he looked back at Mick then me.

'This is a mistake; the man will bring two more chairs tomorrow.'

I looked at all of the delivery men. 'Nikolay, can you also ask the men about the double oven, it should have been fitted with the kitchen.' Nikolay spoke to the men. 'Please can you ask him about all the missing soft furnishings that we have paid for as part of the furniture package?'

Nikolay had another long conversation with the men then he turned to Mick. 'The furniture man will bring everything tomorrow.'

As much as Nikolay tried to reassure both of us, I felt myself getting a bit stressed about all of the missing furniture and the soft furnishings. I left Mick to see everyone out of the apartment, and I started to walk around to the pool to phone Anastasia, the Bulgarian solicitor.

When I made my way to the pool, Lillian asked if all the furniture had arrived. I told her that the furniture company had only brought two chairs and that I was going to call Anastasia. I sat on the sun bed and got my mobile phone out of my bag and called her. As soon as she picked up the phone, I started to tell her about the two chairs, the missing oven and that there were none of the soft furnishings that we had paid for. I advised her that Nikolay had charged us for extra bedding and towels because none of our soft furnishings were at the apartment as she promised, then I informed her that we only had one week to sort everything out!

Anastasia remained very calm while she was listening to all my ranting on the phone. When I had finished saying what I wanted to say, she replied in a soft and gentle voice which actually made me calm down. Within five minutes of listening to her reasoning, she had managed to reassure me that all of the missing items of furniture on the list would be delivered before I returned to the UK, because she was going to sort everything out herself. With this additional reassurance from Anastasia, I put the phone back into my bag, then I went for a long swim in the swimming pool.

Do You Do Eggs?

The water in the swimming pool was very cold, which made it quite refreshing when I first got in and just what I needed after the furniture fiasco. When Mick returned from the apartment, he looked a bit annoyed too.

When he saw me swimming in the pool, he asked me, 'If the water was lovely and warm?'

I told him that it was nice and warm so that he would join me for a swim. Within a few seconds, he pulled his t-shirt off and dove into the deep end of the pool. When he swam up from the freezing cold water, he shouted, 'You little liar, it is bloody freezing.'

He started to swim towards me to get back at me. When he got close, he splashed a load of cold water over me because I lied to him about the temperature. I turned around as fast as I could to swim away, but he soon caught hold of me.

I started to scream. 'Please don't do it, Mick, I don't like getting my hair wet.'

He grinned at me then he splashed loads of very cold water over my face and hair. After he had finished punishing me, we both swam towards the steps at the top of the pool.

When we got to the steps, we both sat down next to the children's pool, admiring the apartment. Mick laughed at my wet hair.

'Janet, aren't you glad that I went to the toilet at the Thistle Hotel?' He moved my long wet hair away from my face.

'Definitely, Mick, I think this is one of the best investments we have ever made.'

We both sat on the steps in the morning sunshine admiring the apartment, then all of a sudden, Mick gave me a big wet hug then he pushed me into the freezing cold pool.

Mick and I started to mess around in the water for a while, we were having a wonderful time. When I looked towards the sun beds by the apartment, I could see that Lillian and Melvin were sitting up on their sun beds trying to get our attention.

'Look, Mick, something is wrong.'

We stopped messing around and swam back to the top of the pool to see what they wanted. I noticed that Lillian had put her shoes back on and her dress was covering her costume. 'Are you hungry, sis, do you and Mick fancy going to the beach for something to eat?'

Mick pushed my head under the water again, then he answered. 'Yes, Lillian, I am famished with all this morning's exercise.'

When I popped my head above the water, I could see that Mick had put his hands onto the tiles around the top of the pool and he was trying to pull himself up out of the water, instead of using the pool steps. When he got out of the pool, he stood up and offered to help me out. I grabbed both of his hands and he started to pull me out of the water. When I was halfway out, he let go of me and I fell back into the pool with a big splash that wet Lillian's dress.

When I finally got out of the pool, by the steps, it did not take me long to dry myself, but I had to leave my hair soaking wet. I got my bag from under the sunbed and we all started to walk together towards the beach. When we walked out of the complex by Apollon 1, I noticed that there were a few shops on the right-hand side of the road next to the mini supermarket. They were opposite the garden where I first saw the man watering the plants, when Christopher, Mick and I were trying to find the complex on our first adventure, but I did not remember them being open at the time.

When I looked across the road, I could see that there were a number of lovely hotels overlooking the beach, they all looked beautiful. We all managed to cross the main road together without any hesitation from the ongoing traffic. Mick suggested we walk towards the Dolphin Hotel to see what was at that side of the beach. As I walked past the hotel, I noticed that there was a restaurant at the other side of the reception. It looked very nice and clean. Lillian caught my attention. 'Did you see that man eating the big pizza? It looked gorgeous.'

I turned around to look inside the restaurant. 'Wow, that does look lovely, sis. Shall we go in?'

Mick opened the door for all of us and Melvin found a table by the window. We all sat down and waited to be served.

While I was looking through the Bulgarian menu, I started to listen to all the people talking around me. I could hear a number of Bulgarians talking, then I heard a few Irish people chatting together. It was great to hear their Irish accents. They sounded so warm and welcoming. It was good to know that we were not the only tourists. I looked at the Irish woman and smiled, she smiled back at me then carried on eating her meal; it looked delicious. I looked through the window to see what was in the surrounding area. There was a little side road that led to the beach and a small supermarket opposite the restaurant.

I was daydreaming about walking to the beach in my swimsuit when the waitress came over to serve everyone. I noticed that she was very slim, with lovely brown eyes and dark brown hair. She looked at Mick first.

'*Dobar vercher.*' Mick smiled at her then asked for the drinks menu. She smiled back at him then asked if we were English. We all said yes at the same time.

The waitress left the table. When she returned, she brought some English menus. They looked very professional and they had a great selection of pizzas for Lillian and me. Mick ordered all the drinks and food without any language problems, and it did not take very long for the drinks to arrive. While we were waiting for the meals to arrive, I looked out of the window again to watch all the people as they walked past the hotel. Some of the people were making their way to Ravda, a little village about half a mile away, and some of them turned left to walk along the road at the side of the restaurant that led to the beach.

The small supermarket across from the Dolphin Hotel looked very busy. I noticed that it sold lots of lovely fresh fruit and vegetables.

'Listen, everyone, we need to get some supplies in for tonight, because we have run out of wine, beer and snacks.'

Lillian opened up her bag and pulled out a pen and paper.

'Right, sis, what do we need?' Melvin shouted.

'Lager, wine and crisps for when we play cards later.'

Lillian started to write a list. 'We need to get some eggs, bread and butter for breakfast in the morning.'

Mick grinned and took a sip of his beer. 'That is brilliant, thank you, Lillian. Janet and I will nip to the supermarket when we have finished our meal, this is our treat for yesterday's birthday party.'

Lillian handed the list to me. 'Thanks, sis, you are a star.'

I continued watching all the people going in and out of the supermarket with their shopping bags to get a better idea of what types of food they were buying (Bulgarian or English). Then all of a sudden, a small boy appeared from the entrance door of the shop, he started to position an old plastic table just outside the main door, then he pulled a dirty dish cloth out of his pocket and started to wipe the top of the table. But no matter how hard he rubbed, the dirt on the top of the table would not budge. Undeterred by this, he spat on the cloth, then he continued to clean the table. After a while, I could see that he was running out of spit and his arms were getting very tired as a result of all the rubbing. He looked to his right, then to his left and then back into the shop window as if he wanted to give up, but he was not allowed to because he had not finished what he was supposed to do. When he was sure that no one was watching him, he picked up a box of vegetables and placed them on top of the dirty table to hide all of the dirt.

When our meals arrived they looked delicious. Within a few seconds of the plates being put on the table, we all started to eat, it did not take us long to devour everything. When we had finished our food and drinks, an Irish couple started to ask Lillian and Melvin where they came from and what they were doing in that location? Lillian told them about the apartment on Apollon 4 complex.

The Irish couple seemed to be happy that we had bought a property on Apollon. Then the women started to talk about the Apollon Complex. She informed us that a number of Irish families had bought properties on Apollon 2, 3 and 5 a few years ago which was brilliant news. She continued to tell us about the who, what, where and when on the complex, which was a fantastic induction. I was so happy that we had called in the Dolphin and we had met some wonderful people.

One of the Irish men started to tell everyone about some of

the experiences he had when he first moved into his apartment on Apollon 3. I was disappointed to find out that he had gone through some of the same issues that we were going through regarding the furniture package and the soft furnishings, but it was great to learn that everything had turned out right for him. When we paid for our meal and drinks, Mick thanked them for taking their time to talk to us, and I thanked them for all their reassurance that everything will turn out right in the end.

When we left the restaurant, Mick and I made our way across to the small supermarket while Melvin rested his feet and Lillian had a cigarette. Mick picked up a small basket from inside the main door and passed it to me. We made our way around the shop to find all of the items on the list. Mick placed each item into the basket and I ticked them off the list.

'Beers, yes; wine, yes; crisps, yes; snacks for later, yes, that is all tonight's essentials Janet. Now we need to look for tomorrow's breakfast.'

We made our way towards the back of the shop. Mick got hold of the basket because it was getting too heavy for me. I started to place some of the breakfast items in the basket. 'Bread, yes; butter, yes; I wonder where the eggs are, Mick.'

Mick carried on looking around all the shelves within the store. 'Sorry, Janet, but I cannot see them anywhere.'

We both walked up and down the shop looking for eggs but they were nowhere in sight. I took the basket from Mick and placed it on the floor in front of me.

'Go and ask that man behind the counter if he has got any eggs.'

Mick walked up to the Bulgarian man behind the counter. The man looked up from what he was doing and smiled at Mick. Mick smiled back at him.

'Hello-do-you-do-eggs?'

The man got up from his wooden stool. 'Please come with me.' He took Mick by the hand and led him behind the counter. Mick looked back towards me; he looked a little bit bewildered.

Mick let go of the man's hand. 'Do-you-do-eggs!' Repeating it for the second time and because the man was taking him to the very back of the shop.

Then the man stopped at what looked like a medicine cupboard that was hanging on the wall at the far end of the shop, he got a key out of his pocket and opened the door, then he handed Mick a large box of Durex.

Mick looked shocked then he pulled his hand away. 'No, no, I want six eggs, not Durex.'

Mick could not believe what the man was holding out towards him. 'No thanks, mate, I wanted SIX EGGS, not Durex!'

Then Mick made the sound of a chicken clucking and he motioned his arms up and down to imitate the flapping of chicken's wings. The man stood watching what Mick was doing for a second or two, then he burst out laughing for a while, then he looked at me as if to apologise.

I pretended to look shocked. 'Six eggs, please.'

He grinned at me then he laughed at Mick, he returned the Durex back into the cabinet and locked it with his key. Mick looked towards me and we both gave the man a funny look, but it did not stop him from laughing at us. By the time Mick and the man had returned from behind the counter, we were all in tears of laughter.

When the Bulgarian man had managed to compose himself for a moment, he started to pull at Mick's hand again. 'Please, mister, please you must come here with me.'

Mick stopped laughing. 'Here we go again.'

The man took Mick towards a fridge where several eggs lay next to the cheese and butter. Mick looked relieved. 'Please, mister, please how many for you?'

Mick smiled at him then he replied. 'Six eggs, please.' Then he burst out laughing. 'I want six eggs, not SEX!' and we all burst out laughing again.

By the time we had all finished laughing, the Bulgarian man managed to place six eggs into a brown paper bag, then he handed them gently over to Mick, as they walked towards the counter, the man picked the basket up off the floor and apologised to me for the misunderstanding. When he was back behind the counter, he took everything out of the basket and placed each item on the counter, then he used a tiny calculator to add up the cost for each item.

When he picked up the eggs, he looked at Mick then me and we all started to laugh again, then he looked back at Mick. 'EGGS not durex, SIX not sex I must remember this for the next time you come here.' And we all started to laugh again.

When the man had finished adding everything up, he handed Mick a receipt for twenty lev. Mick opened his wallet and paid the man in full. Mick picked up the shopping bags and made our way to the main door. When we left the shop, Mick handed the receipt to me.

'Janet, please check this. I do not think he has charged us for everything.'

I counted all of the items and it was correct, we could not believe how cheap everything was in the supermarket. I looked at Mick. 'Wow, Mick, that was great value for money and it was one of the funniest moments I have ever had in a supermarket.'

The Three Amigos

The apartment was becoming the dream holiday home that we had always dreamt of. The furniture package was almost sorted, except for the double oven. Anastasia had fulfilled her promise to sort out the soft furnishings and furniture before we returned to the UK. All the worry of moving into a new home had diminished like a sandstorm on a hot summer's day.

Mick and I had started to build new friendships with a few of the Irish, English and Welsh property owners during the evening when they all gathered for a drink or two at the Apollon pool bar. We also discovered that one of the residents on Apollon 4, used to live in the same village where my little sister Michelle and her husband Paul lived.

With the apartment almost sorted and the orientation of the Apollon Complex completed. Mick suggested taking Lillian and Melvin to visit Sunny Beach for a nice meal, to thank them for helping us to move into the apartment, and he wanted to watch a football match on the big screen. Lillian and I were made up that the boys wanted to watch their football team on Sky TV. This would give us some time for a bit of retail therapy after all the stress of moving into the apartment.

We caught the local bus from just across the road from the complex to take us to Sunny Beach. When we arrived at Sunny Beach, the resort seemed much bigger than when we had first come with Christopher. It actually looked like there had been a lot of new property investment, because of all the new hotels along the Black Sea coast.

The midday sun was shining on the beautiful emerald green sea, and all the sunseekers were lined up on the sunbeds along the miles of golden sand. I stood still for a moment admiring the view, then I noticed that everyone's sun tan looked so much better than mine. I think this was the first day that I had managed to get into the "holiday mood".

Mick and Melvin found a lovely bar with Sky TV, and they settled down to watch the match. Lillian and I walked along the lovely paved walkway that linked the beach to all the hotels. I looked at Lillian and smiled. 'I would like to live like this all the time sis, wouldn't you?'

She looked great in her wonderful black and white sun hat and her beautiful blue summer dress. 'Yes, Jan, it's lovely here. I cannot wait to tell everyone how much fun we have had when I go back to work.' We spent most of the afternoon looking around the shops for some nice gifts for the family, especially Michelle, Paul and Cerys.

After a lovely day shopping, we decided to join the lads at the Sky Sports bar. When I walked towards them, I noticed how nice Mick and Melvin looked in their summer clothes and their fabulous sun tans. It did not take us long to find out that they were both over the moon, because their favourite football team had won the game. I sat opposite Mick, to avoid getting in the way of the TV. He ordered us a couple of well-deserved drinks, and we spent the rest of the afternoon relaxing in the lovely sunshine.

It was late afternoon by the time we got back to the apartment. I put the gifts for Michelle, Paul and Cerys into the suitcases to make sure I did not forget to pack them. Mick and Melvin decided to play a game of cards, and enjoy a few more well-deserved drinks before we had to get ready to go out for the evening.

During the game of cards, I noticed that the Apollon Complex had a number of maintenance staff and there were a number of security guards patrolling the complex during the day and night. We had only been at the complex for a few days and we had already gotten to know some of the names of the staff, but there were a few people we were yet to meet. As a result, we had decided to create a few of our own names for them, as a way of passing time while we were watching them work.

Vanya was the manager of the Apollon Complex. She was a lovely woman and she made everyone feel very happy and welcome.

Chunky one (made up name) was a stocky Bulgarian man and the head gardener at Apollon 1, 2 and 5. He looked very strong, he was not very talkative, but he always smiled when you walked past him.

Chunky two (made up name) was also a stocky Bulgarian man, he was the gardener for Apollon 3 and 4. He also looked big and strong, he was always nice to everyone when they came near to him.

Cuckoo (made up name) was a small electrician, who lived in a section of the roof above Blodwyn and Knobby. They were our new friends from Surrey. Cuckoo was always very friendly and he liked to have fun while he was working.

Johnny Walker (made up name) was a very tall Bulgarian man. He was one of the men that came to check out the taps when we first moved into the apartment. He was also the painter on the complex.

There was a pool man and his girlfriend. They seemed quite different from the rest of the maintenance workers. She was very pretty; she had long black curly hair, olive skin and dark brown eyes. She was always very pleasant when I walked by her. The pool man was quite tall with light brown hair, green/blue eyes and a light tan. He always looked very serious when he was working on the swimming pools, which made me feel very safe and secure.

During the evenings, I noticed that there were three mature security guards they would always take over from the much younger daytime security guards. The daytime security guards were always young Bulgarian men, showing off their muscles and smart clothes; however, when the evening came, the young guards would handover to three very mature men. They reminded me of "three amigos" because they were all quite old and they spent most of their time sitting on the bench outside the toilet block at Apollon 4.

They sat there most of the evenings smoking and drinking small cups of coffee from the vending machine situated just behind the shop. They did not have big muscles and their clothes were never fashionable. The only time they ever got up from the bench was to use the male toilets or if they needed to light one another's cigarette or put them out in the bin. When I watched them, I noticed that their movements were always very slow and the only thing that made them stand up for more than a few seconds was when Vanya, the complex manager, did her regular inspections of the complex.

Before we went out for our usual drinks at the pool bar, then onto a restaurant for our evening meal, we sat on the balcony playing cards and talking about the lovely day we had at Sunny Beach. While Mick was pouring our drinks, I watched and laughed as the "three amigos" took over from the three younger Bulgarian men.

'Bloody hell, Mick, how are they going to protect us during the night?'

Mick laughed. 'Let's hope that no one tries to do anything bad during the night, Janet, because they will either be fast asleep on that bench or even worse, dead.'

Melvin looked over to where the men were sitting. 'To be honest, Mick, they do not look like they are able to run anywhere, never mind chase anyone.'

We stopped playing cards and started to analyse the state of their health and our safety. Mick whispered, 'God help us if someone tries to break into the complex. The best that we could hope for, is for Vanya to be doing one of her regular inspections, she is the only one who could sort out any unwanted intruders.'

Then all of a sudden, the day light started to fade and it suddenly became very dark outside, and the rain started to pour down. We watched as the three amigos had to get up from their comfy bench to take shelter under the walkway in the middle of Apollon 4.

Mick put his glass down and shouted, 'Bloody hell, Janet, keep an eye on them to make sure they don't get lost, they have never been any further than the male toilets.'

Everyone stopped what they were doing and we watched in amazement as they made their way slowly towards the shelter away from the pouring rain.

Within a few seconds, the weather had started to get worse. 'Janet, I do not fancy walking far in this rain, how about you?'

Lillian looked a bit concerned about the dreadful storm. I got up from my chair and looked up towards the sky. 'Wow, Mick, look up at the sky, it has gone jet black.'

Mick stood up and looked at the black sky. 'Let us go back to the fresh fish restaurant, the one that Nikolay recommended, you know the one with the freshly caught fish.'

Then, all of a sudden, it turned very cold on the balcony as the torrential rain poured down onto the sunbeds and into the swimming pools.

Lillian got up from her chair and she started to make her way into the living room to take cover. 'That sounds good to me, it will save us from getting wet tonight.'

Melvin started to pour the last bit of beer into his glass. 'That's great, I have been looking forward to eating a freshly caught rainbow trout.'

Lillian and I got a shower first to warm ourselves up. When I was dressed, I walked onto the balcony to check on the storm. The rain was still quite heavy, but nothing was not going to stop us from going out for tea. When everyone was ready, we decided to make a run for the fish restaurant which was only up the road by Apollon 5. As Mick locked the apartment door, I could hear the wind and rain howling outside.

'Can you hear the sound of that storm everyone?'

Mick put the key in his pocket. 'Come on, Janet, how wet can you get? It's only up the road.'

Lillian looked a bit worried to me. As we made our way towards the pavement, I could tell that none of the new roads had not been designed for lots of rain, because all of the water was gathering along the road, there were lots of big puddles forming everywhere and there was only one small hole in the middle of the road helping the water to escape.

Mick and I started to navigate our way through the deluge of water, it was like walking in a shallow lake. Lillian and Melvin took their time because Lillian did not want to fall into one of the big puddles of water. When we arrived at the house of the fish restaurant, I ran into the garden as fast as I could to find a place to sit out of the rain. Mick sat next to me while we waited for the others to arrive. Within a few seconds of Lillian and Melvin arriving, the young girl ran out of the house.

'*Dobar vecher.*' She pointed her finger and encouraged us to move inside to the small wooden table next to the bar and miniature toilet.

Mick was the first to sit down. 'Hello again, we are back.'

She handed him four homemade menus then ran back into the house. As soon as she had run through the door, the older woman came out to take our food and drinks order.

Melvin was the first to order. 'Please can I have the freshly caught rainbow trout? What time was it caught this morning?'

She looked at Melvin, but she never answered his question. Mick ordered the drinks and his meal, Lillian ordered chicken and chips. Then it was my turn. 'Please can I have the freshly caught rainbow trout too?'

Melvin smiled at me. 'I can't wait to eat it, Janet, I bet it is delicious.' He rubbed his hands together when the women placed a fish knife and fork on the table next to his drink.

I watched as she walked towards the side of the bar, because she did not go into the kitchen like the last time. Then to my amazement, she opened the top of a freezer. I could hear her moving a few boxes, then she pulled out a bag of frozen fish, just like the ones you would get from Iceland, the frozen food shop. I looked at Melvin. 'Did you see that, Mel?'

'I don't believe it, Janet.'

We looked at each other as if we were in shock!

'Fresh fish of the day, my arse, Janet; the only thing fresh around here is the bloody rain.' Mick laughed at me and Melvin.

Melvin moved his fish knife and fork to the side of the table then he took a big sip of his beer. Lillian picked up her glass of wine.

'I am glad we ordered chicken, Mick.'

Mick laughed. 'I hope it is fresher than their fish, Lill.'

Melvin and I waited nervously for our freshly caught frozen trout to be defrosted, then cooked.

While we were waiting for the food to cook, I noticed that the terrible storm was getting worse, the noise of the rain was getting louder and louder on the wooden bars' plastic roof. Then I saw a man come running from the house. I had not seen him before and he did not look happy. He ran past the bar towards what looked like a garden shed and I could see him pulling out some plastic sheets. He started to put the plastic sheets around the bar to protect tables and chairs from the storm. Each time he tried to cover a table, a gust of wind would blow it off, so he got some plant pots from around the garden and sat them on top of the plastic. Then he rolled a sheet of plastic from the wooded roof of the bar, then he fixed it to some hooks within the garden path. The wind and rain kept blowing the sheet, it looked like wet bedding on a washing line. We talked about all the effort he was putting in to keeping us and our frozen meals dry. Melvin and Mick tried to thank him, but he just kept on covering his wooded bar. Then we soon realised that he had no intention of keeping us dry, he was only interested in protecting us from the dodgy electrics along the ceiling of the bar, because he carried on working as if we were not there.

After a while, the garden floor around the bar started to flood.

'Oh my god, sis, the rain is getting worse.'

I knew Lillian was starting to get a bit worried, she was

always very good at doing risk assessments. 'How are we going to get back to the apartment?'

I tried to make her smile. 'It is a good job we haven't got too far to walk, sis, because I have not noticed any life boats for hire around here.'

Mick pointed to a tiny child's rubber dinghy that had been left at the back of the garden. 'Look, Lillian, that's my taxi home. Would you like a lift?'

She laughed. 'I will never get in that dingy, never mind the two of us.'

When the man returned to the house, the woman came running out of the kitchen with two big dishes in her hands. The young girl was holding an umbrella over the woman's head and the plates, trying to protect everything from getting wet from the pouring rain. When they got to the table, the women placed a plate of soggy chicken and chips in front of Mick and Lillian.

'I am so sorry the rain is very wet tonight.'

Then she ran back into the house with the young girl running behind her, trying to keep the umbrella up in the very bad storm.

Melvin and I waited for a while for the freshly caught frozen fish to arrive. Then the kitchen door opened and the woman made her way through the pouring rain and waterlogged garden, without the shelter of the umbrella. She placed the wet fish plates onto the table.

'So sorry for the delay, the rain is very bad here tonight.'

Then she ran back into the house. I looked down at the plate, it looked like the rainbow trout had been dead for years.

'Oh my god, Melvin, this fish looks awful. Do you think we should eat it?'

He did not answer straight away, I think he was in shock.

'Please, Melvin, what do you think, you are the only professional fisherman here.'

Melvin looked over to my plate. 'Listen, Janet, you can always tell by the fish's eyes if it is safe to eat.'

I leant towards him. 'What do you mean, Melvin, I do not want to eat anything that is bad for me, you don't want to know what happened to me the last time I had stomach problems at Sunny Beach!'

Mick shouted, 'No, nor do I, I do not want to have to take you back to that room with all of those hungry mosquitoes and that dodgy doctor.'

Melvin's face became very serious then he looked into the eyes. 'Well, Janet, it is like this; if that fish winks at you, it is a good sign.'

I looked back into his eyes. 'And what happens if it does not wink at me, Melvin?'

He dropped his serious look. 'Don't eat the eyes, you will just have to eat the body because there is nothing else left to eat; all of the chicken and chips have gone.' Then he stuck his fork in his fish.

I picked my fish knife and fork up and moved them towards the fish to cut into the body. When Mick shouted, 'Stop it, Janet, I think I have just seen it move, it's not dead. Please do not kill it.'

Then Melvin sat up laughing. 'Do not be daft, Mick, the last time that fish was in water was tonight when it got wet from the rain; it's been frozen for at least a year!'

I was starving. I placed my fork just below the head of the fish, then I dug my fish knife in just at the top of the gill and pressed. Then all of a sudden, the fish's tail flipped up towards the sky.

Mick shouted out, 'Look out, Janet, it is trying to swim away. Don't let it jump into that puddle of water around your feet.' Then everyone burst out laughing.

The mature woman came to the door because she could hear us all laughing, she made her way through the bad weather to find out what was so funny.

'*Kakvo e tova?*' (what is that?)

We all stopped laughing and looked at her soaking wet face and hair.

Mick smiled at me. 'How do you tell someone that their so-called fresh fish of the day was not fresh at all, because she had just got it out of a freezer and my wife thinks it's still alive because it winked at her and now it is trying to escape into the rain water to swim away?'

I had to hold back my laughter. 'Mick, please, do not try to explain anything to her, just tell her that the chicken and chips had none of the drama like the 'freshly caught' frozen rainbow trout.'

He did not say anything about the food, Mick ordered another round of drinks and she left.

While the lads were talking about football, I noticed that the rain storm was becoming horrendous. The mature woman came out of the house and she started to use a washing line pole to push the big puddles of rain water from gathering on the top of the homemade plastic roof before it collapsed on top of us and the dodgy electrics! While she was pushing the water off, she kept smiling and reassuring us that the torrential rain was going to stop soon, so that we could leave the bar.

Mick whispered, 'There is no way this rain is not going to stop yet.' Then he stood up to get the woman's attention. 'Please can we order some more drinks while we wait for the rain to stop?' She smiled at him then she ran back into the house.

We waited and waited, drink after drink, but the torrential rain never stopped. The storm was just getting worse. The garden had become a small lake and it was getting very late into the night.

When I looked towards the house, I noticed that all the lights were turned off. The man who had fixed the plastic roof had started to come out of the house. He was wearing a big housecoat and it looked like he was ready for bed. He walked past us up to the bar, then he turned all the lights out from behind the counter, then he walked off again as if we were not there. I knew then that we did not have any option but to go home, and we needed to leave the restaurant in the pouring rain.

To encourage us to leave, the woman went inside the house and turned on the kitchen light for a few minutes then it went off again. When the woman came outside, she was holding four black plastic bin bags, one for each of us to cover our heads and clothes. We grabbed a bag each, I made a hole in the top of mine, then I pulled the bag over my head, shoulders to protect some of my clothes from the rain. Everyone else did the same. The woman handed Mick the receipt. Mick and Melvin paid the bill, which included a big tip, because she had tried her best to keep us dry. None of us wanted to leave the bar, never mind the garden. We stood together on a little dry island in the middle of the lawn, each of us hesitating to make the plunge into the water.

Then the woman pointed to the road and shouted, '*Licanosh*' (goodnight). Please go now.'

When I left the shelter of the bar, I felt the rain hitting my head and face, then it started to run down my protective black bag. There were big puddles of water everywhere and within a few seconds, my feet were ringing wet. When we made our way to the road, I could see that it had become like a wild river, all of the rainwater was running onto the main road from the apartments and surrounding fields. I looked at Mick, Lillian and Melvin.

'My god, it looks like one of those documentaries that you see on TV, the ones about floods wiping out local communities.'

Mick grabbed my hand. 'Hold on tight, Janet, it looks like we might have to swim back to the apartment.'

With that bit of encouragement, we all started to wade our way through the water.

'Bloody hell, sis, this rain water is up to my knees.' Lillian was trying her best to walk along the road, but the sheer volume of water kept pushing her back. Melvin held on to her hand so that he could pull her through the river that was once the road.

The black plastic bag that was used to cover my body was preventing my shoulders from getting wet, but all the water from the road was gushing up and under the bag, stopping me from moving my legs.

It seemed to take ages before I could see the lights from Apollon 4 in the distance. 'We're nearly there, everyone, keep going, we can have a nice hot shower when we get home.'

Mick pulled my hand to encourage me to walk faster. 'I am going to have a large glass of beer when I get in, how about you, Melvin?'

I heard a voice coming from behind me. 'That sounds like a great idea, Mick.'

When we got to Apollon 4, Mick opened the apartment door and we all piled into the living room. I caught my reflection in the large mirror by the door. When I turned around, I could see Lillian, Melvin and Mick dripping wet in the kitchen, and I had to laugh.

'We all look like gothic Teletubbies, dressed in these black bin bags.'

They looked at each other then they burst out laughing. Mick pulled his bag off. 'I think it was a good idea at the time, to keep our shoulders dry, but my feet and legs are soaking wet.

Lillian took her bag off. 'So are mine, it has even come up to my knickers.'

As I pulled the black bag over my head and all the rainwater fell into a big puddle on the floor. Mick passed me a towel and I dried my head, hands, legs and feet. By the time I had finished drying myself, Lillian had made a nice cup of coffee for everyone. I put my PJs on and settled down in the living room with a warm cover over me, to watch a bit of Bulgarian TV before going to bed.

It did not take me long to fall asleep, however, I was woken during the night by some very loud bangs coming from outside the apartment; it sounded like something heavy was hitting all of the plastic sun beds and tables from around the swimming pools. Mick jumped up out of bed to take a look out of the window. I moved the warm covers over to the middle of the bed to join him by the window to see what was causing all of the noise?

When I looked out of the window, to my amazement, I could see hundreds of massive hailstones, the size of golf balls, falling from the midnight sky. When the giant hailstones hit the surface of the sun beds and tables, it destroyed them and everything else it landed on.

'Oh my god, Mick, I have never seen anything like this in my entire life.'

He carried on looking out of the window. 'Wow, Janet, I

am so glad that we managed to get home when we did, we could have gotten hurt or even killed if one of those giant hailstones landed on you!'

I could hear Lillian and Melvin talking in the next room, they had also been woken up by the sound of the hailstones destroying the sun beds and tables. We all gathered in the living room. Mick opened the balcony door to see if we could get a closer look, without getting hurt. Together, we watched helplessly as the storm of giant hailstones smashed everything it came into contact with. The damage around Apollon 4 was immense; all of the beautiful whitewashed walls and manicured gardens were being pulverised by massive frozen balls of rain. I watched as the water in the swimming pool kept jumping into the air as the snowballs made their crash landing, it was frightening! We spent most of the night watching the storm damage the beautiful complex.

When the storm had passed over, I was left feeling helpless, because there was nothing that I could do to prevent the amount of destruction. Mick and I made our way back to the bedroom. There was a silence in the air, the sound of laughter had well and truly gone, which was very unusual for the four of us. I struggled to get back to sleep. I kept thinking about all the damage to the complex, swimming pools, sun beds and tables.

The following morning, I got up very early to take a look outside. When I opened the window blind in the living room, I could see that the sun was shining again, as if nothing had happened during the night! I stood on the balcony and I looked around the complex. It was very busy, lots of people were standing outside their apartments assessing the storm damage to their properties.

As I looked across the pool, I could see that the Bulgarian

man who owned the Apollon Hotel, was outside checking all the damage to their guests' motor cars which had been parked outside the hotel overnight. It did not take him long to see where the hail stones had made big massive dents in the bodywork of every car. The roofs, bonnets and boots of the cars looked like colanders. The look on his face was inconsolable.

I did not know what to do; all the sun beds, tables and umbrellas from around the pool were smashed into pieces. The whitewashed exterior walls of the Apollon 3 apartments looked like they had been pebbled dashed, because there were big black spots all over the front where the hail stones had crashed landed onto the walls.

I went back into the bedroom to wake Mick up.

'Mick, please get up and come outside with me to see if our apartment has any damage from last night's hailstones.'

He slipped his shorts and t-shirt on and we went outside to see if there was any damage. When we walked around the corner towards the swimming pools, we started to take a good look at the exterior walls. Thankfully, the walls of the apartment were undamaged; however, when we looked over to Apollon 4, we could see that the lovely white walls looked like they had been covered with black and white polka dots.

Vanya the complex manager was very busy ensuring the maintenance team were repairing all of the surface damage around the pools. I could tell that she wanted to get the complex back to normal as soon as possible. The maintenance team was removing all of the damaged sunbeds, tables and sun shades. The gardening team were sorting out the bedding plants, and cutting back the broken trees and bushes. When she had finished instructing the maintenance and gardening team, she moved onto the next job. Mick and I stood watching as she worked her magic and the team started to return the complex back to normal.

I could hear the noise of machinery coming from the road, then a massive cherry picker stopped in the middle of the driveway by Apollon 3. I watched as she walked over to Johnny Walker (Ivan the painter). She spoke to him for a while, then she passed him a big paint brush and a large white plastic tub. Without any hesitation, Ivan climbed onto the cherry picker and made his way towards the platform. When he was ready, he pressed a few buttons and the platform started to rise up into the air. Once he was positioned along the polka dot wall, he started to dab out all of the black spots where the hail stones had landed with his big white brush. It was like a giant dot to dot. I watched as all the giant black spots disappeared.

Mick and I walked back to the apartment to talk with Lillian and Melvin. They had been watching all of the devastation from the balcony, as a result they thought it would be a good idea to go somewhere else for the day to allow the maintenance team to do their jobs. I went into the bedroom to change out of my sunbathing gear. I could not believe what had happened to the beautiful complex.

When I was ready, we left the apartment and made our way to the bus stop. As we walked up to the main road, it was as if everything was back to normal; there was nothing left of the river of rain that we had to manoeuvre through last night. All of the rain water seemed to have disappeared down the tiny little drainage hole. As I walked across the main road to the bus stop for Old Nessebar. I could see the severity of the damage; every car around the complex was damaged and they all had massive big dimples in the body work where the hail stones had crashed landed onto them. Some of the glass windscreens on the cars were shattered into tiny pieces of glass, I could see that all of the owners were devastated.

When the bus arrived, I took some time to look at the sides of the bus, and I could see that some of the body work on the bus had been slightly damaged, but it was not as bad as the cars around the complex. When we got on the bus, we all sat silently on the back seats staring out of the window at the extent of the damage from the hailstorm; there was a quietness all around us.

When the bus stopped at Old Nessebar, it felt much hotter than usual. I walked up to the thermometer at the side of the minimarket. When I looked at it I could see that the temperature was in the high nineties. I could not believe my eyes. There had been a massive storm with hailstones as big as golf balls during the night and now it was scorching hot.

We spent the morning walking around the wonderful cobbled pathways of Old Nessebar trying to find a few last minute gifts for the family and something different for ourselves to take home. After an hour or two, the midday heat was becoming more and more unbearable. Mick and Melvin decided it was time to go for a nice cool drink and something to eat. We carried on walking along the pathway facing New Nessebar, when Lillian found a lovely restaurant overlooking the Black Sea. It looked amazing.

The waiter was very welcoming, he showed us to a lovely table overlooking the emerald sea. I sat down and started to look through the menu. When I opened the first page, I could see the price lists. Mick looked at me, then I looked at Lillian and Melvin. The price for food in this restaurant was extremely expensive when I compared it with all the restaurants that we had visited around the complex and Sunny Beach.

When I looked up towards Lillian, I noticed that the waiter

was hovering around the table and he was ready and waiting to take our food and drink order. Then just before he got his pen out, a young couple with a baby walked into the restaurant. The waiter had to leave our table to help them with the baby's pram. Mick stood up from the table.

'Bloody hell, Melvin, have you seen these prices, I am not paying twenty lev for a shepherd's salad.'

Everyone jumped up and ran out of the restaurant before the waiter had time to come back to the table.

When we knew it was safe to stop running, we all stood on the pavement outside a clothes shop, waiting to get our breath back.

Lillian looked at me. 'I am so glad that we did not eat at that restaurant because Melvin and I were going to pay for the meal as a thank you for letting us come on holiday with you.'

I was taken by surprise by their kind offer. 'You don't have to pay for anything, we have had a brilliant time together and you helped us to move in.'

But she would not accept. 'No, sis, this is our way of thanking you and Mick.'

I was delighted that they had offered to pay for a meal.

When we got our breath back, we made our way along the sea wall that took us to the other side of Old Nessebar. I started to watch all the fishing boats in the harbour, I noticed that they did not seem to have any damage from last night's horrific hailstorm that hit the Apollon Complex. I watched as all the tourists were relaxing on the beach in the sunshine on the undamaged sun beds.

'It looks like Old Nessebar missed last night's horrific storm.'

Mick looked at everyone relaxing in the sun. 'They are the

lucky ones, Janet.'

We started to walk towards the pathway that led to the bus stop when Melvin found a lovely restaurant in a fabulous location. When I looked at the menu that was positioned on a sign outside the main door, I could see that the food looked great and the price was just right for Lillian and Melvin's thank-you meal. I put my arm through Mick's arm and we walked into the restaurant.

The waiter smiled then he showed us to a lovely long table overlooking the beach and New Nessebar. Mick ordered the drinks and we all settled down in the big wooden chairs for our last meal in Old Nessebar.

The view from the restaurant was stunning. As I sat looking over the beach, I felt a sadness coming over me, then I realised that we would be going home soon.

'I don't want to go home yet, I would like to stay a little longer, it has been a great holiday.'

Mick put his hand on my knee. 'Don't be sad, it will not be long before we are flying back to Bulgaria.'

I looked around the table to see what everyone was doing and it felt like everyone was feeling the same as me. I knew that none of us wanted to return home because it had been such a fabulous holiday. No one mentioned anything about flying home the following evening, we just made the most of our special holiday time together.

By the time we arrived back at the apartment, it was late. I went into the bedroom to get changed into my bedtime clothes to watch a bit of Bulgarian TV. Mick got changed into his PJs, then he left the bedroom to make a goodnight drink for him and Melvin. I had not had any time to hang my clothes in the wardrobe when he came running back into the bedroom and closed the door. The shock on his face was very evident.

'Janet, please go and have a word with your Lillian.'

I stopped hanging my dress in the wardrobe and looked at him. 'Why what has she done?' Mick looked very serious. 'She is having a cigarette on the balcony, but her long blue dress is tucked inside her knickers and I don't want to say anything just in case I embarrass her.' Then he burst out laughing.

'Oh no, Mick, she will be mortified. Stay here, I will have to go and have a word with her, please don't move until she is decent.'

When I walked into the living room, I could see that she was stood on the balcony with the light of the moon shining down on her, the smoke from her cigarette was creating a mist around her face and she looked like she was in one of those old-fashioned movies where the leading lady always looked like they were glowing in the moonlight, she could have gotten away with it except for her lovely blue dress being stuck in her white knickers.

I walked towards her, then in my softest voice, I whispered, 'Good evening, sis.' I surprised her. 'Please, can you take your lovely blue dress out of your white knickers?'

She turned around and looked at me in horror. 'What are you talking about sis, it's not is it?' When she looked behind her, she could see it. 'Oh no, sis, how long has it been like that?'

I smiled at her as she was pulling the dress out of her underwear. 'I am not sure, sis.' But before I had time to say anything else, Mick came out of our bedroom into the living room. 'It must have only just happened, sis, because it was not like that earlier. Thank God!' Mick and I looked at each other and started to giggle.

After a while, Melvin came out of the bathroom, Lillian

couldn't wait to tell him about her little indiscretion and we all started to laugh out loud, then Mick whispered, 'Shush, everyone, you will wake up the three amigos.'

We tiptoed to the balcony to see if the three old men were sitting on their bench outside the toilets to ensure they were keeping us safe. But when we looked over to their bench, it was empty and they were nowhere in sight. There were no more puffs of smoke or any Bulgarian chatter.

I whispered, 'I wonder what has happened to them. Do you think last night's hailstones may have seen them off?'

Lillian looked towards the walkway. 'I hope not, sis, they were nice men.'

Mick started to grin. 'I did not see any coffins around the pool this morning so they should be OK.'

The following morning, we finished packing our suitcases ready for the flight back home to Manchester. We were all sad to be leaving, but we knew that we would be coming back to have some more fun in the sun.

When Nikolay picked us up from the apartment to take us back to the airport he spoke about the horrific thunder storm and all the damage around the complex, he didn't mention anything about anyone dying that night to our relief? We left the apartment not knowing if the three amigos were dead or alive?

Dream Holiday Home

The thirty-minute drive back to Bourgas Airport seemed to take longer than before, because everyone was so very quiet in the car. There was no laughing or joking, just the odd word or two to break the silent atmosphere. Nikolay talked about some of the new developments around the complex, but I think we were all wishing we could stay a little while longer, we were all so very sad to be going home.

The check-in at Bourgas Airport was slow because the customs officers were being very strict. Lillian and Melvin seemed to be far less worried because they were not carrying any funny birthday presents, because Mick was happy to leave Lucy and the grooming kit in the apartment until we came back in July, just to be on the safe side.

When I walked towards the duty-free shopping, my heart was longing to turn around to go back to the apartment. It had been such a lovely holiday I just did not want it to end. I looked across the duty-free perfume towards Lillian and I could tell that she was feeling the same sadness.

'Sis, do you fancy coming up to the rooftop with me? I can have a cigarette up there.'

She started to smile. 'Let's go and find Mick and Melvin.' We made our way up the stairs to the fabulous airport rooftop. Mick opened the door to the roof terrace of the airport, it looked beautiful with all the fancy night lights shining from the above. The night sky was pitch black. When I looked up towards the stars, they looked so close, it made me feel like I could touch them. The boys found four white plastic chairs for us to sit on while we waited in the moonlight for our flight back to Manchester to be called.

We spent most of the time reflecting on the wonderful holiday. I mentioned all the fun we had at Mick's birthday afternoon with Lucy and the near mishap with the two Bulgarian builders. Mick laughed about the Durex... I mean the egg moment in the supermarket and how he felt when the supermarket assistant grabbed hold of his hand and pulled him towards the medicine cabinet... Melvin spoke about the so-called fresh fish restaurant selling frozen rainbow trout as the fresh catch of the day, and Lillian talked about the massive storm with the big hailstones and all the damage. We could not believe so much had happened in one week. It felt like we could make Bulgaria our second home.

Then all of a sudden, Lillian went very quiet as she pulled another cigarette out of her fag packet and started to light it. 'I have just remembered something, sis, and I am beginning to feel a little nervous about the flight taking off because of the bumpy runway, Mick!'

Melvin stood up, 'I will get you something to calm your nerves down, love.'

He went to the bar and bought her a big glass of white wine and offered her another cigarette.

Mick pulled his white plastic chair towards her. 'Listen Lillian, this is the second time Janet and I have taken off from Bourgas Airport, and we are hoping to do it again in July; therefore, we will be paying towards the new runway so that it will be ready for the next time you and Melvin come to Bulgaria.' She took a big sip of her wine and a long drag of her

205

cigarette. 'Can we come back with you?' She smiled at me.

'Absolutely, it has been one of the best holidays.' And I gave her a big hug.

Then we heard the departure call for our flight. 'OK, everyone, we will be back soon.' We held our drinks towards the beautiful night sky and toasted. 'To the next time.'

We did not have to wait very long in the departure lounge. When we got on the plane, the air hostess showed everyone to their seats. I sat down and put my seatbelt on, while Mick placed the hand luggage in the overhead locker. Then within a few minutes the plane took off without any problems, there were no bumps or side to side movements, it actually felt like the runway had been resurfaced. Then I heard a voice from the seats in front of us. 'Wow, Mick, I did not expect that, that was quite a smooth take off.'

Mick looked through the gap in the chairs. 'See, Lillian, our flights have already started to pay off.'

She burst out laughing.

Knowing that we were all settled down for the journey home, I fell asleep feeling very happy because the apartment had actually become our dream holiday home and I knew that Mick and I would be back there within a few weeks.

When the plane landed at Manchester Airport, it did not take long for the cold air to wake me up and for me to realise that I was back home. As I made my way through UK customs then towards arrivals, it felt like I was in a bit of a daze (I am sure it was my body telling me to go back to Bulgaria).

The next thing I heard, 'Hurry up, Janet, the taxi is here to take us home.'

I could not believe that I would soon be back home hugging Christopher in our lovely clean house in Widnes.

When the taxi stopped outside our house it looked massive compared to the apartment in Bulgaria, but this was 'home sweet home' to me, and Bulgaria was our dream holiday home. Mick went to get the suitcases out of the boot of the car while I opened the front door. He carried the two cases over the doorstep and I opened the front door, as I walked into the hallway, a terrible smell hit me. 'What has happened to our beautiful, clean home, Mick'? It smelt terrible, like something had died or gone off.

'Christopher. Christopher, love, what is that horrible smell?' There was no answer from Christopher.

I opened the kitchen door and walked into the kitchen. The first thing I saw was one of the big roasting tins hanging out of the sink. As I made my way towards the sink, I could tell that it had been there for days, then I heard a voice behind me.

'Welcome back, Mum, oh you have found it. Well, Mum, it was like this, Mum, me and my mates wanted to have a BBQ with the big leg of lamb you had in the freezer.'

As I opened the kitchen window, I looked towards Christopher. 'The one that I have been saving for a special day?'

He looked at me and smiled. 'Yes, that one, Mum, it was lovely, we all really enjoyed it.'

I looked at the big roasting tin hanging out of the sink, then back at him. 'OK, why did you leave this roasting tin in the sink, with all of the bits of meat that have gone green mouldy.'

Christopher made his way over to the sink and looked at the roasting tin. 'Well, Mum, it was like this, me and my mates tossed a coin to see who would wash the roasting tin and I am sorry to tell you that you lost!'

I looked at him with piercing eyes. 'I lost, how can that happen? I was not even here so how could I lose the bet?'

He looked down at the roasting tin. 'It wasn't my fault that you weren't here, you should not have left me on my own.' Then he gave me a big hug.

Feeling guilty, I turned the hot tap on and tried to clean the roasting tin, but the bits of leftover meat had gone mouldy and it was ground into the tin. I stopped running the hot soapy water over the roasting tin and passed it over to Christopher. 'Please go and throw it in the bin before your dad sees it, I cannot wash it now.'

Christopher would not take the tin from me. 'I thought it was one of your best ones, that's why I left it in the sink.'

I passed it back to him. 'It's OK, son, I will buy a new one at the weekend, just throw it in the bin please.'

Mick could not believe the smell; he had to open all of the windows in the house before he could turn the TV on, to find out what had been happening in the world of sport. When I entered the living room, he was sitting on the couch with Christopher. Mick turned away from the TV and looked towards me.

'I think we had better order fish and chips from the chippie for lunch, because I am not going to eat anything out of that kitchen until that horrible smell goes, do you know where it is coming from?'

Christopher replied, 'It was only some food that I had left in the sink. I have put it in the bin outside now.' Then he winked at me. Thank's son, the house is looking nice and tidy. You have done a good job of looking after it while we have been away.

Happy Holidays

The following day when Mick and I woke up, we could not wait to book our return flights to Bulgaria. However, before I booked them, I telephoned Michelle and Paul to see if they wanted to join us; but unfortunately, they were still not able to join us at this time because they still had a few financial commitments. We were all disappointed. Mick and I decided to go on our own; this would give us some time to do everything we wanted to do to the apartment before they would join us next year.

I unpacked the suitcases and started to wash all the summer clothes, ready to iron and pack again. I could not wait to return to our dream home in the sun. Mick and I needed to sort out the maintenance cost, water charges, electricity and the community charge with Vanya, the complex manager. We did not want to do any of that while we were with Lillian and Melvin, because it would have taken up so much time.

On the day of the flight back to Bulgaria, we left our home in Widnes in the capable hands of Christopher and his mates again, but this time I made sure that there were no big joints of meat for them to BBQ, and I hid all the roasting tins, just in case.

When Mick and I arrived at Manchester Airport, he checked all the big cases into the check-in, then we made our way through security, customs, then into duty-free before settling down for a nice meal and a bottle of wine.

The flight to Bulgaria was lovely. Nikolay picked us up from Bourgas Airport, and as we made our way to the apartment we passed through a number of small towns and villages again. I noticed that there had been some new structural investment along the main road and the infrastructure surrounding Bourgas airport.

When Nikolay drove along the main road that led to the apartment, I could see that the road had been covered with tarmac and there had been some additional drainage built in to prevent the roads from flooding again. When he drove past Apollon 1, 2, 5 then 3, I could still see where the hailstones had damaged some of the residential buildings and their parked cars, it all looked quite surreal.

When Nikolay pulled up outside Apollon 4, the apartment block looked wonderful, the sun was shining and I could hear children's laughter from the swimming pools. Mick pulled the big suitcases from the car and we made our way up the steps to the front door. Before he turned the key to open the door, we looked at each other and smiled.

'We have bought this, Janet; all our hard work has finally paid off!'

When he opened the door, everything was just how we left it. 'It's good to know that our dream holiday home is only three hours away, Mick.'

I rolled the suitcases into the bedroom and started to unpack while Mick sorted out the patio table and chairs on the balcony. When I had finished unpacking, I joined Mick in the living room. We cleaned the kitchen sink, the bathroom toilets and shower, then we both walked onto the balcony and sat around the table with a nice cup of coffee. I could see lots of people sunbathing and swimming in the pool. Mick looked at me. 'Let's get changed and go outside to sunbathe, we are on holiday.'

It did not take us long to get into our swimwear, then we made our way around to the sun beds and swimming pools. While I was tanning up, a few English people came over and started to chat with us. We soon found out that they were also property owners from Apollon 4. They were really nice people, they guided us through the dos and don'ts regarding travelling on local buses, and asking for the price of a destination before getting into a taxi and the best places to exchange UK sterling into lev. We learnt about all the lovely places to eat out, the best supermarkets nearby and they spoke about the pool bar on Apollon 3.

When they had gone for lunch, I lay in the sunshine outside our dream home. I thought about all the wonderful things Mick and I could do on our two-week holiday. We spent most of the day relaxing by the pool and getting to know a few more of our new neighbours. When the sun started to set behind the apartment block, Mick suggested that we should make our way to the little mini market next to Apollo 5 to buy some essential food and drink. I put my summer dress on and we walked towards the shop. When I walked into the shop, the cool air from the air conditioning hit me. It felt like a cold winter breeze cooling down my whole body.

Mick picked up a basket to carry the essentials; bread, butter, cheese, ham, beer, and a nice selection of wine, Savoy vodka, coke and six freshly laid eggs (not Durex). Mick paid for the shopping then we made our way back to the apartment. I unpacked the shopping, while Mick poured the lovely white Bulgarian wine into our glasses. We sat together on the balcony watching everyone having a good time swimming in the pool.

211

'Do you realise, Janet, that this is the first time we have been in the apartment on our own?'

I loved spending holiday time with Lillian and Melvin, because they were always so much fun, but it was also good to spend some holiday time alone with Mick.

Mick poured another drink while I went into the kitchen to prepare some snacks. When I returned with the bowls of crisps and nuts, he went to get the pack of cards out of the wall cupboard at the side of the TV to play our favourite card game.

When I sat down, I could not stop myself from smiling. 'It is great to relax and not worry about work, Mick, for the next two weeks.'

He looked at me. 'Janet, this is the first time in a long while that I have felt really relaxed.' We sat on the balcony playing our favourite card game until it was time to go out for tea.

'Mick, do you fancy getting a nice shower in the wet room? This will be the first time we have had the chance to use it. Lillian and Melvin said it was great.'

He looked up from his cards. 'That would be good.' I started to walk towards the bathroom. 'It feels strange going into the wet room after Lillian and Melvin; it feels like this is their wetroom.'

Mick came walking in behind me. 'What they don't know won't hurt them, now take your shower.'

The wet room shower was lovely and it was nice to finally use it. Mick and I changed into our best summer clothes and we made our way to the Cat's restaurant on Apollon 3. When I looked through the main door, I could see that it was empty. 'Would you like to go for a walk along the beach, Mick, because there is no one in the restaurant.'

He looked through the window. 'That would be nice, we

can try one of the restaurants overlooking the Black Sea coast.'

When we left the complex, we made our way towards the Dolphin Hotel to see if the restaurant was open, but when we looked through the window, it was full of happy people, eating their meals. Mick decided to turn left by the supermarket, to see if any of the bars at that side of the beach were serving meals. We walked along the rugged road until we came to a paved walkway that separated the beautiful golden beach from the hotels. There were lots of small restaurants all along the seacoast wall, each of them offering a lovely selection of Bulgarian food, and they all had a fantastic view of the beautiful Black Sea coast.

We walked to the end of the pathway towards what looked like a three-storey restaurant. I looked inside to see what the customers were eating and it all looked delicious.

'Shall we go in here for something to eat, Mick?'

He grabbed hold of my hand. 'Yes, I am starving.'

And we walked into the restaurant. The waiter showed Mick and I to a small wooden table by the window. I was delighted because I could see the reflection of the moon over the sea and I could hear the noise of the waves as they rolled across the sand. It was such a beautiful location.

When I looked around the restaurant, I noticed that a lot of the customers were sharing what looked like a large wooded dish which was full of hot meats and vegetables, the food looked delicious. I looked through the menu as fast as I could to see what the dish was called. When I turned to the middle page of the menu, I could see a picture of the same dish. I searched the page to find the name of the dish.

'Do you fancy a Bulgarian Sach, Mick?'

He looked up from his menu. What is in it, Janet?'

I read out the English narrative from the menu. 'It includes four types of BBQ meat; pork, chicken, beef and veal, and a mixture of fresh vegetables, it says that it is served on a hot clay tile, not a dish. It looks delicious!' He looked at the middle page of the menu. 'Go on then, Janet, let us give it a go.' When the waitress came to take our order, Mick ordered a nice bottle of wine and I pointed to the BBQ Sach, she smiled and left.

Mick and I enjoyed eating the delicious Sach, and we loved spending our time together. After the meal was over we sat under the moonlight holding our glasses of wine talking about all the wonderful things that we wanted to do during the two weeks' holiday. When we had finished our drinks, we walked along the beach in our bare feet.

The night sky from the beach was fabulous. I stopped to take some photographs of the amazingly vivid moon and bright stars in the black sky. When we were halfway along the beach, Mick decided to have a drink in the Elizabeth Hotel and restaurant. We brushed the sand off our feet and toes, then we sat at a lovely table overlooking the sea. The full moon in the sky and the noise of the waves crashing over the sand made it feel like one of those romantic films from the old days.

There was a man playing music in the corner of the Elizabeth bar, he looked very happy singing along to all the Karaoke songs. Some of the people in the restaurant were up dancing to the music. I watched as the waiters dodge all of the dancers on the dance floor and the people dancing in between their tables. This manoeuvring ensured that they could carry on serving all of their customers. It looked like everyone was having such a wonderful time. 'Shall we have a few more drinks here, Janet, it looks great fun?'

I smiled. 'Absolutely. Do you fancy a dance?' We joined

the dancing party on the dance floor, for an evening of fun and laughter.

When I woke up the following morning, I felt a little bit hungover after the wonderful Karaoke night in the Elizabeth's. I decided to spend the morning sunbathing and watching some of the hotel's holiday guests, enjoying the swimming pools and the sunbathing area surrounding the children's pool. I turned around to talk to Mick.

'Look, Mick, that was us. How many years have we spent travelling the world looking for that perfect place to buy a holiday home and we ended up here in Bulgaria?'

He took his sunglasses off and smiled. 'Yes, Janet, who would've thought that we would end up in Bulgaria, this place was never on my radar, it was a good job that I went to the toilet when I did!'

The midday sun was shining directly down onto the pool. I noticed that all the tiny crystals of water made from the children splashing in the swimming pool were evaporating as soon as they landed on the stone floor. It was like drops of water hitting a red hot flame. I soon realised that it was becoming far too hot for me, and that it was time to get under the shade of the umbrella before I got sunburn. When I stood up from the sun bed to reposition my bed under the umbrella, Mick turned towards me.

'Wow, Janet, this is becoming far too hot for me too. Would you like to go for a nice walk along the beach to Ravda?'

I knew that I had enough sunbathing for one day. 'That would be lovely, Mick.' I picked up the beach towels and went inside the apartment to cool down.

When Mick and I had had a long cold drink and we had given ourselves enough time to cool down, we decided to explore Ravda. It was a small village about half a mile from the complex. I put my comfiest walking shoes on and we walked along the Black Sea coast. The whole of the coastline was unspoilt and very natural; it was quite stunning. There were lots of small bars and restaurants along the pathway and they were all run by Bulgarian families.

As we continued walking towards Ravda, I realised that everyone was so very friendly, none of the bar or restaurant owners or staff pressured you to go inside for something to eat or drink. This was not like some of the places Mick and I had visited in the past. They just wanted to make sure that you were having a lovely time in their beautiful country.

When we arrived at the end of the coastal path, we came to a long manmade path that was overgrown with tall grasses, bushes and shrubs. I began to feel a bit worried.

'Mick, stop, I am not walking in there, what if there are some snakes in that tall grass?'

He stopped walking and turned to look at me. 'OK, you can go first, Janet, just scream if you see anything so that I can get out of the way. They can bite you first!' I stood still 'No way you can go first.' 'OK' Then he carried on walking like "Mick Dundee".

I tried to walk as fast as I could to get through the urban jungle, but I had to keep stopping to get the long grass and tiny stones out of my shoes. Every time I had to stop, Mick started to make a hissing noise that sounded like a snake to frighten me and to make me walk faster. When we finally made it out of the jungle, we continued to walk past a few hotels and restaurants. We carried on walking along the coastal road. When I looked up I could see that there was a beautiful little cove at the bottom of a small cliff along the Black Sea coast.

As we got closer to the cove, I could see that there were some man made steps leading down to the golden beach which split into two directions, East and West. The steps on the left-hand side led to three little emerald rock pools surrounded by a small, beautiful, secluded beach. The steps on the right-hand side led to a number of tiny beaches and coves reaching out into the Black Sea towards the end of the cliff face.

We stopped at the top of the cliff top, to look at the beautiful emerald sea. As I looked down, I could see that there was a plush blanket of seaweed covering all the sandstone surrounding the rock pools; it looked like an emerald green shag pile carpet changing colour from light green to dark green, as the sea brushed it up and down and the gentle waves rolled over it, it was so relaxing

My moment of relaxation was suddenly broken by the sound of children playing in the rock pools. They were having so much fun trying to catch some of the small fish and crabs that had been left behind by the sea as it rolled away. I stood and watched a number of people swimming in the lovely clear water, then I noticed that a few of them were able to walk across the emerald green seaweed carpet to get in and out of the sea. It looked so idyllic, I knew I did not want to leave this beautiful place. There was a big old wooden table and two benches positioned at the side of the cliff.

'Shall we stay for a while and have a cold beer from the bar, Mick?' He sat down on the wooden bench next to me.

There was a little wooden bar just set back from the cliff edge. It was a fantastic place to rest after the walk through the scary jungle and to find this wonderful little oasis in Ravda. The sea breeze was strong, as soon as it blew over my body it cooled my skin down after the intense heat of the midday sunshine. I

217

knew that I had had enough sun on my face for one day and I did not want to end up bright red like the time on a sunny beach, so I decided to sit with my back to the sun facing the small beach to the west.

Mick ordered two beers from the waiter and he smiled at me. I grabbed hold of his hand.

'This is my favourite place in Bulgaria so far, Mick, I could stay here forever.'

He took a sip of his cold beer. 'So, could I, Jan. This pint of beer is amazing.' We sat together for a few hours watching all of the people playing games on the beach below, they were all having such a fantastic time. I thought to myself, *Out of all the places Mick and I have visited in the world, Bulgaria feels more like home.* It was as if I had been here before.

That night, Mick and I spent the evening at Fagi's, a little restaurant hidden away from the passing traffic on the main road. Their home-cooked food was one of the nicest fast foods that I had eaten in Bulgaria. The owners of the restaurant were very friendly to all of their customers. Mick sat by the TV watching his football team play their match, while I spent my time catching up on my emails and making a few telephone calls to Christopher and family. When the football game was over, we walked back to the apartment to settle down for the night.

Sadness

That night, it did not take long for Mick and I to fall fast asleep, it must have been the strong sea breeze from the wonderful little oasis in Ravda, or it may have been the cold drinks from the bar at the beautiful cove by the cliff. I was having a lovely dream then all of a sudden, I was woken up by the sound of the ringing tone on my mobile phone. The ringing tone was so loud it woke the two of us from a deep sleep. I turned the bedside light on and looked at Mick.

'Oh my god, that is my mobile phone, who could be ringing us in the middle of the night?' I sat up in bed. 'Bloody hell, Mick, what if something has happened to Christopher? I would never forgive myself for leaving him with his mates!'

He sat up in bed. 'We won't know anything if you don't answer it!'

I took two deep breaths to build up the courage to answer the phone. 'Hello, who is it?' I recognised the voice on the other end of the phone immediately, it was Christopher, I was so relieved. Then in a quiet voice, he said. 'Mum, Paul is dead.'

I thought I was dreaming. 'What are you saying, son, please can you say that again?'

His voice was so quiet and I could hardly hear him. 'Mum, Aunty Shell has just phoned, she said that Paul is dead.'

I could not believe what I was hearing, I must be still asleep, this must be a nightmare. 'Do not be daft, son, Paul cannot die, he's far too young. Please phone her back,

Christopher you must have got it wrong?' He put the phone down.

Mick and I were wide awake, we sat up in bed waiting for Christopher to call us back, to tell us that everything was all right. *Ring, ring,* the phone rang again. I answered it.

'Mum, Paul is dead. I have just spoken to Aunty Jean, because Aunty Shell was too upset.' His quiet words were so devastating. 'Oh no, son, this cannot be true. How are you, are you OK, are you upset?' The phone went silent. 'Christopher, are you all right, son?' I waited and waited for a reply.

'Mum, I am not sure, can you come home? I could hear him breathing in the background. Please can you ring me back in a little bit.' Then there was nothing but silence in the air.

Mick knew that something was very wrong, he put his arms around me. 'Paul is dead, Mick.'

His hands dropped as if he was in shock. 'That cannot be true, Janet. Phone your Michelle, this cannot be right. Paul cannot die, he is far too young!'

I took several deep breaths again, then I picked up the mobile phone and called Michelle. The phone only rang once.

'Hi, sis, it is me Janet, Christopher has just phoned me. What has happened?'

I will never forget the sadness in her voice when she told me that Paul had died. The tears of sadness started to pour down my cheeks onto my nighty. I could hear the sound of total devastation in every single word she spoke, and I heard the sound of her heart breaking as she tried to explain what had happened.

'Paul went into hospital yesterday with terrible pains in his chest. The nurse did some routine tests, then after a while she sent him home with a box of tablets and some Gaviscon, and they told him that he would be fine.' Then she burst into tears ; I could hear her sorrow within every single breath that she took.

She went quiet for a while. All I could hear was the sound of silent grief, then she took a deep breath and she tried to talk again. 'When we came home from the hospital, he spent all day on the couch with Cerys. I knew he was still not very well, but I was waiting for the medication to start to work. Later that night, he decided to go to bed to get some rest so I joined him, to make sure he was OK. It did not take long for Paul to fall asleep next to me. Then I was woken up by a strange noise. As I turned over towards Paul, I knew straight away that there was something terribly wrong.' Then she broke down completely. I could hear her deepest sorrow crying out over the phone. I felt so helpless, because I was unable to do anything to console her. I just wanted to hold her next to me, to take away as much of the hurt and sorrow as I could.

The next minute I heard Jean, my older sister on the phone. 'Janet, where are you?'

I had to stop myself from crying. 'Hi, sis, Mick and I are in Bulgaria. I will try to get a flight home tomorrow.'

There was a moment of silence. 'OK, sis, that's great, I will see you tomorrow.'

The sounds of sadness on the phone were only broken by the noise of Jean consoling Michelle, then there was a complete silence.

I turned to Mick. 'Paul has died.'

He put his head down towards the sheets. 'No, no, this cannot happen, what about little Cerys and Michelle?'

I could not answer him, I just broke down in tears. Mick and I held each other throughout the night. I hoped that it was a terrible nightmare, one that we would wake up from in the

221

morning. But the black clouds of total devastation did not end with the morning sunrise. The reality of what had happened to Paul had left us with an unbelievable sadness.

By the time we had managed to pull ourselves together, Mick tried his best to find us a flight home, but we soon realised that all the flights were full and there were none available until the one that we had booked to return home. We had no option but to stay until our existing flight returned to Manchester. I knew I had to phone Michelle to break the bad news to her.

'Hi, Michelle, it is me, Janet.'

As soon as she answered the phone, I could hear that she was inconsolable. 'Why Paul, Janet, what are me and Cerys going to do? How will Cerys and I go on living without him, he was everything to us!'

I knew her heart was broken and there was nothing I could do; my little sister was hurting so bad and I was stuck in bloody Bulgaria. With tears of sorrow running down my checks, I turned towards Mick, and he held me tight.

'Poor Michelle and Cerys, who's going to catch their tears of sadness now, Mick?'

'They will be OK, Jan; all your family will be with them.'

When I managed to stop crying, I told Michelle that we were unable to get a flight home, it was one of the hardest things that I had ever said to her. She was very upset, but I told her that as soon as I got home, I would be there with her and she would not be alone. Then she put the phone down.

Even though the sun was shining and the children were laughing around the pool, it all felt grey and quiet, it was like my senses had been turned down to their lowest point. Then I got this strange thought in my head. I wanted to buy some flowers as a token of our love for Paul. Then I wanted to throw the flowers into the Black Sea, as a way of saying sorry to Paul.

I told Mike what I was thinking, and he felt that it was a lovely idea. We searched everywhere, but we could not find any flowers in any of the local shops. I did, however, notice that the Apollon Complex walkways were covered in lovely roses and the walkways along the Black Sea coast were lined with beautiful wild roses and lots of lovely flowers.

Mick came up with a good plan to get some free flowers, and nothing was going to stop us from throwing the best local roses and flowers into the black sea for Paul.

'Right, Janet, go and get the scissors from the kitchen.'

I opened the kitchen drawer and pulled out the new kitchen scissors and I grabbed a shopping bag.

'Right, let us go, Janet, and I will get you some flowers.'

We walked along the paved area of the complex towards the beautiful red, white, yellow and pink rose bushes.

'Right, Mick, I will keep my eyes out while you cut some of those beautiful roses on that bush.'

We did not like the fact that we were planning on taking some of the nicest flowers from other people's gardens, but we knew Paul would have done the same for us. This made me feel like we were doing the right thing for him and Michelle. Mick hid the scissors in a plastic bag until he was ready to cut some of the loveliest rose bushes on the complex. But as we got close to the best rose bushes, I saw Chunky one and two, they were both on garden duty, which made it impossible to cut any of the roses under their watchful eyes. Undeterred, we made our way along the coastal path towards Ravda.

When we arrived at the town centre, I noticed that one of the restaurants across from the main road square had some gorgeous roses all around their children's play area. Mick and I

223

looked at the colour of the roses to make sure they were right for Paul. We knew we could not take any of the bright red ones because Paul was a true blue. We only wanted the white and yellow ones. With the scissors in his hand, Mick grabbed the first stem of a beautiful white rose ready to cut it when we heard a loud voice. 'Hello, can I help you?'

Mick stopped what he was doing and placed the scissors back into the bag, he looked around slowly. The voice was coming from a waiter in the restaurant. I was a bit upset because he had prevented us from cutting one of their best white roses. I looked up towards him as Mick was folding the plastic bag around the scissors.

'Hello, yes please, do you know where I can find a florist in Ravda?'

The man looked at me then back towards Mick. 'Sorry, there aren't any flower shops in the whole of Ravda.'

I do not know why, but his words made all of the tears of sadness reappear in my eyes then they rolled down my face onto my dress. Maybe it was because he had stopped Mick from doing the only thing that was keeping me going.

Mick could see that I was crying so he held me close. 'Let us order a cup of coffee, Janet, I will wait for the waiter to go back into the restaurant and I will cut those roses for Paul.' We sat down at the table next to the rose bush and Mick ordered the drinks. We waited for the waiter to go into the kitchen, but he did not move, he just stayed next to us. Then within a minute or so, another waiter brought our coffees out and placed them on the table. As he put the cups down, he asked if we would like anything else.

Mick replied, 'Nothing for me, thanks, mate, we are looking for a florist.' He did not mention anything about a florist, he just continued to tell us that the restaurant did one of the best Sunday roasts in the whole of Ravda and that people from all over the UK came to his restaurant for a great Sunday lunch.

Mick looked at the waiter. I knew we hadn't had anything to eat and their Sunday lunch sounded lovely. 'Why not? We have not had anything to eat yet.'

The waiter smiled. 'OK, I will go and book your meal with the chef.'

As soon as he left the table, Mick and I looked at each other.

'Quick let us get those roses while he is booking the meal,' but before he could get the scissor out of the bag, another waiter returned (I'm sure they knew that we were going to take some of their best roses).

'Sorry, mate, we are full for lunch today, but you can always book for next Sunday if you want?'

I had to stop myself from crying again, then I looked up at the waiter. 'No, thank you, we are hoping to go home soon.'

I knew that there was no chance of getting any roses or flowers from Ravda. Mick had tried his best to cut some flowers from outside the fence of one of the resident's gardens, but it was as if everyone was on flower patrol. Every time we saw a lovely flower or rose, someone would sit next to them or they would stand by them watching as they grow. This meant our only option was to walk along the coastal path to the cove of Ravda, where I knew there were lots of beautiful wild flowers.

On the way to the cove, we walked past lots of lemon, apple, pomegranate, pear, plum, peach, walnut and even one or two fig trees, but there were no suitable flowers or roses to cut. I felt myself getting upset again so I grabbed hold of Mick's hand for some comfort.

'Let us try down here, Janet, these flowers look promising.'

When I looked through the big fencing, I could see that there were lots of beautiful white roses, they were just perfect for Paul.

'Quickly, Janet, pass me the scissors.'

Like a true criminal, I handed the scissors to Mick.

'Keep your eyes out for any of the locals, Janet, I could be hanged for this, you know.'

With the fear of him getting hung or getting into any trouble on my mind, I scanned the pavements and gardens for the slightest movement. I was like a radar scanning everything that moved, then I heard a loud noise.

'Hurry up, Mick, someone is coming.'

With a few fast snips, Mick opened the plastic bag and dropped the flowers and scissors into it and we walked off as if nothing had happened like two professional thieves.

Then we walked quickly towards the beautiful cove. I was looking for somewhere peaceful to stay when I noticed that there was a long manmade jetty just up the coast from the cove. It was built of big grey rocks to prevent the high waves from the Black Sea covering the walkway. Mick and I both looked at each other, we knew that this was the perfect place to throw Paul's lovely roses into the sea.

With a new spring in our steps we made our way along the coastal path. When we got to the ideal location, we were faced with another challenge, because the jetty was set far away from all the tourist pathways, the route down to it was very overgrown and dangerous, I struggled to walk on the uneven rocks and to make my way through all of the tall trees and very prickly shrubs; I knew it was going to be very difficult, but I did

226

not want to give up.

When we finally got to the ideal position, Mick opened the bag of roses and I looked up to the sky as if I was looking for Paul.

'Wow, Mick, look at that.' I could not believe my eyes; just above our heads was a massive big white cross, which must have been made by two planes crossing in the bright blue sky. This made the moment even more special for Paul. Mick threw the flowers into the sea while I said the Lord's prayer for Paul, Michelle and Cerys. I sat on one of the big grey rocks and waited for the white cross to fade away with the heat of the sun. When the flowers had floated out to sea and we could not see them any more, Mick and I tried to retrace our steps back through all the challenging overgrowth back onto solid ground again. The rest of the holiday was a complete blur, I could not wait to get back home to hug Michelle, Cerys and see the rest of the family.

This time when I arrived home, it did not matter if Christopher and his mates had eaten everything in the house, and they had left all of their dishes smelling in the sink. I just wanted to hold him and give him the biggest hug and a big love you to the moon and back kiss.

When I walked into the house, I made my way towards the kitchen door to drop the cases off, but before I could open the door the house phone rang. It was Jean, my sister.

'Great, Janet, you're home. When are you coming over to Michelle's?'

I looked over towards Mick and he put the suitcases down in the hall and nodded his head. 'Hi, sis, we are leaving now.'

'Good. See you soon, love.'

When we arrived at Michelle's house, nothing felt the

same. It was one of those moments when I wished that I had a magic wand or a genie in the bottle to make everything all right. As soon as I saw Michelle, I could see that she was broken up with grief. I ran towards her and gave her a big hug. I felt her body crumble in my arms, so I held her close to me until she regained her strength, but I knew at that moment that I could not stop all the hurt inside her.

As I held her up, I told her that everything would be OK, but I knew deep inside that her life and Cerys' world would never be the same again. I wished that I could turn back time to prevent this horrible tragedy from happening. What if I had not gone on holiday? What if I had come over when Paul was sick? Could I have done anything different? I spent most of the day with Michelle, trying to understand why God would have let something so tragic happen to such a lovely family.

The following week was just so unmentionable, how do you plan a funeral for someone who had everything to live for? How do you console two beautiful people who deserved to have the man they love with them for the rest of their lives? How do you tell his little daughter that her daddy will never see her grow up? How do you tell a wife that she will never grow old with her husband?

The day of the funeral was one of the worst days of all our lives. I remember the local church was packed full of Paul's and Michelle's friends and family. There were so many people standing outside the church because there were no spaces left inside, and as the coffin was carried into the church they lined the pathway with silent peace and sorrow. Cerys was amazing, she played. "This Little Light of Mine I'm going to let it shine." on the keyboard for her daddy. Everyone cried as her little voice sang the song so perfectly. Jean read out a wonderful poem for

Paul, which would have made him laugh in heaven.

But most of all, I think he would have been so very proud of Michelle and his beautiful little daughter. I don't know where they got their inner strength from on that day or in the weeks and months that followed his funeral; it must have been very difficult for both of them.

Good Friendships

The following year, Michelle and Cerys were starting to live their life without Paul, a deep sadness had stayed with them and sorrow was always waiting in the shadows for the right moment to make them cry. But there was a bit of good news, Michelle had managed to save enough money to buy both of their passports and they were ready to go on their first holiday abroad to Bulgaria. Michelle asked if they could spend a week with Mick and me in the apartment. I was so overjoyed. Without any hesitation, I booked the flights, we packed our suitcases and we headed off to Manchester Airport.

Michelle was a little bit like Lillian when it came to flying. She did not like to fly, she was also very nervous about the plane landing and taking off properly. I knew it was Cerys' first flight and she did not know what to expect. Mick and I did our best to keep Michelle nice and relaxed, and Cerys happy.

Michelle had brought a "Paul the bear" for Cerys. He wore a blue and white t-shirt and blue shorts just like Paul, and the bear was always close by when Cerys needed to hug him. Mick and I managed to support both of them through the check-in process and throughout customs, everything was going really well until we started to board the plane.

When we sat down and put our seat belts on, then when we were ready to take off, the pilot made an unexpected announcement.

'Due to the high number of empty seats on this flight, we

will be landing at Southampton airport to pick up some additional passengers before we continue the flight to Bulgaria.'

Michelle turned her head towards me, I could see by her face through the seat in front of me that she looked petrified!

'What does he mean, Janet? Do we have to go through two landings and two take offs before we get to Bulgaria?'

I felt like it was my fault. 'I think so, Michelle, we will take off from Manchester, but we won't be in the air for very long before the plane will land at Southampton. When the new passengers will get on the plane, it will take off again for Bulgaria, don't worry, everything will be OK.' I tried my best to calm her down, but before I could finish off my next sentence she shouted. 'Let me get off this plane now! I am not going anywhere, let me off this plane now!' Her face was full of fear.

'You will be OK, sis; just think about all of the fun we will have when we arrive in Bulgaria.'

She steered back at me with her piercing blue eyes. 'Yes, I know, but that will only happen if we get there in one piece!'

Then the plane took off, I could still hear her voice shouting as the engines roared. Then there was nothing, we were not in the sky for very long before the pilot announced that we would be landing soon. 'Oh my God Janet, I hate this, I'm never going to fly again.' When the plane landed at Southampton. The landing was not too bad, I think Michelle was expecting much worse! But to make matters worse we had to wait for ages for the plane to take off again because some of the passengers were missing. This delay was causing a lot of people to get annoyed with the air hostess, which did not help Michelle and Cerys!

As soon as the missing passengers were on the plane, the pilot prepared the crew for take-off. I looked at our Shell and smiled. 'Not long now, sis, we are halfway there now.'

She looked back at me. 'Do you think we will be stopping anywhere else sis, because the seat next to Cerys is still empty?'

I laughed at her. 'Definitely not, sis.' Then I settled down for the in-flight entertainment.

The holiday to Bulgaria with Michelle and Cerys was going to be wonderful and different. Mick and I spent most of the time trying helplessly to make the pain of Paul's death go away if only for a few moments. We knew that it would be impossible to mend their broken hearts, but we tried our best to cheer them up.

The first thing we did after we unpacked the suitcases was to set Michelle the six-pool challenge. This meant that she had to jump into every swimming pool on the Apollon Complex. I knew Michelle was always up for a challenge because she was very sporty in school. However, as she got older, it was normally the game of pool or snooker where she thrived and not in the swimming pool, but she wanted to give it a go. On the day of the first challenge, she made her way into the bedroom to get changed into one of her lovely new costumes, a t-shirt and shorts. When she was ready, we made our way to Apollon 2 to start the contest.

As soon as we had made our way through the gates we walked towards the far side of the pool. The pool was in the shade which made it feel a bit cooler than when the sun was shining on it. I could see that she was having second thoughts, so I had to give her a little bit of encouragement to jump in.

'Go on, Michelle, this is only the first one. Mick will pay for both of your meals tonight if you do all six of them.'

Within a second, she jumped into the water. As soon as the splash of the water cleared, I could tell that she loved it. Cerys and I joined her shortly after and we had a lot of fun playing in the pool.

Mick stayed dry because he was the judge of the challenge. 'Right, everyone, we need to move over to the next pool challenge, you have had enough fun for now.' He passed us the towels and we got dried. 'Where do you want to go next, Michelle? Apollon 5 or 3?'

She did not care. I think she was enjoying some fun time with Cerys. The pools at 5 and 3 were very easy for her to jump in, because she was getting used to the freezing cold water and the hot sun. She also knew that Cerys and I would join her to have a laugh together in the pools.

However, when we got to Apollon 4, she made a big jump into the pool and the splash from the water went all over Mick, which made him dive into the pool to get back at her. After a while, Cerys and I joined her to play before we made our way to Apollon 6, for the final challenge, which she completed without any hesitation.

We spent the afternoon talking to our new neighbours, around Apollon 4. Michelle met the couple who once lived in the village nearby where she lived, and I sat on the pool steps talking to a wonderful woman called Blodwyn and her husband Knobby (Barabara and Robin), while Cerys played in the children's pool. It was a day that I will never forget because it was the only time Michelle allowed herself to have some fun like we used to have when we were younger.

As the days went by, we spent some time sunbathing around the pools, talking to new friends and eating out at the local bars and restaurants. Throughout this time, I noticed that my little sister Michelle had changed so much, but the beautiful essence of what made her so special had disappeared. My little sister was gone! She was now a grieving widow. I watched her as she tried her best to have some fun, but there was always something missing. All the joy and laughter that we had throughout the years,, eating meals in the conservatory and playing cards together with her and Paul had now been replaced with the deepest of sorrow. I could feel that there was an overwhelming sadness with every breath she took and every tiny smile she made. I knew there was nothing anyone could do to mend her heartache, but I was never going to give up trying to make her happy again.

Michelle and Cerys only stayed in Bulgaria for one week, then they were ready to go back home. Nikolay's son and I dropped them off at Bourgas Airport. I gave both of them the biggest hug to make sure they felt safe and secure before boarding the plane. When I was making my way back to the apartment, I got a phone call from Michelle informing me that Cerys had left "Paul the bear" in their bedroom. I could hear Cerys crying in the background. She was devastated. Michelle made me promise to Cerys that I would look after Paul the bear, and that I would take really good care of him, and I would not leave him on his own for too long, and I would make sure that he was always nice and warm.

When I got back to the apartment, I made sure that "Paul the bear" was tucked into Cerys bed to keep him nice and warm. I wished him a goodnight sleep and kissed his fluffy forehead. I pulled the covers up to his shoulders, then lifted his arms out of the covers like I used to do with my dolls when I was a child. I turned the bedroom light off, then I phoned Michelle to let her and Cerys know that "Paul the bear" was nice and warm and fast asleep in bed. Then I went to bed and I fell into a deep sleep.

The following morning when I woke up, I was feeling quite thirsty. I got out of bed to put the kettle on. When I looked into the room where "Paul the bear" had been sleeping, I noticed that all of the covers had been pulled down towards his little feet. I could not believe my eyes (if Cerys had seen him without any covers over him she would have been very upset). Mick was still lying in bed.

'Michael, why have you pulled the covers off Paul the bear?'

Mick lifted his head up from the pillow and looked across the bedroom towards me with disbelief. 'Janet, I have been in bed with you all night, I do not know what you are talking about.'

I looked back at him. 'Paul the bear looks cold now because he has not got any covers over him. I thought that I had tucked him into bed last night.'

Mick got out of bed. 'Janet, are you going bloody stupid, it is just a teddy bear and why are you tucking him into bed?'

I walked towards the kitchen. 'Because I promised Cerys that I would keep him nice and warm and that I would not let him get cold.'

Mick followed me into the kitchen. 'Well, Janet, he might have been roasting hot last night, because he must have kicked all of the covers off by himself, you silly woman.'

Stonehenge?

Mick and I spent most of our time together that week getting to know everyone at the complex. Blodwyn and Knobby were a lovely couple who lived in one of the top apartments. Norris and Noricina lived across from our apartment, they had moved to Bulgaria permanently, they were really helpful people. Mick and I also managed to all pay the utility bills and explore most of Ravda, Old Nessebar and New Nessebar; it felt like we were beginning to settle in Bulgaria.

Everyone that we spoke to on the complex were very nice, the local Bulgarians were also starting to get to know us too, they always smiled and said dobur den (good day) or leka nosht (good night). There were so many lovely people living or holidaying in the Apollon complex. We had started to learn a bit of the Bulgarian language to help when we were shopping or eating out. There were also lots of wonderful Irish families who had bought apartments on Apollon 2, 3, 4 and 5. Every time we met someone new, we always had lots of fun in the sun or around the pool bar. Not only had we found our dream holiday home, we were also developing fabulous friendships.

These new friends told us about all of the many places to visit in Bulgaria, including lots of the local attractions and some of the best restaurants, which resulted in Mick and I spending some of our evenings away from the pool bar and Cat's restaurant. We used to just walk past the bar on our way to discover something new. Then one night while we were talking to Blodwyn and Knobby, I noticed that the pool man (Jose) and his girlfriend (Bella) were serving behind the bar. Blodwyn told me that they had taken over the lease.

Bella was always lovely and very attentive to everyone she spoke with around the complex. I knew that Jose spoke excellent English, because I heard him talking to Norris a few days ago. Jose was having lots of fun with some of the Irish men around the bar. Bella, his partner, smiled at me as she was cleaning the bar tables, everyone looked like they were all having a great time, as a result Mick and I decided to go to the local restaurant for something to eat then join Blodwyn and Knobby later that night for a wonderful evening of fun and laughter.

Blodwyn told me that Jose and Bella's customer service was brilliant, as a result, the pool bar had become a great place for everyone to meet up, because it was the central point for everyone from the Apollon community. Everyone would gather there for a few drinks and a laugh before going out for their evening meal. I also heard that on Tuesdays and Thursdays, Budgie, one of the Irish men, did a pub quiz, which was great entertainment.

Mick and I really enjoyed spending a few evenings at the pool bar, then one night while everyone was having a few glasses of wine and beer, Bella asked if anyone would like to name the bar.

Without any hesitation, Blodwyn shouted, 'Happy Bar.' Then she stood up. 'Let us name this place the Happy Bar because that is what it is.'

Everyone agreed with her and we all toasted to the new "Happy Bar".

The following night when we arrived at the pool bar, Jose

and Bella had a new sign hanging at the front of the bar with neon lights flashing. "Welcome to Happy Bar". Mick and I spent that evening celebrating the official opening of the bar with all of our new friends, it was great fun. I ended the night by dancing around the swimming pool on Apollon 3 with Bella and Pat, while the boys played their air guitars around the bar to the sound of Jose's rock music.

Mick and I loved spending time at the Happy Bar, because there was always someone nice to talk to and they always had a funny story about the things that had happened to them while holidaying in Bulgaria.

One night when we were having a laugh with Blodwyn and Knobby, Bella asked if I wanted to join them the following day to go for a trip out of the complex to visit one of Bulgaria's prehistoric sites. Without any hesitation, I said. 'Yes please, that would be lovely.' Then I just carried on drinking. Before Mick and I left the bar, Bella said they would pick us up around twelve p.m. at the bar the following day.

When I woke up the following morning, I thought it was just going to be like a normal day relaxing by the pool, then going for something nice to eat. I lay in bed thinking about all of the fun we had the previous night, then I remembered! *Oh my god, we are going sightseeing with Jose and Bella today, but Mick does not know about it yet.*

'Good morning, Mick. Look out the window, it is lovely and sunny today. Do you remember when I told Jose and Bella that we would go for a day out with them today?'

He looked at me with doubt in his eyes. 'No, Janet, I do not remember anyone asking me if I wanted to go out for the day with them.'

I smiled at him. 'Well, Mick, they asked me last night and

I said yes.'

He looked straight into my eyes. 'What on earth were you thinking, we have only two days left before we have to go back home.'

I knew he was right (but I always seem to agree to things that I shouldn't when I have had a few drinks). 'I know, love, I wasn't thinking, but we could have a lovely day out with them because they are such a lovely couple.'

Mick and I spent the morning around the pool thinking of ways to avoid going sightseeing, but we could not think of any good ones. At eleven thirty a.m., we got changed and made our way to the bar just before twelve p.m. When I turned the corner at Apollon 3, I could see that Jose and Bella were waiting by their car to go out for the day. Mick and I said hello then goodbye to all of our friends at the bar and we got into the back of Jose's car.

The journey that took us far away from the complex. Jose talked about some of the Bulgarian history which was very informative. When Mick and I spoke to Jose in English, Bella would ask him to translate it back to her in Bulgarian. Therefore, every time we said something in English, he had to translate it back to her in Bulgarian before he replied back to us; it was lovely to experience his translations and her laughter. Jose drove us through so many wonderful little villages, we saw so many beautiful locations on our journey away from the complex, Nessebar and Ravda.

When we arrived at the prehistoric site, Jose and Bella got their bags out of the boot of the car and we started to walk through a beautiful tree-lined path, then Bella stopped at the side of a big stone square at the edge of the pathway then she pointed towards a big hole in the middle of this square. My first impression was that it looked like a big stone grave or a secret entrance to someone's special tomb, but when I asked Jose what it was he was unsure whether it was a grave, or where the hole in the ground led to.

We carried on walking through a large grassed area, then all of a sudden, Mick and I found ourselves standing inside Bulgaria's equivalent to Stonehenge. It was set up differently from England's Stonehenge, but there seemed to be some correlation between the both of them. Whatever had happened in Salisbury, a long time ago, had also happened here.

Unlike the UK's Stonehenge, you could actually climb up, sit on, stand on, go under or over all of the giant Bulgarian stones, without anyone shouting at you or chasing you for a payment. After I had experienced walking over and under a few of the massive stones, I realised that there were lots of Bulgaria families enjoying this prehistoric sight.

Parents were showing their children the wonderful shapes of the stones. There were two big stones that lay on top of each other and from a distance it looked like a big dinosaur in the sky. I could hear a number of children making the sounds of dinosaurs as they ran towards them. As we made our way around the site, I noticed that everyone was so very friendly, everyone kept smiling at each other then they would say 'zdraveyte' or 'dobar den' (hello or good day). When Mick and I spoke to each other or to Jose, a few people stopped and looked at us then they smiled, I think me and Mick were the only two British people there.

Mick and I spent a lot of time taking pictures of the stones and videoing some of the prehistoric sites. This was a place that we would have never found on one of our discovery walks. I felt quite privileged to be shown one of the best sites in

Bulgaria.

It was mid-afternoon by the time we had finished exploring the prehistoric site. Jose asked if we were hungry and if we would like to try some traditional Bulgarian food. Mick and I were both starving, but we told him that we had not seen any cafés or restaurants at the site.

Jose smiled. 'Come with me and I will show you where we are eating.' He walked towards the car then he stopped. 'Bella wants us to go over there and have some food.' He pointed his finger to lots of trees just past one of the big stones.

Mick and I were expecting to go for a lovely meal at a nice restaurant close by, but we were wrong; we were now walking towards a wild forest just behind the prehistoric stones. Jose led us towards a big rock in the middle of the trees. It was very peaceful, there was no one else around and we were all alone. I could not hear anything except the birds in the trees

Bella pulled the rucksack off her shoulders and laid it on the ground. Jose opened up the zip then he pulled out one of the biggest knives I had ever seen. I went white, my suntan must have evaporated within seconds. Mick and I looked at each other, then I grabbed his hand. Within a moment or two, Jose looked at the pair of us.

'Please come and help me to find some wood for the fire, we need it to build the BBQ.'

Mick let go of my hand. 'Stop it, you silly woman, there is nothing to be frightened of.'

We both walked off in different directions, to ensure that we stayed just behind Jose and Bella to find the BBQ wood.

Jose went into the wild forest first then he disappeared. I could hear him cutting the branches from the trees with his big knife, then I heard his voice. 'Come over here, please, help me,

241

I am over here.'

Mick and I hesitated at first, then we walked over towards the big tree to find him in the forest. When we got close to him, I started to pick up some branches from the ground. Jose shook his head. 'No, Janet, not them, they are damp, the branches need to be dry or they won't burn.'

Bella grabbed my hand then she started to show me the right twigs and leaves to light the fire. Once we had got enough kindle, twigs and wood Bella and I made our way back to the opening in the forest. Shortly after, Jose and Mick returned with some long branches. I watched quietly as Jose removed the outer layer of the branch with his big knife to reveal the untouched wood underneath, then within a few minutes Bella had filled them with chicken pieces and vegetables ready for the BBQ.

Mick and I sat watching in amazement, it was like something out of Bear Grylls. Don't get me wrong, we have had lots of BBQ sets from B&Q, but we had never eaten food cooked on the ground or eaten meat from the branches of a tree. When the tree kebabs were prepared, Jose used an old-fashioned flint, some tiny pieces of wood and some fluff that Bella pulled from the bag to light the fire.

The smoke from the wood and fluff started to rise into the air, then within a few seconds the wood was alight and the BBQ was starting to burn bright. Bella placed some bigger pieces of wood on top. I could see that Jose was delighted, it had only taken him about ten minutes to chop and gather all the wood from the forest, and to light a fabulous BBQ using a flint and some fluff. He looked at Mick and smiled.

'Mick, would you like a drink of Bulgarian wine with your meal?'

Mick sat down next to the fire. 'Yes, please, Jose, that would be lovely.'

Bella pulled a bottle of wine from out of her bag along with some plastic glasses. I sat down next to the fire to drink my first glass of Bulgarian white wine within a wild forest.

When the fire was red hot, Jose positioned the chicken kebabs on the hot wood that lay on the big stone. Bella prepared all the vegetables, cheese peppers and bread, then she placed them on a cloth next to the BBQ, it all looked lovely. I sat for a while watching the fire while drinking the beautiful wine. It did not take very long before all of the food was cooked, ready for eating. Jose passed the tree kebabs to Bella and she served them on a white paper plates. We all tucked into the delicious food. I was enjoying eating one of the stuffed cheese peppers when Jose just stopped eating his chicken kabab, then he sat up straight as if he had been alerted about something coming towards us, he stayed very still. '*Shush,* everyone, did you hear that noise, Bella? It sounded like a wild boar.'

Mick and I stared at each other; Jose pulled out his big knife then he looked towards Bella. Mick and I stood up like two meerkats waiting to see if we were going to live or die, then the two of them ran off into the forest, leaving me and Mick alone next to the burning fire.

I sat down close to the fire and held the BBQ stick in front of me and a plastic cup of wine as my only protection against the wild boar. 'Oh my god, Mick, what have I done; we could have been murdered here.'

He looked at me. 'Don't be silly, Janet, we could be having some fresh pork instead of this chicken if they are lucky enough to catch that wild boar.'

Jose and Bella were gone for ages, the fire had almost gone

out, all that was left were little puffs of smoke every time the wind blew through the ashes. Mick and I were left sitting in the middle of nowhere, talking about how I had managed to get us into the middle of a wild forest with two Bulgarians, and why the hell had I put my trust in two locals to take us on a trip into the unknown, then leave us for ages to chase a wild boar.

'What would Christopher do if anything happened to us?'

Mick just laughed at me. 'I thought about calling out for help, but how would anyone understand what I was saying if they did not speak English?'

I started to pack everything away into the rucksack just in case we needed to run. Mick and I kept laughing with each other about our dilemma, but I think it was just fear of being attacked by a wild boar that made me giggle.

By the time Jose and Bella had got back to camp, it was going dark. By this time I was ready to go back to Apollon, everything was packed tidy and the fire was out. They smiled at us then Jose spoke. 'Sorry it took so long; the wild boar kept getting away from me. Would you like to go back to the pool bar now?'

Mick and I grabbed some of their things and without any hesitation, I said, 'Yes, please.'

Jose took the rubbish bag from me. 'Come, I will show you the way back to the car, please come this way and follow me.'

The journey back from the prehistoric site was quiet. Mick and I were glad to be going home to our apartment. Jose and Bella must have been very tired from chasing after the wide boar. When we got back to the pool bar at Apollon, Mick bought four big drinks for all of us to recover from the lovely day.

Later that night, I thanked Jose and Bella for such a wonderful day. Mick and I sat down at a table next to the bar and Mick told some of our friends about how Jose made a fire from flint and fluff, the tree kabab, our delicious BBQ and when Jose and Bella went into the forest to catch wild boar. Bella sat next to me then Jose joined her to join in the conversation. I started talking about how scared I felt when Jose got his big knife out, then he burst out laughing. 'I didn't mean to scare you, Janet, the knife is only for the trees and wild boars.' Then he translated it to Bella. She held my hand and Jose translated. 'You are a lovely woman, we only wanted to show you how we made the BBQ in Bulgaria. We never meant to frighten you.' I spent the night talking to both of them about Mick and me, our BBQs back in the UK, Christopher, our extended family and what we did for a living back home. Jose spoke about his family and their two children, the village where they lived in the winter which was called Devin and the work he did around the complex during the summer. It was wonderful listening to Jose and Bella, and finding out what it was like to live in Bulgaria. On our last night we decided to go for a meal at Fagi's then have a few drinks with our friends around Happy Bar. When I sat down next to Blodwyn and Knobly, Jose and Bella came over to the table to join us. Within a moment or two Jose asked if I would help them to develop some additional tourist opportunities in Devin, which was located within the Rhodope mountains. Where Jose, Bella and family lived in the winter when the Black Sea coast closes down for the season. I did not hesitate. 'Yes, I am willing to do whatever I could to develop new opportunities for Bulgarian tourism.' Before leaving the pool bar, I offered to keep in touch with both of them when I returned to England.

Heart Broken

When I got back home, I could not wait to return "Paul the bear" to Cerys, and tell Michelle about the giant stones and the "scary BBQ moment" with Jose and Bella. However, when I entered the house and I started to talk to her about Bulgaria I could tell that Michelle was not very well. Don't get me wrong, her voice was as I remembered, she smiled like she used to and she laughed the same, but there was an emptiness inside her that she could not hide. I knew then that the heartache from losing Paul was just too much for her to cope with, and as a consequence of her broken heart, her health and well-being had started to deteriorate.

Cerys was growing into a beautiful young girl; she was very intelligent and creative like her dad. Michelle cherished her so very much, her love was endless and her support was constant, but all the love and support in the world could not change how Michelle was feeling on the inside.

Over the next few months this deterioration kept getting worse. Our family and some of the friends of Michelle and Paul kept telling me that they were so very worried about her health and wellbeing. They had all tried their best to make her feel better, but it wasn't enough, despite all the good intentions nobody could help to heal her broken heart. As a result, I made an appointment at the doctor's to try and get her some professional support.

The following week, I took Michelle to the doctor's to see

if they could do anything to support her through this horrific time. When Michelle spoke to the doctor, she explained what had happened to Paul and how she was coping with the heartache. The doctor offered her some bereavement counselling and blood tests, which were supposed to help, but it was no good. Michelle ended up in hospital a few weeks later and she died before she got the first appointment for counselling through the post!

Everyone was totally devastated! Cerys had lost two wonderful parents within such a small space in time; She would never be able to hug and kiss them again. Who will be there for her when she needs her mummy and daddy? I had lost an amazing sister and a fantastic brother-in-law; both of our families were completely traumatised and the local community where they lived grieved for the sad loss of such a fabulous couple.

I thought that I would never get over the sudden death of Michelle and Paul, and the passing of our beautiful young nephew Mark, who died from cancer within a year of each other. My life could not have gotten any worse. The tragic deaths of so many beautiful people had hit me like a thunderbolt, my life was in a darkness that I could not explain to anyone, it was one of the worst experiences that I had ever had to endure. It was only then that I started to understand how Michelle had been feeling and her silent broken heart.

I tried to spend as much time as I could with Cerys, to help her cope with the pain of losing both parents. I knew I had to be close to her because she reminded me so much of her mum yet she looked just like her dad, and she had both of her parents' funny sense of humour. We spent some wonderful times together, learning how to cook and going for lovely days out.

Within a few months, Cerys had settled in nicely with Paul's eldest sister, her husband, son and daughter, they became her second family. She did excellent at school and her time at university is going extremely well. All of her lecturers are delighted with her progress. She has made lots of lovely new friends, and our times together have become less and less as we both tried to rebuild our lives without two very special people.

I am so immensely proud of Cerys because she has shown everyone around her that no matter how bad life gets, there's always hope.

Throughout all of this sadness, Mick and I tried to keep in touch with Jose and Bella. I think they were our little escape away from all of the sorrow during the cold winter months. Most weekends, Mick and I would sit in the conservatory with thick covers around our legs to keep them warm. Mick changed the normal clear ceiling light bulbs with three bright orange glowing lights so that they would shine down on us like the sun, and we would pretend that we were back in Bulgaria where it was nice and hot. Mick and I would always talk to Jose and Bella via Skype. They did not know that we had brightened up the conservatory with glowing lights or that we had to cover our legs from the cold, because we always pretended to be nice and warm. We made it feel like it was just like having one of our conversations around the pool bar at Apollon 3.

Throughout our weekend conversations, I noticed that Bella's English was improving. She did not need Jose to translate as many of our conversations. Mick and I talked to Jose and Bella about developing tourism for the little spa village in Devin. This was the place where Bella was born and where they lived with their two children and Bella's parents during the winter. From our discussions, I knew that I could help them to develop tourism in their village, and that I could ask a few of my business contacts in Merseyside to help the municipality of Devin, to grow their little spa village into a tourist attraction for British visitors. With this in mind, I arranged to meet them at the Apollon Complex the following year.

When I arrived at the Apollon Complex, it was the middle of the night. When I opened the door to the apartment, I felt very alone because Mick was not with me (he had to stay at home and work). Our dream home had not changed, it just felt empty. While I was unpacking the suitcase, I remembered all of the fun we had at Mick's fiftieth birthday and it helped to make some of the emptiness fade away. As soon as everything was sorted, I went to bed and I fell into a deep sleep.

The following day, I spent some time cleaning the apartment and sunbathing by the pool. I made my way around to Happy Bar early that evening to meet up with Jose and Bella. When I walked around the corner towards Apollon 3, Bella came running towards me with her arms open wide ready to hug me, it was a lovely welcome back and just what I needed. Jose poured a drink for me and we sat together at the bar talking about the journey to Devin, as I listened to Jose and Bella talking about the little spa village. I started to look forward to spending some time in the mountains.

While we were talking about the journey, a group of Irish apartment owners started to settle at the bar. I recognised one or two of them from the previous holidays, but I did not know if they would remember me, but this didn't matter because they were all so very nice and friendly, and all of their conversations were full of joy and laughter. Two of the men started talking about a job they had undertaken for a friend who owned a property in Bulgaria. Their task was to smarten up the garden for when their friend returned to Bulgaria in the summer. Then they started to show everyone around the bar their hands; when I looked, I could see that they were full of cuts and blisters.

'When I spoke to the two men, they told me that the owner of the property had only asked them to sort out the garden, he told them that it might be a little bit overgrown, but when they got to the property, it was like a jungle. What seemed to be a two-day job had now become a six-week challenge.' Then everyone burst out laughing.

They continued talking about the night they decided to stay at the property because it was getting too late to drive back to the complex. However, when they settled down for the night, they heard lots of little noises coming from all around them, but they thought it was nothing to worry about so they turned all the lights off. Then the noises started to get louder and louder and when they turned the lights back on in the room, it was full of jumping spiders – they were coming from everywhere; the roof, floorboards, ceiling, windows and doors, and they had nowhere to run. When they spoke about all of the spiders jumping all around them, they started to run and jump around the bar to show everyone how they reacted to the spiders jumping towards them. The spiders ended up in their hair, all over their faces and under their clothes. Then they started to run and jump again to show everyone how they had to get them out from under their clothes and their hair. Alex the smaller man was jumping up and down and pulling his shirt and shorts left and right to show how he stopped them from getting into his underwear. Big Duncan the taller man had sat on the bar stool waving his hands in the air and over his body to show how he managed to stop them from biting him. Their re-enactment of this dramatisation was one of the funniest things I had ever seen, everyone at the bar was laughing their heads off at their misfortune and hilarious performance. This moment of fun and laughter reinforced the reason why it was good to come back to Bulgaria.

The Balkans

The following day, Jose and Bella came to the apartment to pick me up to start the journey to Devin, which would take about four hours. When I got into the car, it felt like I was going somewhere very exciting. Jose told me lots of little stories about each of the towns and villages, as we passed through them. The journey through the Rhodope Mountains was outstanding.

When we arrived in Devin, there was an amazing hotel at the edge of the village. My first impression was that it looked like some of the pictures you see of the Swiss Alps. However, as Jose drove into the village, it started to look quite old and grey. There were a lot of concrete buildings which looked like they were built in the late forties, after World War II, but I was not going to let any concrete buildings prevent the chance of any new business opportunities developing in the little spa village called Devin.

Jose and Bella drove me to the hotel where I was staying. They helped me to check into the room because no one spoke English and my Bulgarian was still rubbish. When I got the key to my room, they showed me the way to the stairs then they left. Once I was settled in the room, I unpacked my little suitcase. When I was finished, I looked outside the window over the village. It looked amazing; all I could see for miles was the beautiful Rhodope Mountains surrounding the village. I stepped outside onto a small balcony and the view was breath-taking; however, the tranquillity of the stunning mountains was broken by the sounds of a few stray dogs barking in the street, but that did not stop me from taking lots of photographs of this amazing location.

That night, Jose and Bella took me out for a wonderful meal in one of the local restaurants. They told me about all their exciting plans for Devin and some of the meetings they had arranged in advance with some of the local businesses. Bella told Jose to tell me about some of the tourist attractions they had also planned for me to visit with some of her cousins – it all sounded fabulous.

That night, I lay in bed thinking about how I could develop the village, and who would be the best business contacts to talk to when I got home. I found it difficult to sleep that night because of all the business development strategies and stakeholder engagement developing in my head, however these ideas were broken by the sounds of dogs barking in the streets. It sounded like the dogs were trying to warn their owners that something was wrong, but no one was listening.

The following day, Jose and Bella met me at the hotel. I asked them if they had heard the dogs barking during the night. Jose said no, but he would mention it to the receptionist. When I got into the car, Jose informed me that we were going for a drive into the Rhodope Mountains to show me one of the smallest churches in Bulgaria. I could not wait to spend the day with them.

The journey into the mountains was astounding, I watched as the beautiful landscape kept changing around me. I found myself thinking about Michelle and all of the wonderful times we spent laughing together as children, teenagers, then adults; it hurt so much to think about her. She was so much younger than me, yet she was no longer here.

When we got to the top of the mountain Jose parked the car under a large tree to keep it in the shade. There was a small wooden church and to the left of the car park, as I looked out of the window I could see that there was one of the biggest man made crosses that I had ever seen, it looked similar to the cross Jesus was crucified on. Jose explained that this location was the place where Christianity was born in the Rhodope Mountains; it felt very spiritual. I helped Jose and Bella to get their bags out of the car then we found a lovely place within the wild mountain flowers to relax in the sunshine. Jose gathered some wood from the nearby trees and shrubs, then he made a fire within a circle of stones. Bella got the meat and vegetables ready and we had a lovely BBQ together. While I was eating the delicious food, I thought about the time when Mick and I were in the wild forest when I was worried about dying, and now I was sitting in the middle of the mountains with the same people wishing he were here with me, because it was such a special place.

After we had finished eating, Bella and I washed the plates in a little sink at the side of the church. We picked some wild flowers and made daisy chains in the midday sun. After a while, Jose made sure that the fire was out, then he asked if I would like to go and see the smallest church in the Rhodopes. I looked at him.

'I thought that was the church that you were talking about.' Then I pointed to the small church by the giant manmade cross.

He looked at me then Bella and smiled. 'No, that is not it, the smallest church is at the top of the peak. Would you like us to take you there?'

Without any hesitation, I said, 'Yes, please!'

Jose made sure that there were no hot ashes left in the fire, then we made our way up to the peak of the mountain. When I got to the top of the summit, all I could see was 360 degrees of mountains and thousands of enormous trees stretching high into the sky. It was breath-taking. But I could not see the smallest church anywhere? Jose started to move towards the right-hand side of the mountain.

'Please follow me, Janet.'

I could not take my eyes off the magnificent views. I could not stop looking all around me. It was spectacular. Every time I stopped to take in a new aspect, Jose would stop walking and whisper, 'Please follow me, Janet, it is not far now.'

We made our way through some small trees and bushes and there it was, an old grey wooden door fixed between two giant oak trees. At first, it just looked like an out-of-place wooden door. Jose looked at me and pointed at the door.

'Here it is, Janet, come and take a look.'

As I walked towards the grey wooden door, Jose smiled at me. 'Yes, Janet, please open the door and go in.'

Bella also smiled at me and pointed towards the door.

When I opened the wooden door, it made a slight noise as the old wood rubbed against the oak trees. As soon as the door opened, the sunlight hit the ground and the small room radiated Christianity from all of the Christian artefacts. I noticed a small alight candle flickering with the gentle breeze. This wonderful place of worship was not what I expected at all; it felt very spiritual and soulful.

On the floor in front of the door lay a beautiful fresh flower display. There was a tray of golden sand for the tiny white candles that someone had left glowing in the sunlight. When I looked up, I could see that there were a few small wooden shelves that were holding sacraments of Bulgarian Orthodox Saints.

I stood in the church for a little while, praying for all the people that I had loved and lost. Then Jose asked me if I wanted to light a candle and he handed me his lighter. I picked up a candle from a tiny little box next to the golden sand and flicked the lighter. When the light from the candle started to brighten up the church, all of my deep sadness and sorrow made it feel dark again; it was as if the big grey wooden door was closing behind me. I knelt down and placed the candle into the sand. Then all the tears of despair started to roll down my cheeks onto my summer top. Within that moment, I realised that I was never really going to get over the loss of so many beautiful people.

When I left the church, Bella walked inside the church to light a candle for her loved ones. I left Jose and Bella in the church while I walked into the mountains to have a quiet word with God. I stopped walking at a small opening where the trees made way for the sun to shine on some wildflowers.

Then I looked out onto the mountains and whispered, 'Christ, why did Michelle, Paul and Mark have to die? Why would you do this, God, why have you left me all alone?' Then the strangest thing happened. I heard a majestic voice that sounded like it was coming from the actual mountains. *I am with you; I am always with you.* Then the whole of the mountains seemed to fold around me like a big warm hug.

Those few words sounded extremely peaceful, but they took me by surprise, yet I felt very safe and secure for the first time in years. I turned around to find Jose and Bella, but they were only just leaving the church. I ran towards them.

'Jose, did you hear that voice?'

He stood by the church door looking at me. 'What voice, Janet, I did not hear anything. Who was it, there is no one else here?'

I looked all around the forest to see if I could see anyone, then I looked back towards Bella. 'Jose, I am sure I heard a voice!' I made my way towards them.

Jose closed the wooden church door then he looked at me. 'Janet, this is the place where Christianity was born in the Balkans. There are many voices in the mountains, just accept that this voice was for you.' Then he smiled at Bella. 'Let us go back down the mountain to the car.'

While I was walking back down the mountain back, I kept going through what the voice had said and what it meant. *I am with you; I am always with you.* Where did it come from?

By the time we had got back into the car, the sun had stopped shining and within a few seconds of putting my seatbelt on, the heavens opened. First came the rain, then the hail and finally the snow started to fall down all around us.

Jose started the engine and he manoeuvred the car away from the church. While he was driving down the mountains, the weather continued to get worse. I could not hold back my feelings any longer. All of the sadness inside my heart started to pour out. I tried to stop it, but it just would not stop; the floods of tears came pouring down my cheeks like the rain on the windows of a car. It was as if all of the sorrow that I had been holding back since the passing of Mark, Paul and Michelle was leaving my body and soul because there was no place left for it inside me.

Jose and Bella must have thought that I was going crazy. First, I was hearing voices, then I was sitting in the back of their car expressing my painful grief all over my clothes, and the sound of my pain had made the weather change from a beautiful sunny day into a dreadful winter storm. Bella played some Bulgarian pipe music to drown out my crying and she kept turning around to look at me to see if I was all right. But it did not matter, all of my sorrow just would not stop pouring out of me!

When Jose dropped me off at the hotel, I made my way to the room to phone Mick. When I told him about my experience in the mountains, he thought that I was going mad.

'You must be hearing things, woman; don't worry, you can get it sorted when you get home.'

I knew deep down inside that what I heard was for real and it was a wonderful moment in my life and one that I would never forget.

Earthquake

That night when I lay in bed reflecting on the wonderful time I had in the mountains, I could hear lots of stray dogs barking outside the hotel. I knew that there was nothing I could do to stop them. Jose had already complained to the receptionist and she had called the local dog warden. My wonderful day was being ruined by the sound of dogs barking; their barks kept getting louder and louder with every passing second, it was becoming unbearable. I turned the TV on and waited for the darkness to cover the room. I managed to fall asleep while listening to Bulgarian MTV, which helped to drown out the noise of the dogs.

Then all of a sudden, I was awakened by a very loud noise. When I opened my eyes, I could see that all of the bedroom walls were shaking around me. When I looked up towards the ceiling, I could see that some of the lights were still on but they were swinging backwards and forwards above my head on a tiny pole that kept hitting the ceiling. Then the bed started to move across the wooden floor, it was sliding from one corner to another corner over the floor of the room. The bedroom lights started to flick on and off, as if someone was playing with the light switch, but there was no one else in the room.

All I could think about was that I was going to die in a hotel room in the middle of Devin, and I was on my own. Then it went quiet and everything came to a stop. The bed came to a standstill in the middle of the room, the lights above my head slowed down to a stop, the room lights stopped flicking on and off, they just stayed on. I lay quietly in the bed thinking of what on earth was going on. Then it registered that it must have been some kind of earthquake.

Devin must have been hit by a big tremor. I turned the TV on to watch the news. The noise from the TV sounded very loud then I realised that the whole village was in complete silence. The dogs had stopped barking and there were no other sounds either. I got out of bed and walked across the room to the window. When I looked outside, there was no one to be seen, not even a dog. I waited for a while to see if anyone appeared but everywhere was empty. I returned to the bed to watch the news and waited for the morning to come.

The next day when I went downstairs for breakfast, I looked out of the ground floor window to see if there was any damage. But to my surprise the village seemed like it was back to normal, everyone was acting like nothing had happened. When I looked towards the village centre, I could see that the dog warden was rounding up all of the stray dogs.

I started to shout. 'Stop it! I think they were only trying to warn us about the earthquake, please don't take them, please leave them alone.'

Then a woman at the reception desk stared at me with dismay in her eyes. I felt awful, it was my fault that the dogs were being rounded up and taken away. When I looked out of the window again, the dog warden was driving past the hotel with all of the dogs in cages. As he drove past me, I could see the sadness in the dogs' eyes.

When Jose and Bella arrived at the hotel, Jose asked me if I liked the earthquake. Then Bella laughed.

Then he shouted. 'We arranged that earthquake especially

for you.'

I turned towards him. 'Thank you, Jose, it was very frightening, but I managed to get through it.' Then we all laughed and smiled together.

When I made my way to Jose's car, I could see a little bit of damage to some of the flowerpots along the road, but there was no major damage. When Jose drove out of the village, we went past the dog warden's van with all of the stray dogs in their cages.

'Jose, I feel awful, those dogs were only warning us about the earthquake.'

Jose looked at me and smiled. 'Don't worry about the dogs, Janet. Once you leave the village they will be free again.'

We spent the whole day looking at some of the wonderful tourist attractions within the Rudolph Mountains. At every site that we visited; I was fortunate to meet one of Bella's cousins. They would take me on a personal sightseeing tour; it was such a lovely day, there were so many beautiful places to visit and so many wonderful things to do in the mountains. I came away from the sightseeing tour thinking when God made the Earth, Bulgaria may have been the first place He started to develop the landscape, because everything within the mountains was just how natural nature was meant to be.

That evening was a very special occasion because I had been invited for a traditional home-cooked meal at Bella's mother's house. This would be my first time in a Bulgarian home, with a beautiful home-cooked meal. Jose met me at the hotel and we walked through the village towards her home. When I walked through the front door, I was met by a beautiful mature woman; she was very happy, warm and welcoming. Bella introduced me to her mama and their two daughters, then she showed me where to sit in the living room. When I sat down, I could smell the wonderful aroma of fresh home cooking coming from the kitchen.

When the food was ready, I sat behind a lovely long table just across from the kitchen door. I could see that Bella and her mama were cooking lots of lovely fresh food. When everything was ready, they served a traditional Bulgarian meal together with a lot of grace, harmony and love. While we were eating the beautiful meal there were a lot of different conversations. Jose translated all of my communication to Bella and her beautiful mama. There was so much joy in the room, the food was fantastic and mama's homemade cakes were so delicious I asked if I could keep some for when I got back to the hotel room.

Jose and Bella's children were beautiful, they spent the night watching a version of the Bulgarian X Factor. After the meal had finished, we spent some time talking about the earthquake. I asked mama how she felt when the tremors started. She replied to Jose, then he translated.

'I was worried about the colour of my hair because my dark roots are starting to show, so while the earthquake was happening, I was sitting in the bathroom colouring my hair just in case the Bulgarian TV showed up.' Everyone started laughing.

During the evening, all of my communications and Jose's translations merged into one. We were all having such a great time together, language was no longer a barrier, because we all seemed to understand what each other was saying. It was the universal language of joyfulness.

Before I left to go back to the hotel, Mama started to talk about a popular supermarket in Bulgaria that was named after me. I was a bit disappointed so I asked her. 'Mama, why a supermarket and not a mountain or a wild forest?'

She smiled at me. 'You're lucky, Janet, mountains and forest are not in every town, but there's always a Janet supermarket.' Bella nodded her head and Jose laughed.

That evening was one of the nicest times I had in Devin. When Jose and I walked back to the hotel, I noticed that all of the dogs had been returned to the village, but instead of them barking their heads off, they were all fast asleep outside their owner's front doors.

Secret Island

Our friendships in Bulgaria were evolving with every holiday. Mick and I looked forward to returning to the apartment whenever we could. It was as if we were going to another place in time, far away from all the hustle and bustle of everyday life at home.

Lillian and Melvin decided to spend two weeks at the apartment with Mick and me. It was the first time they had joined us for a two-week holiday and we were all looking forward to having lots of fun in the sun. The flight to Bulgaria was brilliant, there was no effing or jeffing from Lillian this time, just a smooth take-off and delicate touch down at Bourgas Airport.

Nikolay picked everyone up from the airport, then he dropped us all off at the apartment. When Mike opened the front door, it felt really good to be back in our dream holiday home. Lillian and I unpacked the suitcases while the boys sorted out the TV and fridge. It did not take us very long to settle in. Melvin and Mick went to the supermarket for the much-needed essentials, beer, wine, snacks, eggs and bread.

Lillian and I walked around to the pool to find four sunbeds for a nice relaxing afternoon in the sun. When we had sorted out the sunbeds and tables, Mick and Melvin passed two white wines and two large glasses of beer over the balcony to drink while sunbathing. I introduced Lillian and Melvin to our new friends Blodwyn and Knobby, while Mick went back into the apartment to pour them a large beer and a wine. Everyone got on so well, it was as if we had known each other forever.

Later that afternoon, Mick and I walked around to a Happy Bar to see Jose and Bella. They were delighted to see both of us. Jose told Mick about a wonderful island location at the other side of the Black Sea coast, where some of the local Bulgarians went to get away from all the tourists in the summer. He offered to take us for a day out when it was convenient. I informed him that Lillian and Melvin were spending their holiday with us and we were also with Blodwyn and Knobby. Jose smiled. 'This does not matter, the more people the merrier.' Then he spoke to Bella in Bulgarian. 'Bella will ask her sister to drive Lillian and Melvin to the island, and we will take everyone else in the people carrier.'

Mick and I went back to the pool to tell everyone about a new wonderful location and the trip out with our Bulgarian friends. Blodwyn and Knobby were delighted they had only stayed around the complex and visited New Nessebar, Old Nessebar and Ravda to pay their bills. This was a great opportunity for them to finally see more of Bulgaria. Lillian and Melvin could not wait to meet Jose and Bella, and have a day out to a wonderful location, it was just what they needed after working hard all year.

We spent the next few days having lots of fun around the pool, drinking at the Happy Bar, and eating out at all of the local restaurants. Then the day came when we were visiting the mystery island with Jose and Bella, everyone was so excited. We all made our way around to Happy Bar to start the journey. Lillian and Melvin got into Bella's sister's car with her husband, and the rest of us got into Jose's people carrier and we were off on our journey into the unknown.

On the way to the island, Jose stopped off at Janet's Supermarket to pick up some supplies for the BBQ. Lillian and I waited outside with Blodwyn and Knobby while Mick and Melvin went inside to help Jose and Bella with the shopping and to make sure there was enough alcohol for everyone. The sun was shining and it was a glorious day. When everyone came out of the supermarket, I could not believe my eyes; they had two big trolleys full of food and drink, it looked like they had bought two weeks' worth of shopping. Jose and Mick placed everything in the boot of the car and we were off to spend the day in a Bulgarian paradise.

When we arrived at the location, it did not resemble any beautiful paradise islands that I had imagined. There was only a small beach that was located at the end of a village. I felt a little disappointed and a bit worried about what everyone else would think. Jose helped everyone out of the car, then Bella started to hand everyone a bag of food or drink. 'Please, you will need to carry them to the Island.'

I looked around but I could not see an island anywhere. 'Where is the island, Mick?'

He looked around. 'I don't know, it has got to be somewhere around here.'

As I looked around, I could see that Lillian and Melvin were talking to Blodwyn and Knobby. Mick and I walked over to join them. 'I can't see any island, can you?'

Knobby looked around. 'Maybe it is a mystery island and it only appears at a certain time of the day.' We all laughed and waited for the island to appear somewhere within the Black Sea.

Then Jose called us over towards a big long concrete partition that was situated between the car park and the beach. 'Please come and see, the island is over here.'

I grabbed the shopping bags and walked towards him. Mick and I managed to climb over the large partition without any problems, but Lillian and Knobby needed a little bit of assistance from Jose and Bella's sister's husband to get them over the concrete.

When I landed at the other side of the partition, I could not believe my eyes; there was actually a beautiful deserted beach with a small island located about thirty metres off the coast. I looked at Mick. 'Wow, this is amazing! We would have never found this location on one of our discoveries.'

Bella waited for everyone to get over the partition before she found a lovely place for everyone to relax in the midday sunshine.

Jose started to build a beach BBQ with old pieces of wood that he had found scattered along the sand. Blodwyn and Knobby waited by the shopping bags, while Bella and Mick looked for a safe location within the small rock pools that lined the partition wall to keep all of the alcoholic drinks cold. Lillian and I started to collect some small pieces of kindle that had washed up on the beach for Jose.

'This is lovely, sis, I never expected it to be this nice.'

I looked up from the sand. Lillian looked radiant in her black shorts, white t-shirt and sun hat. 'I know, sis, I was a bit worried when we stopped at the car park, but once we got over the concrete partition, I could not believe my eyes.'

When we got back to Jose, we handed him the kindle and he placed it under some of the large pieces of wood. Blodwyn was helping Bella to prepare the fresh salad and Lillian offered to help.

I sat down on the warm sand and looked around the beach, the sound of the waves crashing against the small rocks and the massive partition wall was extraordinary; it sounded like the beautiful emerald sea wanted to tell everyone on the other side of the concrete partition that it was still here, and it was trying with all of its might to remove the wall with every powerful wave.

The noise of the waves was broken when Bella asked me to help her and Mick carry some of the beer, wine and a giant watermelon to the safe place that they had found within the rock pools. I watched as the waves crashed against the wall. Bella started placing all of the alcohol into two big string bags, then she placed the bags under the waves into a little rock pool. Mick handed her some large rocks and she positioned the rocks on top of the bags to hold them in place. I handed her a bag of bottled water and the big watermelon, she placed them into another little rock pool next to the concrete partition, and Mick placed some large rocks on top of the bag to keep everything cool and safe. Then we made our way back to everyone.

When we got back, all of the salad was ready, the food was cooking on the BBQ and the drinks were cooling in the sea.

Mick grabbed my hand. 'Fancy going for a swim before we have our lunch?'

I looked at him. 'That would be lovely.'

Bella and Jose stood up. 'We will come with you.'

'Do you want to come for a swim, Lillian and Melvin?'

Melvin looked up at the sun in the sky. 'No, thanks, I'm going to top up my tan today.'

Lillian sat up and looked at the sea. 'Not today. Thanks, sis, I'm staying nice and dry today.'

When I walked into the sea, the forceful power from the emerald waves started to hit me; it felt so invigorating, my body felt like it was being re-energised with every crashing wave. I dipped the whole of my body under the water to ensure that all my flesh and bones benefited from the sea's invigorating energy and the constant boost of nature's wellbeing.

Mick came swimming towards me. 'Would you like to swim to the mystery island?' The island was about twenty metres away.

'That would be lovely.'

As we swam together in the sea, it felt like we were in our own little paradise. When I walked out of the sea, it reminded me of the movie "From Here to Eternity." It was such a beautiful location. Mick and I sat on a large rock at the edge of the beach to rest for a while and admire the amazing views. While we rested, the waves from the sea kept crashing over the rock to remind us that it was still there. I was glad that the heat from the midday sun was providing some warmth from the constant rolling waves.

After we had rested for a while, we made our way back to the others. Melvin was watching Jose as he rubbed two flints together to catch a spark to light the little piece of cotton wool. When the wool was ignited with little flames, Jose carefully positioned the dry wood onto the second BBQ.

When the smoke from the burning wood died down, Melvin started to place some small potatoes around the edges of the fire to make sure they had plenty of time to cook. Bella, Lillian and Blodwyn were arranging a makeshift table in the sand, it was lovely to see everyone working in harmony.

Mick and I started to walk back towards the sea to get some of the bottled water from the rock pool, when I noticed that there were a few beer cans floating out to sea. 'Oh look, Mick, someone has thrown an empty beer can into the sea, isn't that terrible!'

He looked for a while. 'Look, Janet, there's another can of beer.'

I looked towards the strong waves that were crashing against the concrete partition. 'On my God, Mick, there are loads of beer cans and a watermelon floating off to sea.'

Mick ran off like a bolt of lightning, then he started shouting, 'Jose, Melvin, hurry up, we are losing all the beer to the sea.'

Everybody stopped what they were doing and looked out to the sea and the powerful waves trying to steal the alcohol. Bella got up from the table and she started to run towards Mick. When Melvin and Jose saw the beer cans floating off to sea, they started to place the meat at the edge of the first BBQ, so it would not burn.

When I got to the location where Bella and Mick had placed the bags of alcohol, bottled water and melon into the rock pools, I noticed that all the bags had gone! There was nothing there, the sea had taken everything. When I looked out towards the island, I could see the tops of numerous beer cans bobbing up and down in the waves, then I noticed that there were two bottles of wine floating out to sea as well; It looked like they were carrying a secret message to some unknown place in time. It did not take long before I could see the giant watermelon trying to catch up with all the beer and wine.

I started to shout. 'Hurry, everyone, come and help, we are losing everything.'

Melvin and Jose ran into the waves to rescue the cans of beer. 'Save the wine first.' Then I heard Mick shouting, 'I have got the wine, lads, you save the beers.'

Bella and I tried to get to grab the bottled water, but the force of the waves kept pushing us back onto the rocks. I held

Bella's hand as she tried to grab hold of the string bag, but a big wave took her feet and she fell against the rocks.

Mick swam over to help. He managed to pull Bella up before another big wave tried to take her away into the angry sea. When she got close to me, I could tell by her reaction that she had been hurt by the crushing waves. I put my hand around her to give her some reassurance. 'Are you two all right?'

I smiled at Mick. 'Thank you, that was frightening.'

Bella and I sat down on the warm sand. 'Thank you, Mick, I think the sea is very angry today.'

Mick looked at her. 'No, Bella, I think it is very thirsty, because it is trying to take all of our beers.' Then he turned around and ran back into the sea.

When I looked at Bella, I noticed that her leg was bleeding. I used a piece of tissue to wipe away the blood. She smiled at me then she pointed towards the sea. I turned my head and looked behind me, I could see that Mick, Melvin and Jose were swimming out to sea to rescue the beers. Each time they got close to a beer can, the sea would pull it away with the force of its waves.

Lillian passed me a clean tissue out of her bag to remove the blood that was pouring down Bella's leg. 'Bloody hell, Janet, I hope the lads are OK, they should leave the beer.'

I grabbed the tissues and wiped away the blood to see how bad the cut was. 'I know, Lillian, but they will not let the sea take away their beers, we would never hear the last of it!'

Once all of the blood had been removed by the tissues, I could see that there was only a small cut just below the knee. I held a clean tissue over the cut to stop it from bleeding. While I was kneeling down in the sand, I watched the lads as they fought with the waves to rescue their beer cans.

271

Mick was the first to swim out of the sea with two cans of beer, Melvin followed him with another two cans, Jose was not far behind with a bottle of water and one can of beer. They placed the alcohol next to the BBQ then ran back into the sea to rescue the rest. We watched as the lads battled with the waves to save the day. Jose was the first to return back this time; he had rescued a bottle of water and a can. Mick and Melvin returned shortly after with a few more beer cans.

When I looked at Mick, he looked like he had been swimming the English Channel. 'That's it, Janet, I am not going back into the sea, it is far too dangerous.'

I looked at him and gave him a big hug.

'Pass me a towel, please.'

I went into the beach bag to get a towel for him, when I turned around to give it to him, I saw a big green watermelon near the edge of the water. 'Look, everyone, someone get that watermelon before it goes back to sea.'

Melvin and Jose turned around to look at the sea, then Jose looked back towards me. 'Janet, the angry sea can have the watermelon today and we will keep the beer.'

Then the three lads walked over to Knobby, they opened a can of beer each then they settled down by the BBQ.

After they had drunk the first beer, Jose started to return the chicken to the middle of the BBQ, while Bella cut the bread, cheese and tomatoes. Blodwyn started to talk to Jose about the secret island. Jose told us that it used to be called Snake Island because of the high number of snakes. We all looked at each other, then down towards our feet. 'Don't worry, the snakes have left the island now,' which did not make me feel any better.

'Where are they now, Jose?'

He looked up from the BBQ. 'The snakes.' He stood up and

looked towards the island. 'No one knows, they just disappeared.'

I could see Lillian and Blodwyn grabbing their bags up from off the sand. 'It's OK, everyone, the snakes are not here any more, they have gone away.'

I felt myself relax for a moment, but Lillian and Blodwyn were a little more hesitant.

'Pass me the wine, Mick, I think we all need a big drink.'

Mick passed Lillian the wine and she poured a drink for everyone.

When the food was ready, we all sat around the fire talking about our "international rescue" of the beer cans, each of us giving our own version of what we saw and what we did. We spent most of our lunch time laughing together in the sun. After the BBQ, I started to relax in the afternoon sunshine, listening to the waves as they crashed against the shore (while keeping my eyes wide open for any snakes).

Bella's sister arrived late into the afternoon. She had come to take Lillian and Melvin back to the complex. I felt quite sad because I did not want the day to end. Our Bulgarian paradise was invigorating, energising, dangerous, risky, but above all of this; it was very funny. Feeling a little bit reluctant, I made my way back to the car park to start the journey home. But before I left the secret island, I picked up a small piece of rock to take away with me as a little reminder.

'That the sea can take our watermelon, but it will never take away our beer.'

The journey back to the apartment was very relaxing. Jose spoke about some of his experiences; where he worked as an adult, his education in Bulgaria, his family and friends. I was starting to realise that his life in Bulgaria was not like our life in England.

When we got back to the complex, we all had a nice cold drink at Happy Bar, before going back to the apartment to get changed for the evening. Lillian and Melvin wanted to go to Fagi's for something to eat, the restaurant was only about two hundred metres from the complex. When we finished our meal, we made our way back to Happy Bar to tell everyone about the terrific day we had at Snake Island. Blodwyn and Knobby were sitting at the bar when we arrived, they had been telling all of the regulars about how the sea tried to take the beer and wine. Everyone started laughing when Mick showed them how he and Bella secured the alcohol with lots of rocks, but when they returned to the string bags that they were in, they saw that the sea had taken everything.

Before Mick and I left the bar that evening, Jose and Bella stopped us. 'Would like to come and stay in Devin this autumn for a wonderful winter holiday?'

Mick was delighted; he had always wanted to visit Devin, since the time I had travelled there on my own, but he needed to book a week's holiday when he returned to work.

Blodwyn and Knobby were sitting next to Mick when Jose was talking about going to Devin. 'Would it be possible for Knobby and I to visit Devin in the Autumn too?'

Jose and Bella were ecstatic. 'Absolutely, we will book the hotel once you have sorted out the dates and times of your flights.'

I was very excited. 'Jose, please try to book the first hotel on the way into Devin, it looks amazing and there are no barking dogs around.'

Bella and Jose started to laugh. 'No problem, Janet, it is a lovely hotel and nobody there owns a dog.'

When Bella and Jose went back to the bar, we all made our way back to the apartment with Blodwyn and Knobby. Before we went inside, we said, 'Licanosh' (good night) to each other. Then Blodwyn held my hand.

'Janet, when Mick has sorted out the dates when he can get a week off work, and you know the times of your flight to Sofia from Manchester, please will you phone me and I will try and book the same dates and times for myself and Knobby, so that we will all arrive at the airport at the same time?'

I gave her a big hug. 'Absolutely, once Mick has booked his holidays from work, I will check out the flights to Sofia and phone you.' I wished everyone a good night's sleep. And we all said Licanosh again at the same time.

The flight home from Bulgaria felt very different. I think it was because I knew that Mick and I would be coming back in the autumn to stay in Devin with Blodwyn and Knobby. I could not wait to book our return flights.

Rhodope Mountain Roads or Rivers?

The following Monday morning when Mick returned to work; he could not wait to ask his manager for one week's holiday in the autumn. It did not take his manager too long to give him an answer, because there was only one week free in the calendar. Mick phoned me straight away.

'Good morning, Janet, there is only one week's holiday left, but it is at the beginning of October. Please can you have a look on the Internet to see if there are any flights going to Sofia from Manchester on this date before I confirm the week's annual leave with my manager?'

I put the phone down and turned on the PC. My heart was pounding. 'Please let there be a flight. Please let there be a flight.' I put the first week of October's dates into the EasyJet website and waited. To my surprise, there were several flights leaving Manchester Airport for Sofia that week. I phoned Mick straight away.

'Book those holidays, we are going to Devin.' I could hear him shouting to his manager. 'Book that week's annual leave for me, please, the wife has sorted out a flight, we are going on holiday.'

His manager shouted back, 'It's not even six a.m. yet, how has she managed that?'

Mick put the phone down.

I waited until after nine a.m. to phone Blodwyn to coordinate our flights to Sofia Airport. It only took us about ten minutes to book both flights to Sofia. When I had finished catching up with Blodwyn and Knobby, I telephoned Jose to inform him of the dates and times of both of our flights. Bella was very happy, I could hear her excitement in the background. Jose assured me that they would book our accommodation at the beautiful Ismena Spa Hotel that day. I could not wait to return to Devin to show Mick, Knobby and Blodwyn the wonderful Rhodope Mountains.

When we landed at Sofia Airport, it felt very different then Bourgas Airport; it did not feel like we had landed at a holiday destination, it felt more industrial and business-like. Mick got our suitcases and we made our way out through the arrivals gate. I looked everywhere for Knobby, Blodwyn, Jose and Bella, but they were nowhere in sight. Mick and I walked outside to the car parks to see if we could see Jose's car, but the car park was almost empty.

'What are we going to do, Mick?'

He put the suitcases down and looked at me. 'Phone Jose to see where they are. Knowing you, we are probably in the wrong place.'

Jose answered the phone. 'Hello, Janet, we have just dropped Blodwyn and Knobby at the hotel, we are on our way back, we won't be long.'

'Thank God, Mick, they are on their way.'

Mick and I waited under the shade of the bus shelter.

'I thought we were all arriving at the same time, Janet?'

I thought for a moment. 'So did I, Mick; Blodwyn never mentioned any changes to their flight.'

It wasn't long before I saw Jose's car turning into the carpark. As soon as it stopped, Bella got out of the car. She ran towards me with the biggest smile on her face, her arms were wide open to give me a big hug. Mick and I grabbed the suitcases and walked towards her. When I got close, I dropped my bag and we hugged each other. Jose placed the suitcases in the boot of the car and we were off on another discovery.

When we arrived at the Hotel Ismena, it looked as beautiful as it did when I first visited Devin. Bella showed us to the reception area and helped us to check in. We put the suitcases into the room and went to find Blodwyn and Knobby. The grounds of the hotel were stunning; it was located in an idyllic area of the mountains. The spa facilities looked amazing and the indoor and outdoor swimming pools were outstanding. The dining room smelt of freshly baked pastries, coffee and fresh fruit. When I looked outside the patio door, I could see Blodwyn and Knobby waiting for us with a nice glass of wine and beer. 'There they are, Mick.' We made our way outside to surprise them.

'Hello, everyone.'

Blodwyn jumped up and hugged me. Mick and Knobby shook hands, then I gave Knobby a big hug. We sat down and waited for Jose and Bella to join us. The views outside were stunning, I could not stop looking into the mountains. They looked so inviting. Jose brought out two large drinks, while Bella carried a tray with two small beers and two glasses of white wine. When we sat down, we held our glasses up in the air and toasted "to all the good times we will have together". Jose took a sip of his beer then he started to tell us about all of the wonderful trips they had planned with Bella's family and her numerous cousins. None of us could wait to see all of the wonderful destinations they had organised.

The following morning, Mick and I had arranged to meet everyone in the dining room for breakfast. The food looked delicious and there was plenty of choice. I found a seat on the biggest table, then I walked over to the food counters to get something nice to eat before I went on the journey into the mountains. When I was returning with my plate of breakfast delights, Blodwyn and Knobby had just arrived in the dining room. She smiled at me then she asked if they could join us.

'Absolutely, I have got that big table for everyone.' Then I pointed towards the table. It did not take long before we were all sitting, eating our breakfast wondering what wonderful experiences lay ahead of us.

When Jose and Bella arrived, we were all full of delicious fresh food and ready to go for a day in the mountains. Knobby got in the front seat of the people carrier, and the rest of us made our way onto the seats at the back. Jose started the engine and we were off on a mystery tour. The roads into the mountains were very good, there were a number of tricky bends, but Jose was a professional driver and it was obvious that he had driven along these roads many times before. It did not take long before we were high up into the vast mountain ranges. The views were stunning. He drove through the mountains for a few hours, then he stopped the car in a lovely location for some well-deserved food and drink.

Before we got back into the car, I noticed that Bella and Jose seemed to be having a conversation about the next location, it looked like they were undecided on where to take us next. When we got back into the car, Bella got a satnav out of the glove compartment and she set the coordinates for the next part of our journey.

The satnav guided Jose deeper into the mountains and off the main highway. The quality of the roads seemed to change the higher we went. The views were amazing but the roads became very rough and bumpy, Jose used all of his driving skills to stop the car from tilting to the left then the right. Then all of a sudden we ran out of road, and he was driving along what looked like a very rocky pathway. Then suddenly the car came to a standstill.

Jose tried to drive over whatever was stopping the car, but the car would not move. He went backwards and forwards a few times, but there was no road left to drive on. I could hear Jose and Bella talking to each other in Bulgarian about the satnav, it sounded like they were lost.

Blodwyn looked at me and I looked at Mick. 'This does not look good, does it?'

Knobby turned his head around to face us. 'Jose is a very good mountaineer and driver, he knows his way around the mountains; however, we may just have to wait until it gets dark so that he can follow the stars.' We all laughed then sat quietly waiting for the car to move, but nothing happened.

Bella put some new details into the satnav, then she got out of the car and went for a walk into the forest to see if she could get a good signal, then Jose got out of the car to look at the terrain and to see what was stopping the car from moving forward.

When they had gone out of sight, I whispered to Blodwyn, 'I am dying for a wee, it's because of all of those lovely drinks I had for breakfast and lunch.'

She held onto my hand. 'So am I, but I have not seen any toilets up here, have you?'

I looked outside into the surrounding forest. 'Not yet, do you think they will have any nice toilet roll in them?'

Mick laughed. 'Up here, don't expect any Andrex toilet rolls, you will be lucky to find a bush, never mind a toilet.'

Blodwyn let go of my hand. 'I have never ever had a wee outside in my entire life.'

I grabbed her hand again. 'Me too, I hope we don't have to go behind a bush.'

When Jose returned to the car, he did not look happy; he was scratching his head as if he was looking for a solution. Bella was still out walking around the forest with the satnav in her hand. Jose opened the back door of the car.

'OK, everyone, please get out of the car, we will have to build a new road to get us out of here.'

Mick got out of the car first and he made his way towards Jose. Blodwyn and I got out of the other side of the car like two unwilling assistants. We made our way to the front of the car and waited tentatively for any instructions from Jose.

'Right, Knobby, you stay in the car. I will need you to steer the wheels.'

Then he looked around. 'Mick, pick up some of those large rocks and place them behind the front wheels.' Then he pointed to the front wheel. 'Janet and Blodwyn, grab some of those smaller stones and push them under the back wheels.'

We all did what we were told without any hesitation. I was not sure what I was doing, but I knew we needed to get out of the forest before it got dark.

Bella saw what we were doing and she came back to the car, she put the satnav back into the glovebox and walked over to Jose to update him on our location. While I was picking up a stone, I looked at the terrain.

'This is not a road, it looks like a dried-up river.'

Blodwyn turned around. 'I thought that, you don't get stones like these on a road, but you do find them at the edge of water.'

After a while, Jose came back to the car to inspect our work. 'That looks good. I think we can try to go forward now.'

Blodwyn and I made our way back to the side of the car and I opened the door. 'No, no, stop, you cannot get into the car yet, you will have to push!'

We looked at each other. 'Oh my God, Blodwyn, I cannot push a car. I really need a wee now.'

She looked down towards the ground. 'Me too, this dried up river may be getting some additional water soon.'

We walked slowly to the front of the car. 'Right, Janet, you and Blodwyn can push from the back of the car, Mick and I will push the wheels over the stones while Knobby steers.' Bella joined us at the back of the car. 'Right, Knobby, start the engine.' The smoke from the exhaust made me cough, then my eyes started to water from the fumes. 'Right, everyone, push, push.' But the car stayed still, and it did not move an inch.

'Right, let's try again, this time push harder from the back.'

Blodwyn and I put our shoulders to the back of the car, but every time we pushed, one of our flip flops fell off and we had nothing for our feet to push on. We pushed and we pushed, then the car moved very slightly.

'Stop!' We all stopped and walked around to the front of the car. 'Right, I can see what is stopping the car from moving, can you see that big rock, Mick?' Jose pointed to something under the wheel of the car.

Mick got on his knees to look under the wheel. 'Yes, that does not look very good.'

Jose walked into the forest for a moment or two, then he came back. 'Right, everyone, we are going to have to bump the car over this large blockage.'

We all nodded our heads together. I walked towards the

side of the car. 'We will do whatever it takes to get us out of here.'

Bella smiled then spoke to Jose in Bulgarian. 'Right, Mick, you will have to sit on the bonnet of the car to give it some leverage.'

Mick looked at the top of the bonnet. 'I can't do that, Jose, I am far too heavy. I will dint it.'

Jose just looked at him and agreed. 'Girls, you will all have to push from the back as hard as you can.'

I started to walk towards the back of the car then Mick stopped me. 'If I put a dent in this car, will our holiday insurance cover it?'

I thought for a moment. 'I don't think so, Mick, please try not to put all of your weight on it.' I put my shoulder to the back of the car and waited for Jose's instructions.

Blodwyn looked at me. 'If I push hard again, I know I am going to wee.'

I looked down towards my feet. 'If you see any water running past your flip flops, it won't be the river breaking its banks, it will be my waters breaking.'

Bella looked at me then towards Jose. 'Right, push, push, push. Mick, sit on the bumper and bounce as hard as you can?'

I shouted, 'Not too hard Mick, you are not insured.'

We pushed and we pushed, Mick bounced and bounced, Knobby started to manoeuvre the wheels of the car. After a few minutes, the car started to move forward. 'Don't stop pushing, keep going!'

We continued to push and bounce, then there was a big jolt forward. 'Stop, stop pushing!'

Blodwyn and I stopped, then we ran towards the bushes. I whispered, 'We will be back soon, we have to go…'

When we returned from behind the bushes, Jose, Bella and Mick had started to lay a new road of stones along the dried-up river.

'Please help us, we will need to build a new road out of the forest.' As I walked past the front of the car, I could see a large dent in the top of the bonnet where Mick had been bouncing. I walked over to talk to Mick. 'Have you seen the big dent in the bonnet?'

Mick grinned. 'I felt it go when I did the final bounce.'

'What are we going to do, we are not insured.'

'We will just have to wait and see how much it is going to cost to fix it. In the meantime, let us build this road and get out of here.'

When the road was finished, the light in the forest was starting to fade, so we all got back into the car to join Knobby. 'Well done, everyone, we won't have to wait for the stars to come out now.'

When we got back to the hotel, Blodwyn suggested spending the night in the hotel's restaurant because it had been a wonderful long day. Jose and Bella agreed and they went to the receptionist to book a large table for everyone. We went outside into the garden and waited for them to return.

'Right, the table is booked for seven p.m., we will meet you in the bar around six thirty p.m.' Then they left. Knobby ordered four large drinks from the waiter.

'Oh my god, everyone, I thought we were going to be stuck on the mountains.'

I stood up. 'It was never a bloody mountain road. That sat nav had taken us to a dried-up river bed.'

Mick started to laugh. 'There was no chance of getting the RAC, the AA or International Rescue out, they would never have found us in that forest.'

The waiter placed the four drinks on the table, we all picked up our drinks and toasted to our safe return to the hotel.

We all sat quietly for a while then Blodwyn started to giggle. 'I wasn't keeping my eyes on the road, I was only looking for the ladies' toilets.'

I started to laugh. 'Me too, I can't believe we ended up going behind a bush!'

Knobby put his drink down and he looked really serious. 'God knows where we will end up tomorrow, I think we should take our wet gear and some extra food just in case.'

We spent the next few hours laughing and joking about the day's escapades and what could happen next.

That evening, Mick and I got dressed up to eat in the restaurant. We joined Blodwyn and Knobby at the bar for a drink or two before Jose and Bella joined us. When they arrived, I noticed that their two beautiful children had come with them. We made our way to the dining room and the waiter escorted us to the table. I heard some English music in the background when I looked behind the bar, I could see that the TV channel was on MTV. It was nice to hear some pop music.

The table looked fabulous, it was set for eight people and there was a row of fresh flowers along the centre of the tablecloth. When everyone had sat down, the waiters handed out the menus and we ordered our meals. When the food arrived, it looked amazing. I could not wait to eat mine because I was absolutely famished. During the main meal, Jose told us that we were the first group of tourists to build a new road out of the mountains.

Mick put his knife and fork down. 'Jose, how much will it cost to get that big dent fixed in your car?'

Jose and Bella stood up at the same time. 'We will never get it repaired. It will always be a wonderful memory of our happy times in the mountains with our very good friends.'

Everyone talked about their own experience in the mountains. It seemed to be a lot funnier now, I think it was because we were in a lovely restaurant, surrounded by lots of food and drink and close to some luxury toilets.

When everyone had finished talking, Jose started to talk about a trip that they had planned for us the following day. We all sat quietly waiting to hear if it was going to be as challenging.

'Bella would like me to take you to the cave where one of her relatives works; it's in a lovely location and the road is tarmacked.'

I smiled at him. 'That would be lovely, Jose and Bella, thank you.'

Later that evening, the children said that they had enjoyed their evening, but the youngest daughter was beginning to look a little bit tired. Jose and Bella noticed that she was sleepy so they decided to leave the restaurant to make their way home. While they were putting their coats on, I realised that the background music had stopped and all I could hear was heavy breathing and what sounded like a woman groaning. When I turned around to look at the TV, the MTV music channel had finished and there was a man and woman having sex on the fifty-six inch television.

'Oh my God, look what's on TV.' I pointed my finger towards the bar.

Mick looked up and Blodwyn turned her head. 'Bloody hell, that is terrible, please somebody turn the TV off, there are young children in the room!'

A waiter came running out of the kitchen to find the remote for the TV. But before he could turn the TV off, Knobby shouted, 'Hold on, mate, I have not seen what's happening yet, did someone mention sex?'

The waiter turned the TV off. Knobby was a bit disappointed because he was unable to turn his wheelchair around to catch sight of the couple's romantic moments.

'That's the story of my life... I'm always last to the party.'

Mountain Caves and Dodgy Zip Lines

The following morning, Mick and I joined Blodwyn and Knobby for breakfast. Knobby was still a little bit deterred about missing the naughty moments on the TV.

'Good morning, Mick and Janet, I am not sitting with my back to the TV again.'

Mick burst out laughing. 'You did not miss much, Knobby.'

Blodwyn grabbed hold of his arm. 'Knobby, Janet and Mick don't want to know about your disappointment, they want to eat their breakfast in peace.'

We spent our time in the restaurant laughing and joking about Bulgarian sat navs, dried-up rivers and fifty inch TVs. When Jose and Bella arrived, we were all sitting outside in the sunshine. Jose looked at our feet to see what shoes we were wearing.

'Janet and Blodwyn, please can you change out of your flip flops into something a bit sturdier?'

'No problem, Jose.' I left everyone to change into my trainers. When I got back, the men were having a nice cold beer and there was a glass of wine waiting for me.

When everyone had drunk their drinks, we made our way to the car. When I looked at the bonnet of the car, I could tell that Jose had tried to get the big dint out of the bonnet, because it looked like an upside-down wok.

'Hold on a minute, everyone, there is something I need to do before we go anywhere.' I ran to the toilets to have a "just in

288

case wee," then I sat in the car waiting for Blodwyn and Bella to join me.

The start of our journey into the mountains was different this time. Instead of turning right at the bottom of the hotel, Jose drove through the spa village of Devin. We went past the hotel where I stayed the year before.

'Mick, that is the hotel where I was sleeping when they had that earthquake!'

He looked out of the car window. 'It looks solid to me.'

Blodwyn looked towards me. 'It is a good job, you would not have liked to die here on your own.'

I smiled with relief. 'Absolutely not, it would have been awful for Mick and Christopher!'

Knobby laughed. 'It would have been worse even for you!'

I sat quietly thinking about how lucky I was to survive an earthquake.

Jose drove the car up the other side of the mountains into a massive forest of beautiful wild trees. He drove for a few more miles before stopping at what looked like a bus stop. I got out of the car to see why he had stopped.

'Look, Janet, you can see the spa village of Devin from here, it looks like the shape of a dragon from above.'

I walked towards the edge of the road. 'Wow, yes, Jose, it looks like the Welsh dragon.'

When I got back into the car, Jose started the engine to continue our journey. He must have driven for over an hour before we came to the next stop which was the "Devil's Throat Cave."

This cave was located near the border with Greece in southern Bulgaria. This was not a typical cave like you would visit in the UK. Instead, it was called a "precipice cave" because of all the water from the Trigrad River running down into the 42-metre ravine. Blodwyn, Bella and I decided to complete the full tour of the cave. The tour guide was one of Bella's cousins, he informed us that the cave descends straight in the depths of hell, with the waters of Trigrad Rivers plunging 137 ft. into the Hall of Thunder. The second largest cavern in the country, the Hall of Thunder houses a funnel through which the water escapes, flowing 500 more feet before joining with the underground river. I stood still with amazement. It was enormous yet fascinating at the same time. Then he continued, 'It is this underground river that presents the most interesting feature of the cave-nothing carried into the Devil's Mouth Cave by the river ever surfaces from it on the other side?' It felt amazing to be standing so close to the tallest underground waterfall in the Balkans. Then the tour guide showed us to the 220 plus steps that we had to climb to exit the cave. Blodwyn and I looked at each other. 'I can't climb up there Janet, it's too difficult for me.' I put my foot on the first step. 'We will do it together, we will take our time and enjoy each and every step.' Bella stayed behind Blodwyn to encourage her to reach the top.

When we had finished the tour of the cave and the hundreds of steps, we were all exhausted and delighted to have been able to complete the tour. Jose took us to a local cafe for a well-deserved lunch. Bella ordered some local food for everyone and a few alcoholic drinks. It was lovely to eat some of the locally caught fresh fish and homemade cheese. We sat talking about how wonderful it was to visit such an amazing cave. Jose spoke about the different experiences he and Bella had had in the cave, given the changing seasons within the mountains.

On the way out of the cafe, I noticed that there was a zip line over a river by the small bridge which was next to the car park. While everyone was chatting away, I made my way over the bridge to watch the local people take a ride on the zipline. When they stood at the top of the zip wire to start their journey to the other side of the river, it did not look like much of a ride, but it was quite exhilarating to watch them fly across the big white rapid waters.

It wasn't long before Blodwyn joined me on the other side of the river. 'I am going to have a go on this zip line, Blodwyn, are you?' I stood watching the next person as they took hold of the safety harness and then they were off to the other side of the river.

'OK, Janet, why not.' While we were waiting in line, Knobby and Mick joined us. 'We are going to have a go on the zip line, are you?'

They watched as the next person flew across the river. 'No way, that harness would never hold my wait.' (I don't think Mick trusted any of the outdoor activities since his bungee jump trip to space and back at Sunny Beach).

I waited at the front of the line to be called up to the top of the step ladder, which led to the top of the wire. I don't know whether it was the nice wine at lunch or the high altitude that was making me feel crazy enough to go on a zip line. When I started my journey up the ladder, my Dutch courage was starting to fade away, and I was having second thoughts!

'Oh my god, what am I doing?'

Blodwyn pushed me up the ladder. 'Go on, Janet, it will be OK.'

With her gentle push, I stepped to the top of the ladders. Within a second or two, the safety harness was on then I was flying over the rapid waters. I felt frightened and excited at the same time, but it was all over within a few seconds.

When I got to the other side of the river, a local man had to pull me away from the water's edge. It was quite scary. He took the safety harness off me, then he pulled on the zipline to the man on the other side of the river. I sat watching as the harness made its way towards Blodwyn. For a moment, it looked like everything was in slow motion, I think my body needed a bit of time to adjust to being back on solid ground.

I stood up to watch Blodwyn as she made her way up the step ladder, she looked like she was the winner of a competition. But instead of getting first prize, the man pulled the safety harness over her head, shoulders and waist and she was off like a torpedo out of a submarine. Then all of a sudden, the zip line started to slow down and her body started to fall towards the white water, her head was tilting forwards towards the rocks below, then her left hand let go of the line and she fell towards the rushing water below. My heart stopped beating as I heard her scream. The man next to me had to pull the line to tighten it up as fast as he could. I watched as Blodwyn flew into the air then back down again towards the rocks. The man pulled the rope again to get her closer to him, then he jumped into the river to pull her back to safety.

I stood watching helplessly as he helped her navigate through the jagged rocks at the edge of the river.

'Are you OK, Blodwyn?' I don't know whether she was in shock or hurt, but she just burst out laughing. 'Please come here, let me take a look at you to make sure you're OK.' I looked all over her body to see if there were any cuts or bruises, but I could not find any.

Then she stopped laughing. 'That did not go to plan Janet!'

'You can say that again, I thought you were going to get hurt.'

Mick helped Knobby over the bridge to the other side of the river towards where we were sitting. 'Bloody hell, missis, what were you thinking? You could have been hurt!' I could tell that Knobby was frightened for Blodwyn and he was angry because the ride had gone so terribly wrong.

'Don't worry, Knobby, I'm OK, but my hands were not strong enough to hold on to the harness.'

I left the two of them to talk about what could have happened, and I made my way back to Mick. 'She was very lucky, I thought she was going to fall into the water and hurt herself.'

Mick stared at me. 'You were both very lucky, that zipline is not safe!'

When Blodwyn felt ready to move, we made our way back to Jose and Bella for a nice quiet drive back to the hotel.

That evening, we went for a meal in the village of Devin. We spoke about the wonderful time we had during the day and the zipline incident. Knobby was still unhappy about the risks Blodwyn and I had taken.

'You could have both been seriously injured or killed!'

Bella looked up. 'No one has died on the zipline yet, but after today they are going to make sure that everyone can hold their own body weight before they are allowed on the ride.'

The following day we decided to have a quiet day exploring the village, we met Bella's mama and papa, mama remembered me from the last time I visited. 'Hello Janet supermarket.' Then she laughed and gave me a big hug. We spent the afternoon sitting in the sunshine eating and drinking with the locals, it was a wonderful experience.

Our time in Devin was coming to an end, everyone had had a brilliant time and there had been no earthquakes. We had, however, built a new road out of the mountains, and climbed hundreds of steps, Blodwyn almost fed herself to the fishes and Knobby missed the naughty movie. The sightseeing trips in the mountains were absolutely stunning and the Devil's Throat Cave was absolutely amazing, but we were all so very sad to be going home. Bella and Jose noticed that we were all unhappy so they decided to arrange a leaving party for us at the hotel.

With a party in mind, we decided to go back to the hotel to get our best clothes on. When we arrived at the restaurant the staff had set a table in the middle of the room. It looked amazing. There were beautiful flowers and decorations all around the table. When everyone had arrived, we sat down to have a perfect meal with all of our Bulgarian friends.

We ended the evening laughing and joking about all of the wonderful experiences we had had in Devin. It was so good that we started to plan our next visit to the mountains for the following year.

The next day, we said goodbye to everyone and left the hotel to make our way to the airport to fly back to the UK. For some reason I did not feel sad or unhappy any more. I just felt so excited about booking our next holiday to Bulgaria.

The End